VOLATILE
PLACES

*To the students, faculty, and staff at the
University of New Orleans who are struggling
to find their lives after the great flood of 2005, with a
special nod to our friends in the Department of Sociology*

VOLATILE PLACES

A Sociology of Communities and Environmental Controversies

VALERIE GUNTER
University of New Orleans

STEVE KROLL-SMITH
University of North Carolina at Greensboro

PINE FORGE PRESS
An Imprint of Sage Publications, Inc.
Thousand Oaks • London • New Delhi

For information:

Pine Forge Press
A Sage Publications Company
2455 Teller Road
Thousand Oaks, California 91320
E-mail: order@sagepub.com

Sage Publications Ltd.
1 Oliver's Yard
55 City Road
London EC1Y 1SP
United Kingdom

Sage Publications India Pvt. Ltd.
B-42, Panchsheel Enclave
Post Box 4109
New Delhi 110 017 India

Printed in the United States of America

Library of Congress Cataloging-in-Publication Data

Gunter, Valerie J. (Valerie Jan), 1961-
Volatile places: A sociology of communities and environmental controversies / Valerie Gunter, Steve Kroll-Smith.
 p. cm.
Includes bibliographical references and index.
ISBN 0-7619-8750-9 or 978-0-7619-8750-5 (pbk.: acid-free paper)
 1. Environmentalism. 2. Human beings—Effect of environment on.
3. Environmental psychology. I. Kroll-Smith, J. Stephen, 1947- II. Title.
GE195.G86 2007
363.7—dc22

        2006016905

This book is printed on acid-free paper.

06 07 08 09 10 10 9 8 7 6 5 4 3 2 1

Acquisitions Editor:	Benjamin Penner
Editorial Assistant:	Camille Herrera
Production Editor:	Denise Santoyo
Copy Editor:	Barbara Coster
Typesetter:	C&M Digitals (P) Ltd.
Indexer:	Kathy Paparchontis
Cover Designer:	Candice Harman

About the Authors

Valerie Gunter is Associate Professor in the Department of Sociology at the University of New Orleans. Following the ravages of Hurricane Katrina, she spent a year as Visiting Associate Professor at Michigan State University, from which she had received her PhD in sociology in 1994. She has spent over 20 years researching the controversial processes by which environmental issues become registered on community and national political agendas. Articles reporting the results from this research have been published in such journals as *Social Problems, The Sociological Quarterly, The American Sociologist, Sociological Inquiry,* and *Rural Sociology.* She is a coeditor of *Illness and the Environment: A Reader in Contested Medicine.*

Steve Kroll-Smith is Head of the Department of Sociology at the University of North Carolina in Greensboro. He was formerly Research Professor of Sociology at the University of New Orleans. He has edited and written five books on environmental hazards and disasters, health and the environment, and sociologists as expert witnesses. He is the current editor of *Sociological Inquiry* and the 2004 recipient of the American Sociological Association's Distinguished Contribution Award in the study of environment and technology. His current work is the problem of race, class, and water in New Orleans in the aftermath of Hurricanes Katrina and Rita. He also regularly contributes to the growing scholarship on the sociology of sleep.

Contents

Preface

It is now commonplace to recognize that people change environments and environments, in turn, change people. More important, these reciprocal effects often occur in neighborhoods, villages, and towns, localities that we loosely call communities. Students of environments and societies soon recognize that a substantial portion of their subject matter intersects with that social arrangement commonly called the community. Hundreds of empirical studies now registered in the literature are organized around the variable effects of environmental changes on the anatomy of communities. In spite of the almost unavoidable presence of community in the human-environment encounter, there are no books that look specifically at the intersections of humans, environments, and communities. This book was written to provide students of all kinds—undergraduate, graduate, and faculty—with an analytical guide to the investigation of community and environmental controversies. It begins with a simple observation, to wit, environmental issues are almost always contested and are likely to transform communities into volatile places. Using dozens of case studies written and organized around specific themes, we develop an array of ideas and orientations that should prove valuable to anyone interested in the spirited public controversies that almost always occur when environments become community problems.

Imagine this book as a trail map of a national park. The purpose of the map is twofold: to prevent you from getting hopelessly lost and to suggest points or places on your trek to stop and look, to examine with some care what is around you or just ahead. As a map of local environmental controversies, this book will help you from getting confused and befuddled by the complexity of environmental troubles and community conflicts. It promises that for all their apparent disorder, these conflicts are not random and unpredictable. On the contrary, if viewed from, say, the *presence of the past, perceptions of fairness,* or *oppositional activity,* significant features of these controversies become visible and knowable.

Chapters 2 through 6 offer five quite different outlooks on local environmental controversies. As a place on the map, each outlook is an invitation to stop and carefully examine a particular set of issues that are both shaping and shaped by social and environmental conflict. Each of these substantive chapters is a place to begin a thesis, dissertation, paper, or book. Taken in their totality, each one of these five chapters might itself serve as a book chapter. Two or more chapters could be combined into a unique study of, say, social and brute facts and perceptions of fairness in a local preservation controversy.

There is a second, more implicit, invitation in this book that cannot go unmentioned. Its basis is a simple, but affecting, observation summed up nicely by Kenneth Burke. "Every insight," he reminds us, "contains its own special kind of blindness."[1] Put another way, each chapter in this book possesses a circumference. It points to where a particular interpretation stops. And here, readers, is where you are invited to toss the map aside and become your own sociological cartographers. Acknowledging the inherent limitations of any insight, concept, theory, or point of view is an invitation to others to add, modify, innovate, or abandon and start anew. By its very limitations, sociological inquiry is pluralistic.

So, in closing, we invite you to examine local environmental controversies through the manifold lenses we provide. Or, should these prove inadequate, we invite you to modify them or create your own and discover something new and different to question, examine, and interpret.

Acknowledgments

This book began several years ago as a mere glimmer of an idea, and we want to thank the folks at Pine Forge for continuing to support us through what proved to be a prolonged birthing process. A special note of gratitude goes to Jerry Westby, senior editor, who renewed Pine Forge's commitment to the project after unexpectedly inheriting it from his predecessor. Our decision to write about a specialized subfield of environmental sociology presented challenges to editors trying to get not only a sense of the market potential for our book but also an understanding about how it related to a broader body of literature. We want to thank Ben Penner, acquisition editor, for seeing us through several rounds of reviews and revisions while providing us with the leeway to write the book we wanted to write.

Feedback from reviewers encouraged our own convictions that we were putting together a unique presentation of material that others in the field would find useful. Reviewers' comments and suggestions allowed us to sharpen our argument and improve the overall quality of the manuscript. We want to extend a special thanks to each of the following individuals, who played a crucial role in getting this manuscript into print: Timothy Bartley, Indiana University–Bloomington; Joan M. Brehm, Illinois State University; Cliff Brown, University of New Hampshire; Diane C. Bates, The College of New Jersey; Stephen R. Couch, The Pennsylvania State University; Furjen Deng, Sam Houston State University; Harry R. Potter, Purdue University; and Steve Scanlan, Ohio University.

I want to extend personal thanks to the sociology department at Michigan State University, especially to Craig Harris, Jan Bokemeier, and Marilyn Aronoff. Craig Harris and Marilyn Aronoff nurtured my interest in environmental and community sociology when I was a graduate student at MSU, and for this alone I would be grateful. A second debt of gratitude is more recent, however. Beyond all expectations, the sociology department brought me on for a semester's teaching after my New Orleans' apartment was flooded in the aftermath of Hurricane Katrina. I want to thank Craig

Harris for taking the trouble to track me down at my sister's house in Texas and for getting the wheels spinning on opportunities at Michigan State. I am also grateful to Jan Bokemeier, chair of MSU's sociology department, for working with the dean and provost to secure funding for me.

Another note of appreciation goes to Michigan State's Kellogg Biological Station, where I was graciously provided with an office, a computer, and a furnished apartment in October and November 2005. I especially want to thank KBS director Kay Gross and computer specialist John Gorentz, though I will never forget the kindness of all the KBS staff.

I am grateful to the folks in the sociology department at the University of New Orleans for providing an unusually hospitable environment for professional matriculation. A special note of thanks goes to Susan Mann, who provided needed social diversions. I would also like to thank my sister, Lauren Brooks, who graciously provided housing for me and my husband in the aftermath of Hurricane Katrina, and also my mother, Ella Olson, who took care of our cats after we fled New Orleans.

A special note of thanks goes to my husband, Tom Andersen, who not only patiently endured the long hours needed to meet deadlines on this project but during the final stages did so under the adverse conditions of being a hurricane evacuee himself.

Valerie Gunter

As always, my work is an extension of my family. Thank you, Susan, Amanda, and Emma.

Steve Kroll-Smith

Note

1. Burke (1989), 8.

1

When Environments and Communities Collide

Writing in 1982, sociologist William Catton made this case for the intersection of environments and communities:

> There can be no exclusively human community. . . . The phrase "human community," therefore, should always be regarded as a shorthand for a biotic community dominated by humans.[1]

Twenty-three years later, a younger sociologist, Michael Bell, echoed and expanded on Catton's observation:

> We need . . . to make the study of community the central task of environmental sociology. Ecology is often described as the study of natural communities. Sociology is often described as the study of human communities. Environmental sociology is the study of both together, the single commons of the Earth we humans share, sometimes grudgingly, with others—other people, other forms of life, and the rocks and water and soil and air that support all life. Environmental sociology is the study of this, the biggest community of all.[2]

Locating Communities in Environmental Controversies

A Place for Community in Environmental Sociology

This book joins Catton's reflection on the inescapable connection of human and biotic communities to Bell's spirited call to center the idea of community in environmental sociology. Using rich and evocative case studies, an experiential or inductive approach to making sense of local environmental controversies, and portfolios highlighting many (but not all) of the key questions students of community and environment are likely to ask, we invite you to read and ponder the always complicated and always dramatic intersections of human settlements and biospheres.

Bell is right in observing the essential place of community in the study of sociology. A strong and vibrant tradition of community studies is at the core of the sociological canon. Missing from this literature, however, is a text that pulls together and advances the rich and variegated studies of communities and environments.[3] Examine the textbooks in environmental sociology, and community is apt to be mentioned, but it will not appear as a key organizing concept.[4] Indeed, Bell himself gives limited attention to local manifestations of environmental problems, focusing instead on the broad structural and cultural factors underlying ecological unsustainable ways of life.

The absence of a text organized around the almost inescapable presence of community in the study of environmental sociology is not a reflection of the dearth of empirical research on communities and environments; there is, in truth, a good deal of it. You will encounter many and varied studies of environments and communities in the chapters to follow. Perhaps it is more the fact that the idea of community has become a commonplace in the study of sociology, so common in fact as to be almost banal or taken for granted. More likely, though, is the overwhelming emphasis placed on emergent protest groups and social movements in the sociological study of environment. A rich and valuable literature is now available in this area. Go to almost any standard textbook in environmental sociology, and the idea of grassroots activism and social movements is likely to loom quite large.

Local activism and regional, national, and international coalitions working in concert toward some common end are dynamic sociological phenomena, but aside these is the almost inescapable presence of community. Shift the focus from local activists to the more inclusive idea of community, and a somewhat different, often more complicated, picture emerges. Here is an example.

A Brief Excursus: The Love Canal From Two Perspectives

In 1982 Adeline Levine published her now landmark book *Love Canal: Science, Politics, and People.*[5] The story of Love Canal is the classic tale of buried toxic waste that everyone forgot until it percolated to the surface and contaminated a school and neighborhoods in the city of Niagara Falls, New York. Levine became aware of the looming crisis by watching a local news feature on the affected neighborhoods. Using the good help of her graduate students in the Department of Sociology at the State University of New York at Buffalo, Professor Levine embarked on a qualitative study of the actions local residents were taking in response to this growing danger. More important, she made the decision to focus on citizen activists, indeed, on one group of activists, the Love Canal Homeowner's Association (LCHA).

Levine's book stands as one of the premier investigations of citizen activism in response to the perils of toxic contamination. We learn firsthand what one group of informed citizens could do to shape the political and medical response to the crisis. What we don't learn is how this dramatic transformation of the local environment interacted with the neighborhood community, which was far more demographically and economically diverse than the homogenous, white, young-adult female population that constituted the LCHA. In contrast to *Love Canal: Science, Politics, and People*, two cultural anthropologists, Martha Fowlkes and Patricia Miller, examined the interchange between the toxins buried at Love Canal and this broader, more inclusive social community.

Their 1982 study, *Love Canal: The Social Construction of Disaster*, is based on extended interviews with a random sample of 63 neighborhood residents.[6] Their goal was to assess people's beliefs, opinions, and perceptions of the risks to health, property, and the viability of the community posed by toxins seeping through the earth's crust into yards, houses, and, perhaps, bodies. Fowlkes and Miller found a far more complicated personal and social response to the contamination than reported by Levine. While essential to the formation of new affiliations within the Love Canal neighborhood and critical to the political outcome of the crisis, the LCHA was only a part of a rich and diverse collective action.

Documented in *Love Canal: The Social Construction of Disaster* is the presence of a Love Canal Renter's Association, comprised of low- to middle-income blacks who took the position that the chemicals posed no immediate threat and should be cleaned up. They fought efforts to relocate them. Age, it appears, also created a certain social segmentation, with late middle-age and senior residents taking the position that the contamination was not a dire threat. Location in relationship to the waste and the presence or absence of children in the household also played key roles in creating a diverse and conflicting array of personal and social beliefs and opinions regarding the scope and degree of danger.

This all-too-brief summary points to a simple conclusion: though there was only one Love Canal crisis, it is possible to tell two quite different stories about it. One story recounts the heroic and dedicated work of citizen activists to acquire important knowledge about the dangers and to face off with local, state, and national leaders who sought to minimize the risks or offered silly and inappropriate remedial measures. Another story narrates the crisis from the vantage point of the community. This latter account shows that the contamination seeping into the neighborhood also seeped into its social fabric, creating multiple groups and conflicting beliefs about the true scope of the crisis.

It is this latter story, told from the vantage point of community, that is underrepresented in most standard texts in environmental sociology. This book is offered as a balance to this literature. It was written to fill a gap. By centering the idea of community in the study of environmental sociology, we invite students of people and biospheres to take a fresh look at an essential dynamic in the social and cultural study of environments. The plain fact is that most of us live our lives in some semblance of community, and human communities are always parts of larger, more complicated biospheric communities. When we wittingly or unwittingly alter the biosphere or even propose to do so, people respond, often with differing interpretations, claims, and solutions. In the chapters to follow, we explore this dynamic, focusing explicitly on the troubles, difficulties, and conflicts that are likely to emerge in the wake of real or proposed environmental changes.

Students of environment, as well as those interested in communities or social conflicts, will find this book a useful guide to a rich and provocative case study literature. And aside from this literature, informing and shaping it, is a conceptual vocabulary. It is our hope this literature and vocabulary will inspire you to engage in some spirited thinking and, perchance, some original research.

A Modern Social Drama

A place to begin this study is with the often turbulent nature of human responses to environmental disruptions and troubles. Indeed, environments and communities are often unwitting actors in what are contemporary social dramas: vivid, emotional, and conflicting portrayals of villains, victims, sacrifices, and, sometimes, redemptions. As we write this chapter, a community conflict of epic proportions is emerging in the "wake" of Katrina as New Orleans struggles to survive.

We use the word *wake* deliberately as a play on words to signal the source of the controversy. It was not Katrina's winds that destroyed 80% of New Orleans' housing, but the powerful wakes and waves roused by its winds that breached at least three levees, pouring more than a third of Lake

Ponchatrain into unsuspecting neighborhoods. Early investigations suggest the levees were not properly built. The conflagrations between the city and the Army Corps of Engineers are likely to continue for years as the city and its residents struggle to achieve a just measure of compensation and a levee system that can withstand the super storms expected in the future.

New Orleans, of course, is an example of community conflict orders of magnitude greater than those discussed at length in this book. But post-Katrina New Orleans and the dozens of cases presented in the chapters to follow are shaped, at least in part, by what William James once called the logic of the "forced option."[7] This idea is based on the simple observation that we can avoid some choices but not others.

A young father might decide, for example, to avoid voting on a local referendum to rename a city street after a local politician. It is not something he feels compelled to do. A referendum to block the siting of a hospital waste facility in close proximity to his daughter's school, however, is a vote he could not ignore. Activities begun by others are seen to pose a threat to his own family; he is forced to respond.

In calling attention to the forced option, James did not intend for us to assume that one choice was innately right and the other wrong. What is forced is not a "true" path per se, but the simple fact that some path must be chosen. Consider the example of the waste facility: another parent might argue vigorously for the siting of a well-regulated plant near a school because plant management promises to build new roads, provide new school buses, and contribute $2 million annually to the school district. The perceived consequences of the siting proposal required a response from both parents, though each chose a different path.

In the aftermath of Hurricane Katrina, New Orleans' officials and residents face a plethora of forced options. Among them, whether or not to return to the city, and if so, when; whether or not to rebuild destroyed homes, and if so, whether to rebuild in the same old style or in one more reflective of vulnerability to flooding (such as constructing houses on stilts or replacing single-family dwellings with high-rise apartments); and whether or not to allow any rebuilding in the most severely flooded portions of the city. Moreover, what will happen if the rest of the nation decides it does not want to spend billions of federal dollars it will cost to repair and improve the levees? It is not that the people of New Orleans want to wrestle with these decisions; circumstances demand that they do so.

On a less publicly visible scale than New Orleans, local communities in ever-increasing numbers are forced to decide how to act toward and make sense of complicated, value-laden environmental problems. Land-use decisions that could alter the quality of environments for generations to come, toxins in local biospheres, species habitats and human needs, and questions about the use of natural resources for market purposes are among the forced options facing villages, small towns, neighborhoods, and cities throughout the United States and, indeed, worldwide.

Emotional and dramatic intensity issue from the forced option, in part because there is a choice, perhaps several choices, and consensus on what to do is not easily achieved. The title *Volatile Places* conveys our appreciation for the high-stakes consequences of many local environmental controversies. Human life and well-being, a house, friendship, a job, a treasured way of life, and justice itself are often endangered when people cannot reach agreement on how to use environments or the kind and degree of danger they pose.

Complementing and enhancing our focus on the human community and environmental conflict are two far more complex and interrelated processes, each of which will have some bearing on the many and varied discussions to follow: global environmental change and the—equally evocative—end of nature.

Community as Ground Zero in a Global World

In spite of Catton's and Bell's counsel on the significance of human community in the sociological study of environments and our own views on the salience of community to environmental sociology, some readers might still ask, Why focus attention on local, community-based environmental problems when the important issues seem to be global environmental change with its worldwide implications? After all, if the polar ice caps melt and the carbon dioxide (CO_2) content of the atmosphere reaches a certain magnitude, life everywhere is likely to undergo massive ecological, social, and political transformation.

We agree. Global environmental change (GEC) promises sweeping alterations in the lives of untold numbers of people, but we also note that people experience their social, cultural, and environmental worlds in groups and communities, not as separate, isolated, autonomous individuals. Even something as potentially massive as GEC will affect people living in villages, neighborhoods, towns, and cities. It will be experienced in part, in other words, as a local community trouble. Indeed, Katrina herself might be a harbinger of this, as there is reason to be concerned that the record-breaking and unprecedented 2005 tropical storm season may be related to warming of the Gulf of Mexico and Atlantic Ocean currents. Interpretations of the various signals of GEC will occur in local settings through media, conversations with friends and neighbors, work group ties, and so on. Community, we suggest, is ground zero in the human experience of environment.

Understanding how communities struggle with, make disputed sense of, and change or accommodate to their local environments is, therefore, of considerable significance regardless of whether the source of environmental disruption is worldwide climate change or leaking toxic waste drums buried near an aquifer. Local environmental disputes are an increasingly pervasive feature of community life. Indeed, we suspect students reading this text know, or could quickly find evidence, of these types of environmental conflicts occurring in their states, or perhaps in their communities.

On a somewhat grander scale, an inquiry into local environmental conflicts is an occasion to examine the making and unmaking of social life. It is an opportunity to observe people who fashion versions of history to make sense of environmental controversies. It is also a chance to encounter the complicated role of expert knowledge in creating both opportunities and obstacles to community formation. Visible too is the awakening of a political consciousness as people encounter the duplicity of corporations and government agencies. Citizens become moral entrepreneurs, posing questions about the distribution of justice and fairness to the ecological and political conundrums of environmental controversies. And local groups form, many with competing visions of the environmental controversy and its solution. Simply put, local environmental conflicts are often volatile human dramas combining both creative and destructive social forces into historical moments of social transformation. They are, following Lévi-Strauss, "good to think."

Taking the community as ground zero, however, does not mean an exclusive focus on the local level. A characteristic feature of modernity is the pervasive interplay between the local and the global. It will be difficult to grasp what is going on in any particular community without an appreciation of the broader regional, national, and extra-national relationships impinging on and shaping local practices, opinions, and beliefs. A quick example. Economic prosperity, increased leisure time, and the development of an "automobile culture" in the post–World War II era resulted in a dramatic increase of visitors to national parks, intensifying long-standing conflicts over whether the parks existed primarily to provide recreational opportunities for humans or to protect species and habitat. To adequately explain local conflicts over who should use a park and how would require a studied awareness of this broader social and cultural context.

Communities, in other words, are affected by technological, political, economic, and cultural developments that originate beyond their borders. Increasingly, these influences are global in scope.[8] Indeed, the close relationship between the local and the extra-local is, itself, a historical occurrence, appearing only in the last several decades.[9] The social activist phrase "Think globally, act locally" expresses the need to recognize the confounding of provincial issues and concerns with far-reaching national, international, indeed planetary trends and forces.

The intersection between human communities and environmental troubles is also underscored in the profound ways in which society is remaking the natural and sculpting the contours along which environments and communities—with increasing frequency—collide.

The End of Nature as We Know It: From the Biocentric to the Anthropocentric

Over the course of time, humans altered nature, transforming it into a reflection of ourselves: from a biotic and physical world, set apart from the flotsam and jetsam of culture, to a human artifact. In more formal terms, nature is now as much *anthropocentric* as it is *biocentric*. No longer standing on its own, nature is the handmaiden of civilization.

Let's start with air. The basic chemistry of our air has changed dramatically in the past 40 years. "If you'd climbed some remote mountain in 1960 and sealed up a bottle of air at its peak, and did the same thing this year, the two would be substantially different."[10] In addition to naturally occurring CO_2, produced, for example, by forest fires, there is a human-produced array of CO_2 emissions that now exceed that produced by nature. Burning fossil fuels, deforestation, and waste incineration is increasing CO_2 at a rate of about 1.2 parts per million each year. But CO_2s are not the only problem. Chlorofluorocarbons (CFCs) are not produced anywhere in nature. They are chemical compounds containing chlorine, fluorine, and carbon and are made by people. Air samples taken anywhere in the world will contain at least trace elements of CFC, though they have been phased out in the United States and other Western countries.

The atmosphere, in short, is now a product of human activities. We could make similar arguments for soil and water. Decades ago Rachel Carson reported the presence of DDT (a pesticide) in soil samples around the world. Indeed, it is now found deep in the ice at both the North and South Poles. Residents from 46% of all counties in the United States use groundwater susceptible to contamination from agricultural pesticides and fertilizers.[11]

This last observation is worth considering. It would appear that just as industrial culture has entered nature, altering its chemistries and ecologies, so too has it entered human bodies, once thought natural. In 1986, an Environmental Protection Agency (EPA) executive summary on chemicals in human tissue reported measurable levels of styrene and ethyl phenol in 100% of adults living in the United States. The study also found 96% of adults with clinical levels of chlorobenzene, benzene, and ethyl benzene; 91% with toluene; and 83% with polychlorinated byphenols.[12] There's more. A few years ago, the federal Centers of Disease Control and Prevention admitted "that virtually every person who has lived in the United States since 1951 has been exposed to radiological fallout . . . [and that] all organs and tissues of the body have received some radiation exposure."[13] What do these figures and observations imply? Bill McKibben views them as signs that nature is ending.[14] Whether it is the nature of the biosphere or the nature of the human body, it would appear that the "nature" of industrial and postindustrial societies is no longer "natural." Nature as a natural phenomenon will survive in our imaginations, of course, but it is no longer the "natural" nature that nurtured us and ensured our survival as a species. It is, to quote sociologist Anthony Giddens, a *socialized nature*.[15] We made it, though unintentionally and without a clear understanding of its effects on human well-being. "Our society," writes Giddens, "lives after the end of nature."[16]

There is no way to know the long-term effects of shifting from a biocentric to an anthropocentric nature, but one thing seems clear: we have set environments (and bodies) on an unprecedented journey toward some as yet to be defined end, and on that journey human communities will figure prominently as the locations for struggling with the changes we've set in motion.

The past several pages introduced an array of complicated and provocative concerns and ideas. The point of these discussions is to alert the reader to the salience of community in the study of environmental conflicts and to set this topic in a broader, more inclusive, dynamic of global environmental changes and the human manufacture of nature. The second part of this chapter shifts to the conceptual and material organization of the book. As we proceed, please bear in mind the continuing relevance of these broader, more contextual, discussions.

Two Organizing Devices

Two devices or motifs work to organize the materials in this primer. One motif is *taxonomic* and focuses attention on three distinct types of local environmental conflicts. A second motif is both *conceptual* and *pedagogical* and focuses on a portfolio approach to studying conflict. A short discussion introduces each motif, and a longer discussion demonstrates how types of environmental conflicts intersect with a portfolio strategy for abstracting and remembering.

The Three Controversies

The three most prominent types of local environmental conflicts are the *conservancy dispute,* the *siting dispute,* and the *exposure dispute.* These are not necessarily mutually exclusive categories, as we illustrate below. Each type is a classic example of the forced option. Conservancy disputes are characterized by struggles over how to define and protect natural areas and animal species, as well as certain human-created artifacts such as prehistoric and historic buildings.[17] A variant of conservancy disputes which has become increasingly common over the last couple of decades is ecosystem restoration. Efforts to restore prairie, urban wilderness, watersheds, and wetlands are among the examples of this relatively new type of conservancy dispute.[18] This variant of local environmental conflicts, then, is comprised of efforts to protect, or restore, a more biocentric nature.

Siting disputes are formed when opposition develops to some proposed land use. They typically occur when communities, or certain people within communities, resist proposals to build new facilities or modify existing ones. Facilities commonly targeted in such disputes include petrochemical factories, nuclear power plants, solid waste landfills, hazardous waste treatment facilities, and large-scale hydroelectric projects. Siting disputes are directed against what are sometimes referred to as LULUs, or locally unwanted land uses. Siting disputes are often driven by concerns about the human health consequences of an industrialized, anthropocentric nature, though sometimes other, more prosaic, concerns, such as property values and the desire to maintain a neighborhood's "character" and "charm," may be equally, or even more, important. Siting and conservancy disputes can intersect if development is being opposed on such grounds as it threatens a "wild, natural" or "ecologically sensitive" area. (For an example of a siting conservancy dispute, see the Orme Dam case in Chapter 2.)

Exposure disputes, in contrast, are comprised of fights against hazards already existing in the local area. These may include factories that emit air and water pollutants, or chemicals leaching into the groundwater. A common type of exposure dispute is controversies over the accidental or negligent release of toxins into local environments. Human health concerns are preeminent in exposure disputes, though occasionally the primary focus is on risks to nonhuman life forms. The result is an intersecting exposure-conservancy dispute, as seen in the 1989 *Exxon Valdez* oil spill in Prince William Sound, Alaska. While the spill did raise health concerns about human consumption of contaminated fish and wildlife, the major issues had to do with effects on the aquatic ecosystem and the flora and fauna in the area.[19]

Typical of each of these three types of conflicts is the seeming imperative most people feel to take a position on the justice or injustice, the rightness or wrongness, or the "facts" of the controversy. Below we provide three short vignettes, each illustrating one of the three types of disputes. Before we proceed to that task, however, we first introduce the idea of the portfolio approach.

The Portfolio Approach

Analysis requires seeing beyond the concrete details of any particular conflict to broader patterns of relationships found in similar cases. Many students find analysis—or theoretical work—challenging. It requires making abstract linkages between the general and the specific, which in sociology is accomplished through the use of theoretical concepts and propositions.

This book is not intended as a highly theoretical treatise, but we do want to provide readers with tools which push beyond the simple descriptive level of who said/did what, when they said/did it, and what happened as a result of what was said/done. Not that we want to shortchange description; it is the basic starting point of any investigation, as we illustrate shortly. Yet sociologists seek to augment description with more complex explanations of why and how things happened as they did.

The approach we take to theory in this text derives from the largely inductive, qualitative, and case study research techniques we use in our own work. Induction means that researchers develop theoretical explanations after they have gained extensive familiarity with some aspect of the empirical world.[20] Deduction, in contrast, involves the researcher arriving to a study with a theoretical model already in hand. We define our own approach as "largely inductive" because we agree with Fine that the best approach is one that combines inductive and deductive elements.[21] Students of local environmental conflicts need to have extensive familiarity with the relevant literature before undertaking empirical investigations and to use that literature judiciously where applicable. This is the deductive move in the research process. What induction contributes to the investigative endeavor is the flexibility to deal with the unexpected.

This dual approach is needed because humans reside somewhere between the extremes of complete free will and complete determination (in sociological lingo we would say human social life is characterized by both structure and agency). To paraphrase Karl Marx, humans make history, but they do not do so under conditions of their choosing. There is certainly a great deal of order and patterned regularity to human social life; this is what allows us to make general observations about local environmental conflicts which transcend the specifics of any individual case. Yet humans also have inordinate capabilities to be innovative and creative; they often behave in ways we expect, but not always. Environmental conflicts, as complex, messy, contested affairs, often involving novel environmental states, are particularly fertile ground for the unexpected.

What we do *not* do in this text is provide readers with an overarching theoretical framework that can be used to explain every local environmental conflict. We do provide readers with an extensive list of questions which can be asked of any conflict and which are designed to encourage students of these conflicts to see beyond the obvious. We separate these questions out in boxes titled Adding to the Portfolio. Each box adds a new set of questions that readers can add to the portfolio, a set of conceptual tools which can be carried into any conflict investigation. Such investigations may take the form of analyzing one of the many published case studies of local environmental conflicts or of gathering original secondary (e.g., newspaper accounts) and primary (e.g., interviews with conflict participants) source material about a particular conflict.

Not every question presented in these boxes will be applicable to every conflict, nor do the lists of questions included in this book (extensive as it is) cover the full range of questions that *could* be asked of these conflicts. Our goal here is not to be exhaustive but to get students started down a path of inquiry. The theoretical ideas informing these questions are discussed in some depth in the analysis section following each case study vignette. The portfolio boxes also double, then, as useful section summaries and study guides.

We turn now to three cases which illustrate conservancy, siting, and exposure disputes, and to accompanying discussions which illustrate how the portfolio approach will be used in this book.[22]

Conservancy Disputes

Scotia, California, is a company town built by the Pacific Lumber Company.[23] At odds with the predominant clear-cutting practices of the timber industry, Pacific Lumber had implemented a policy of selective cutting in the 1930s. The company also adopted a sustainable harvesting policy ensuring that trees would not be cut down at a rate faster than natural replacement. This policy would ensure that Pacific Lumber would own a crop of trees to cut down this year, next year, and every year. As a result of these practices, Pacific Lumber entered the 1980s controlling "almost 70 percent of the remaining ancient redwood forest that was still in private hands."[24]

In the mid-1980s, Pacific Lumber came to the attention of the corporate raider Charles Hurwitz. An associate of the junk bond king Michael Milken, Hurwitz made a career out of taking over publicly held companies with undervalued stocks. Pacific Lumber was just such a firm, the result of its sustainable harvesting policies which reduced short-term profits, making it appear to the short-term investor as a bad risk. In early 1986, Hurwitz succeeded in a hostile takeover of Pacific Lumber. To accomplish this he had borrowed over $500 million, much of it from Michael Milken's outfit, Drexel Burnham Lambert. In order to repay this debt, Hurwitz needed to liquidate as many assets of Pacific Lumber as he could, as quickly as he could.

Clear-cutting stands of redwood was the primary means Hurwitz used to generate high levels of profit in a short period. Once harvested and milled, a single redwood's market value is approximately $30,000. Hurwitz now controlled close to 200,000 acres of prime forest. Pacific Lumber's new clear-cutting policy soon came to the attention of a group of young people who had moved into the area, some of whom claimed affiliation with the radical environmentalist group Earth First! They quickly mounted a variety of defensive actions against the clear-cutting, including tree sitting, protest marches through the streets of Scotia, and lawsuits charging that the California Department of Forestry acted illegally in approving Pacific Lumber's timber harvesting plans.

The environmental activists were opposed by many of the residents of Scotia, who quickly defined the dispute as a Manichean struggle between jobs and a small town's future versus the dispensable luxury of old trees. Moreover, many people in Scotia were now making more money by working overtime to help Hurwitz repay his debt to Milken. Pleased with their new levels of economic prosperity, Scotia residents were angry at those "outsiders" who wanted to take this away from them. That the activists were branded by Pacific Lumber management as long-haired welfare bums without proper respect for authority only served to further fuel the lumber workers' anger and contempt. Anonymous threats of violence and death directed toward activists became increasingly common. In May 1990 the violence escalated when a car bomb exploded inside a vehicle carrying two activists who at the time were on a trip to the San Francisco area. The FBI, which considers Earth First! to be an internal terrorist group, concluded the activists were transporting the explosive material for their own terrorist uses when it accidentally exploded. The activists dispute this claim, though no official investigation to identify other potential culprits was undertaken.

Oppositional activity by environmentalists dropped off markedly in the wake of the car bombing. Life in the town of Scotia returned more or less to normal. The long-term economic effects of Pacific Lumber's clear-cutting policy on the town remain to be seen.[25]

Conflict Participants and Their Claims

The strategy we employ in this book is to take case study vignettes as a starting point from which to extract important concepts, ideas, and themes. In this chapter our portfolio questions are focused on basic descriptive information investigators need to know about a case. While our goal is to move students of local environmental conflicts beyond this descriptive level, more complex understandings need to be built on a solid grounding of the "who, what, when, and where" of conflict. Descriptive questions are also more straightforward than the material covered in subsequent chapters and therefore provide a useful starting point for easing students into the portfolio approach.[26]

One of the most basic descriptive questions which can be asked of a conflict is, Who are the individuals, groups, and organizations involved in it? At the most basic descriptive level, actual names are used, such as the LCHA or Charlie Hurwitz. A slightly more analytic approach locates individuals and organizations within broader participant categories. There are a number of such categories which put in regular appearances in local environmental conflicts. These include grassroots environmental organizations, national environmental organizations, nonenvironmental voluntary associations like labor unions and the League of Women Voters, state and federal regulatory agencies, elected officials, landowners, neighborhood residents, private companies, and university scientists. These categories provide a useful starting point for understanding the words and actions of different conflict participants. For example, a regulatory agency has a different array of possible (and perhaps mandated) responses open to it than, say, a chemical factory or an environmental organization.

A word of caution: do not get too comfortable in assuming that a conflict participant's stance on an issue can necessarily be read from the broader participant category to which the individual, group, or organization belongs. Private companies sometimes voluntarily adopt sound environmental practices,[27] while environmentalists sometimes put narrow organizational interests ahead of viable conservation plans.[28] This is the reason we emphasize the role of human agency; social actors have more options available to them than blindly following the script society dictates. In other words, don't get so caught up in stereotypical thinking that you miss the atypical and unexpected.

Next, it is useful to assess whether conflict participants are local (community insiders) or extra-local (outsiders). We can see the importance of this distinction in the Scotia case, where the Pacific Lumber Company and local residents used young eco-activists' status as "outsiders" to dismiss their concerns and delegitimate their protest. In some cases, insider/outsider distinctions form fault lines along which alliances and hostilities form. Readers will encounter additional examples of such conflict scenarios in Chapter 6. Of course, it is not always easy to clearly classify all participants as local or extra-local. What about a local chapter of the national Sierra

Club? What about a factory which started out as locally owned, was taken over by a multinational corporation, but remains an important source of local employment and community identity? When encountered, such classificatory difficulties should be acknowledged, for a couple of reasons. First, they may become a source of local contention, for example, when long-time residents and ex-urban newcomers quarrel over who counts as a "real" member of a small rural village. Second, participants which span the local/extra-local divide have a unique vantage point and a unique set of network connections which may play an important role in the way the conflict develops, a point we develop further in Chapter 6.

Another important descriptive component is the political agendas of each of the different conflict participants. What are the specific outcomes they are hoping to achieve? In part, this question addresses the basic component of support or opposition for the issues under contention in a conservancy, siting, or exposure dispute. Does the conflict participant want to have the factory built or the species listed as endangered? Yet agendas are often more encompassing than just the stance on one or a handful of related issues; indeed, those stances themselves tend to derive from broader goals and visions. Familiarity with participants' agendas can help students of local environmental conflicts identify potential fault lines of dissension, as well as explain shifting alliances and situations where politics have produced strange bedfellows.

Dizard, for example, studied a conflict over a proposal to allow deer hunting on the Quabbin Reservation, near Boston.[29] An important source of drinking water for the city, the integrity of the surrounding watershed (the Quabbin Reservation) was managed by the Metropolitan District Commission (MDC). A number of critics were united in their opposition to the hunt and in their belief that it was the mismanagement of the MDC that had resulted in an overpopulation of deer. Opponents managed to remain united around these shared concerns, despite other differences in agenda. Some opponents, for example, enjoyed the Quabbin as a peaceful sanctuary in which to take walks and commune with nature; they were appalled at the thought of this wilderness retreat being disturbed by the presence of hunters and the sound of gunfire. Animal rights activists were opposed to all hunting on philosophical grounds; they believed every single animal had a right to be protected from human predation and interference. Environmentalists, in contrast, directed their concern not at the welfare of individual animals but to species and ecosystem integrity. Their primary concern was that the MDC was managing the Quabbin for the purpose of timber extraction, something they opposed. Had the MDC agreed to stop this practice, the environmentalists would have likely dropped their opposition to the hunt.

Participants use *claims* to legitimate and advance their agendas. Claims include assertions of facts ("The city of New Orleans flooded in the aftermath of Hurricane Katrina"), evaluative statements ("The federal response to Hurricane Katrina was woefully inadequate"), and normative directives ("We need to halt erosion along the Louisiana Gulf Coast"). While claims are highly specific statements, such as "This factory will create 400 new jobs for the community," they often resonate with broader themes, in this particular case, economic development. Sociologists often refer to such themes as *frames,* because they highlight salient features of the conflict.[30] Frames connect claims with more encompassing agendas and cultural values and hence are used strategically to win allies. Examining frames also provides a quick lesson in the multiple interpretations that can be given to a singular environmental event. As sociologists are very much aware, there is no automatic or natural sensory appropriation of what humans encounter in their material surroundings. What people "see" when they look out at the environment very much depends on where they are looking from. The "where" here does not refer to a geographic but a structural and cultural location.

To take an example of the way any single event can be subsumed under a number of competing frames, consider the following quotation from the novel *The Buffalo Commons,* which recounts a fictionalized conflict over grassland prairie restoration efforts in the state of Montana.

> Almost every schoolchild in the nation ached to see a National Grassland Trust full of buffalo and elk. For most Americans, the project seemed almost miraculous. Some saw it as a way of preserving the past. Others saw it as a vast petting zoo full of nice animals. A few hunters saw it as a place to safari for Boone and Crockett trophies. Some saw it as a way of preserving and restoring the precious topsoil. . . .
>
> A few others thought that perhaps it would become Indian lands, and the tribes would restore their ancient ways of life in that vast territory that lay adjacent to several reservations. Weird Californians opined that the grassland would emanate a great spirit of tranquility and healing that would affect the psyches of all the world's family and achieve psychic unity and peace so everyone would become brothers and sisters.[31]

If conducting original research, students might well wonder where they would turn to collect information about conflict participants and their agendas and claims. This book is not intended as a methods text, and therefore we are not going to provide an extensive answer to this question (though see Box 1.1 for a brief discussion of case study methods). What we will point out here is that often a useful starting place is with local news coverage of

Box 1.1   A Brief Primer on the Case Study Method

It was the Chicago School of Sociology that introduced the case study method to the social sciences. For more than 30 years, from the early 1900s to roughly 1935, the Chicago School dominated American sociology. Chicago itself was viewed as a complex social laboratory that invited dozens of inquiries into the interstices of urban life. Case studies of hobos, taxi dance halls, hotel lobbies, pickpockets, immigrants, neighborhoods, and more were written as master theses, doctoral dissertations, and books. In the middle of the 1930s, the center of sociology shifted from the University of Chicago to Columbia University, where faculty were far less interested in case studies and more interested in systematic surveys and experiments. The contrasts between these two quite different schools of sociology were handed down to later generations, and exist today, as the differences between qualitative and quantitative sociology.

Case studies in sociology generally share a number of qualities. First, they begin from an investigative space that is descriptive rather than analytic. That is, the task of the case study is to provide what Clifford Geertz would call a thick description of the setting, scene, situation, event, or person. Analyses might occur in bits and pieces throughout the description but more likely comes at the end. Second, most case studies are presented in a diachronic manner. That is, most of them follow the clock and the calendar, moving linearly through time. This gives the text a "first then, then that" character. As a story with a beginning, middle, and an end, the case study reads like a chronicle or narrative. Its narrative style is the basis for a third characteristic of the case study: the reader is invited to make both a conceptual and personal connection to the text. Indeed, where the survey rejects personalization in favor of objectivity, the case study personalizes data, encouraging readers to identify, at some level, with the story.

Finally, the quality of case studies always varies with the quality of writing. It might look relatively easy to write a case study. If so, we encourage you to read a few of the Chicago School studies or other case study classics in the field. We suspect you will be impressed by the quality of the writing. Remember, it is easier to invoke a concept than to describe it in a particular historical situation. Take the concept *status,* for example. It is much simpler to write *status* than to describe in loving detail a particular style, expression, physical arrangement, and so on that gives expression to vertical order.

We wrote more than 15 case studies for this book using previously published case study research. So, in a sense, we mined this cache of case studies to create our own cases. Our goal was to reread the published cases to extract what was useful and necessary to cobble together our own accounts of siting, toxic, and conservancy disputes. We were guided by one simple goal: to present what is known about each of the cases in a manner that would underscore contentious issues, group conflict, and community controversies. This is one of the many ways that sociologists borrow from one another to push the field in new and, hopefully, rewarding directions.

We advise you to read these case studies with a critical eye. What is not said in these thick descriptions? How might you compose a more suitable case? Does the case adequately represent the conceptual discussion that follows it?

NOTE: For a classic work on case study research in sociology, see Yin (1994).

the controversy. We present this advice with qualifications, because we do not want readers to assume media will provide an accurate or objective portrayal of the conflict. Indeed, the local media may be highly selective in which participants and claims it covers, or it may simply ignore the controversy altogether. Yet, as long as these shortcomings are kept in mind, local media coverage can provide valuable information in the early investigative stages. This can include names of conflict participants and perhaps even provide preliminary answers to many of the descriptive questions listed in this chapter (though this information should be verified with additional sources). Analyzing media coverage can allow researchers to re-create a public portrayal of the conservancy, siting, or exposure dispute. While hardly a perfect measure of community sentiment, local media can provide insights into the types of interpretive frames and symbolic imagery circulating through the community.

A summary of the basic descriptive questions covered in this section is provided in Box 1.2. Readers will find exercises which illustrate some of the potential uses of these questions at the end of the chapter.

Siting Disputes

Convent is a small, historically black community located in Louisiana's St. James Parish.[32] In the early 1990s, the Japanese corporation Shintech proposed to build the world's largest polyvinyl chloride (PVC) plant in Convent. Backers argued that the $700 million plant would bring needed economic development to the area, including the creation of approximately 165 new jobs for local residents. One of the staunchest and most powerful of Shintech's supporters was Louisiana Governor Mike Foster. Opposition to the project soon mounted, however.

Convent is located along the 90-mile stretch of the Mississippi River that lies between New Orleans and Baton Rouge. Variously known as "the industrial corridor" and "cancer alley," this region houses almost 25% of the nation's chemical manufacturing capacity. St. James Parish, already host to a number of hazardous facilities, was ranked the 11th most toxic "endangered place" in the United States by the National Trust for Historic Preservation. Convent was ranked as one of the most polluted communities in the world.[33]

Opponents argued that the PVC plant would increase the pollution burden already borne by local residents. According to their calculations, Shintech would release 600,000 pounds of toxic chemicals per year into the air of St. James Parish. Close to 3,000 people lived within a 3-mile radius

---

Box 1.2   Adding to the Portfolio: Conflict Participants and Their Claims

---

1. What are the specific individuals, groups, and organizations involved in the conflict? Under what types of broader participant categories can these individuals, groups, and organizations be subsumed?

2. Which conflict participants are local (community insiders), which are extra-local (outsiders), and which span the local/extra-local divide?

3. What are the specific agendas of the different conflict participants? What possibilities do these agendas raise for alliances and opposition?

4. What are the specific claims made by each of the conflict participants? What are the more general themes or frames reflected in these claims?

5. How are conflict participants and their claims portrayed in local or other pertinent news media?

---

of the proposed plant site; 800 children attended school within that same area. In addition to the potential health threats of chronic exposure to pollution from the plant, narrow streets would make evacuating these people in the event of a major leak or other emergency at the plant difficult, if not impossible.

Convent is a unique American town. It was started as a village of freemen shortly after slavery was abolished in 1863. Since the early 1980s, the U.S. environmental justice movement has sought to raise awareness of the disproportionate siting of hazardous facilities in poor communities and in communities of people of color. These siting practices are increasingly viewed as yet another form of discrimination, another way in which poor people, and peoples of color, are forced to bear the costs of economic growth while at the same time receiving few of its benefits.

To oppose the plant, some Convent residents joined forces with the Louisiana Environmental Action Network (LEAN, an umbrella organization for the state's grassroots environmental organizations) and the Tulane Environmental Law Clinic. The law clinic offered court challenges to Shintech. A particularly novel strategy used Title VI of the Civil Rights Act and President Clinton's Executive Order 12,898 to charge that the siting decision constituted an illegal form of racial discrimination. The air emissions permit issued by the Louisiana Department of Environmental Quality was subsequently revoked by the EPA. In the end, Shintech gave up on the St. James site, choosing instead to build a smaller PVC facility in the town of Plaquemines, just to the east of Baton Rouge.[34]

Developing a Time Line

In this section we continue our focus on basic descriptive questions, this time examining the chronological development of the controversy. Our concern here is with process; the questions presented in this section will help readers set the conflict in motion. We accomplish this through the development of a time line.

Time lines require a beginning point, generally a particular event which precipitated the conflict. Such events stand at the precipice of change, marking a transition between relative quiescence to contentious fighting. The community, in other words, looks different prior to the precipitating event than it looks after the event. Sociologist Ed Walsh captures what is unique about these events in his phrase "suddenly imposed grievance."[35] Something about the local context will change, introducing threats to cherished values and ways of life, disrupting a community or neighborhood setting that residents had previously found an acceptable, perhaps even desirable, place to live.

As in the Shintech case, the precipitating event in siting disputes is generally the announcement of plans to construct some type of new, and at least by some residents unwanted, facility in the area. Exposure disputes may be precipitated by the discovery, and public announcement, of toxic chemicals in a community's drinking water. The U.S. Fish and Wildlife Service listing a species as endangered may precipitate a conservancy dispute. While it is often clear what event precipitates a local conflict, there are times when making such a designation can be tricky, a theme we explore in greater depth in Chapter 2. Sometimes, for example, activity may be going on at a site for quite a while before anyone mobilizes to oppose it.[36] There are also cases where what initially appears to be a novel conflict turns out, on closer examination, to be the latest cycle in a larger, long-running battle.[37]

Conflict ensues because the precipitating event evokes a reaction; individuals and organizations feel threatened and seek to ameliorate or remove the threat through political action. Time lines, therefore, need to record the entry of various participants in the fray, as well as any exits or shifts in alliances. The formation of new groups specifically in reaction to the conflict (such as grassroots environmental organizations) also needs to be noted. We can go back to the language of suddenly imposed grievances to understand why such mobilization might occur in response to a precipitating event. Residents were not mobilized prior to the species listing, siting announcement, or discovery of toxic chemicals in their drinking water because they were reasonably happy with their circumstances. Grassroots groups are a pervasive feature of local environmental conflicts, and when they form are likely to be major players in the unfolding drama.[38] Indeed, grassroots activists and grassroots organizations are so important to local environmental conflicts that the battles between these groups and their opponents are frequently the central focus of sociological investigations. In this book we want to encourage readers to expand their horizons, to situate these conflicts within a broader community context. Even this broader focus, however, still requires extensive knowledge about the activities and concerns of grassroots organizations.

Grassroots activists and other conflict participants engage in various types of strategies (or oppositional activities) to advance their agendas. These strategies can range from lawsuits to public demonstrations. Setting the conflict in motion requires an appreciation of the action-reaction dynamics of controversy: oppositional activity evokes responses from other conflict participants, in turn creating a changed context that may require shifts in strategy. Chapter 6 provides a more focused analysis of this conflict dynamic. For now, we simply want readers to note the need to include a descriptive account of strategic interplay in their chronology of conflict development.

This same set of observations extend to government agencies and officials. Still, we want to stress the importance of documenting key government actions in any conflict time line. The government is being singled out here not because it is considered a more neutral player than other conflict participants but because of its specific, often central, role in local environmental disputes. Many key battles play out in the arenas of government: in regulatory agencies, in legislatures, in courts. The fate of many siting, exposure, and conservancy disputes lie in the hands of government decision makers: whether a permit will be granted, a species listed, a particular cleanup option pursued, a lawsuit allowed to go forward, disaster monies made available, public hearings held, fines levied, or epidemiological studies conducted. To understand any local environmental conflict, it is imperative to know the actions of key governmental players at all levels found in the conflict (community, county, state, federal) and the statutes that both dictate and constrain their behavior. It is equally important to understand the reactions government actions evoke in other conflict participants, a topic we pursue in some depth in Chapter 3.

The final step of creating a time line is to designate an end point for analysis. Ideally, this end point would be the resolution to the precipitating event which sparked the controversy in the first place. As happened in the community of Convent, the end may happen when a siting proposal is defeated. Alternatively, the factory, hydroelectric dam, landfill, or whatever may be successfully built in spite of local protests, providing a different type of ending to the conflict. An exposure dispute may end with removal of the hazard from the local area, or it may end by relocating people away from the hazard. A conservancy dispute may end when one side or the other exhausts its options for appealing an authoritative governmental decision.

Not all conflicts are marked by such clear resolution points, however. Indeed, designating an end to a conflict is an artifice, a way of bracketing an ongoing stream of community life for special consideration. It is worth remembering that where a researcher chooses to end a story is rarely where the story ends for the community.[39] The outcomes of local environmental conflicts may have repercussions, both positive and negative, for years to come. They may strengthen the bonds of communal ties, creating new alliances and feelings of empowerment which are used to tackle other local problems,[40] or they may factionalize and splinter local social ties, creating fault lines of animosity and resentment which divide residents for years to come.[41] Outcomes may undermine the viability of the local economy or result in local hazards which pose threats for decades. Endings may prove particularly elusive in exposure disputes involving radioactive materials and toxic chemicals, since it is almost impossible to completely remove these materials from the environment.[42] Determining when a conflict "ends" may also be made difficult by long-term emotional and psychological problems, such as depression and posttraumatic stress disorder.[43] Some conflicts become entrenched, and the struggles continue for years or decades, becoming "intractable conflicts."[44]

Box 1.3 lists the key questions that will assist in the construction of a time line. Because local environmental conflicts are often quite complex, it can be useful to summarize the highlights of time lines in tabular form. An

---

Box 1.3   Adding to the Portfolio: Developing a Time Line

1. What event precipitated the conflict?

2. When do various participants enter the conflict, and are any of these participants new groups formed specifically in response to the precipitating event and/or the conflict? What is the timing of any exits from the controversy or shifts in alliances?

3. What is the timing of the major strategies nongovernmental conflicts participants use to influence the course and outcome of the controversy? What reactions do these strategies evoke?

4. What is the timing of the major governmental actions undertaken at the local, state, and/or federal level? How do other conflict participants respond to these actions?

5. What event ends the conflict? If there is no clear ending, what event is chosen as the end point of analysis?

example is provided in Table 1.1, which lists the key events in an exposure controversy which occurred in the small town of St. Louis, Michigan. A more detailed discussion of this case is presented in Chapter 2.

Table 1.1   Example of a Time Line: Major Highlights of the Toxic
             Disaster in St. Louis, Michigan

Date	Event
1973	Michigan Chemical/Velsicol's St. Louis, Michigan, factory mistakenly ships between 500 and 2,000 pounds of the fire retardant PBB to a Michigan Farm Bureau feed mill, where it is mixed into feed for dairy cows. By the time the adulteration is discovered, the contamination has spread throughout much of the Michigan human food chain.
1974	The Michigan government finally acknowledges the contamination. The St. Louis plant is identified as a likely source of the contamination, and an investigation is begun.
August 1976	Michigan Chemical/Velsicol signs a consent agreement with the state DNR (Department of Natural Resources) to close its St. Louis plant by September 1978.
March 1977	U.S. EPA discloses that 80 tons of PBB contaminated wastes are buried in the Gratiot County landfill.
Fall 1977	St. Louis officials aid Michigan Chemical/Velsicol in its attempt to keep the chemical plant open.
December 1977	Gratiot County landfill is closed.
Spring 1978	Possible employee takeover of the chemical plant is pursued. This plan fails to materialize due to the failure of the DNR and Michigan Chemical/Velsicol to reach an agreement over liability for area contamination.
Fall 1978	Michigan Chemical/Velsicol plant closes. Michigan Departments of Commerce and Labor conduct studies on the economic impact of the plant closing. A task force with extensive local involvement is formed to aid former plant workers.
November 1978	Former plant workers sue Michigan Chemical/Velsicol.

(Continued)

Table 1.1   (Continued)

Date	Event
December 1978	Gratiot County Development Inc. receives an $8,000 state grant for use in targeting properties suitable for economic development to aid county recovery from the plant closing.
March 1979	Greater Gratiot Development Inc. receives a $640,000 federal grant for redevelopment efforts.
November 1979	U.S. congressional hearing (Water Resources Subcommittee of the House Public Works and Transportation Committee) held in Gratiot County.
June 1980	A series of weekly meetings between St. Louis and the Michigan Departments of Public Health and Natural Resources are held to determine an "official plan of action" to address contamination. As an outcome of these meetings, St. Louis officials initiate citywide testing of soil samples to determine the extent of area contamination. This study is conducted by the Michigan Departments of Agriculture, Health, and Natural Resources.
Fall 1980	A request for an "emergency declaration" for Gratiot County due to PBB contamination is sent to President Carter. This request is rejected twice (an appeal is sent after the first refusal) by the Federal Emergency Management Agency on the grounds that Gratiot County is experiencing economic hardship, not a toxic emergency.
November 1980	St. Louis receives a $2 million Economic Development Administration grant for redevelopment efforts.
June 1981	The state of Michigan names the Gratiot County landfill as its number one priority for receipt of EPA "Superfund" monies.
June 1981	The Michigan Chemical plant is demolished after having been declared structurally unsound by the state DNR.
Fall 1981	St. Louis and Velsicol officials negotiate cleanup arrangements on several smaller contaminated sites in the area.
November 1982	The state of Michigan reaches a $38.5 million settlement with Velsicol for cleanup and containment of contaminated sites in Gratiot County.

SOURCE: Adapted from Aronoff and Gunter (1992a), p. 352. Copyright 1992 by The Society for the Study of Social Problems.

Exposure Disputes

In 1962 a fire started in a seam of anthracite deep beneath the earth's surface on the outskirts of a small town in northeast Pennsylvania.[45] Mine fires are nothing new to the American landscape. At any one time there are typically 150 to 200 fires burning throughout the United States. What was troubling about this particular fire was its potential to burn underneath the town of Centralia, posing severe risks to health and safety. From 1962 to 1982 the federal government spent more than $5 million to extinguish or at least abate the fire. The underground blaze marched on.

In spite of its inexorable advance toward the village, the fire wrought little visible damage over the years. But it posed a subtler kind of menace. In 1969, for example, carbon monoxide gas forced three families to evacuate their homes; seven years later more of the same gas, in a concentration 20 times that of the lethal human exposure, was found pouring from a borehole 27 feet from the doorstep of another house in town. In 1980 the federal government purchased seven houses considered unsafe, and other property sales followed in short order. Increasingly, residents showed up in physicians' offices with headaches, nausea, or respiratory discomforts. Then, on Saint Valentine's Day 1981, a 12-year-old boy walked into his grandmother's backyard and almost dropped off the face of the earth. The earth, apparently weakened by the fire, simply opened up underneath him. As he dropped down, he grabbed an exposed tree root and hung on desperately until a friend pulled him out. He was lucky. The subsidence that opened in his grandmother's yard was over 100 feet deep.

In response to the near tragedy, several Centralians, mostly young parents, formed a community action group to press for more drastic government action against the fire. One might assume that townspeople rallied round their call for a solution to the fire; but quite to the contrary, the militant organization, which drew substantial media attention, touched off rancorous community discord. Many residents dismissed the group as a mob of hysterics and blamed its members for the plague of reports that descended on the town. Public meetings became forums in which residents lashed out bitterly not only at perceived government indifference but also at one another. Anonymous telephone threats, slashed tires, and a fire bombing brought this once peaceful village to the brink of social chaos.

A principal source of the local enmity was the ecological features of the fire itself. Underground, it could not be seen; its poison carbon-based gases were invisible to the senses. Many health and environmental impact studies reached opposing conclusions, with some claiming minimal and others maximal damage. Finally, the geographic configuration of the town ensured that residents living on the south end would experience the fire directly, while those living on the north end could continue their way of life as if very little had changed. Like a Rorschach card, the underground mine fire was sufficiently ambiguous to invite multiple and conflicting interpretations. Indeed, in a mere 5 years, seven grassroots groups formed in response to this conflagration, each representing an opposing view of its scope and degree of danger.[46] This conflict eventually ended through relocation of local residents.

A Focus on Context

Conflict draws and holds our attention. It is dramatic, touches on deeply held moral convictions, generates victims and villains, and motivates deep-seated desires to right wrongs and ameliorate harms. It is the presence of conflict which draws social scientific attention to places like Centralia, and in recognition of that fact, our first two sets of descriptive questions are designed to highlight the key features of local controversies. This final set of portfolio questions is designed to invite students to embrace a cognate goal of this book: a more Catholic or expansive consideration of the community context within which conflict occurs.

Information about local context contributes to both descriptive and analytic endeavors. Attention to context aids description by providing richness and depth, helping readers visualize a place they have never been. Contextual factors can also play an important role in explaining conflict dynamics. This analytic task is the more challenging of the two, and one that we wait to develop in the following chapters.

A good contextual starting place is to capture the character of the local area where the conflict is occurring. Is it a large urban area of several million people? A small city of several hundred thousand? A suburban residential area? A small town of several thousand? A rural area? Does the town lay claim to a unique history or other distinguishing feature, as we saw in the case of Convent, Louisiana, reported earlier in the chapter? If local people had to describe their community to outsiders in a few sentences, what would they say?

Another important contextual factor is the demographic profile of the area. Are most residents working class, or upper middle class? Is the local population predominantly white? Black? Hispanic? Indian? Vietnamese? Some local areas are highly diverse, with a mix of different social classes, racial/ethnic groups, and family types. Other communities (including specific neighborhoods within urban settings) are quite homogeneous. What is the average level of education among the local people? What about the age distribution; are there a lot of elderly people in the community, or perhaps young families with small children? Has there been any substantial population movement (in- or out-migration) in recent decades? Is the community shrinking because young people are leaving due to lack of local opportunities? Alternatively, has a new group of people, demographically distinct from older residents, moved into the area? Basic demographic factors such as these not only provide a sense of who lives in local areas; they also give clues about possible fault lines along which conflict may develop.

Students of local environmental conflicts also need to have a good sense of the economic base of communities of interest. Who are the major employers in the town? Specific companies or firms which are major employers in a local area, such as the Pacific Lumber Company in Scotia, California, need to be identified. Is the local area highly dependent on one type of economic activity, such as mining, agriculture, manufacturing, or tourism? Alternatively, is the local economy highly diversified? What has been the track record of economic performance over the last several decades? Has it held steady, experienced growth, or been plagued by a recession? What are the current rates of unemployment and underemployment? Both the demographic makeup and economic viability of local areas can affect how residents perceive the fairness of various decision outcomes, a point we develop in more depth in Chapter 5.

Another important contextual element pertains to the key features of the local landscape. Alternatively we could ask, What is the visual appearance of the local area? Is the housing stock well maintained or run down? Is retail space located in strip malls or in quaint downtown areas? Does industrial or extractive infrastructure loom large on the horizon? What are the basic topographic features of the local landscape? What rivers and streams run through the area? What types of outdoor recreational spaces are available? What features of the local landscape present risks or hazards to the local people? What aspects of the local environment are aesthetically pleasing? In Chapter 7 we provide some guidelines for using landscape features in explanatory accounts of the local environmental conflict.

One final contextual feature bears mentioning: the key points of contact between local residents and relevant aspects of their surrounding environment. It is not the mundane forms of contact where the environment serves as mere backdrop to action that concerns us, but rather the circumstances and moments where the environment moves to the foreground as an integral part of the action. Anyone engaged in chopping down trees, hunting, fishing, or trying to figure out why the water smells and tastes funny is interacting with the environment in a very direct and purposeful way. It is these points of engaged contact which are likely to generate local knowledge about environmental conditions, and which may become the source of contending interpretations between community residents and outside experts. We address this issue in some depth in Chapter 4.

Questions which will aid students' endeavors to describe the community context of local environmental conflicts are provided in Box 1.4. As with all the portfolio boxes, this list is not exhaustive, though it does cover the basics. Still, the framework we provide in this book is designed to provide flexibility in the face of the unexpected, which means investigative forays into terrain not covered by these questions may at times be warranted.

Box 1.4   Adding to the Portfolio: A Focus on Context

1. What type of community characterization best fits the local area where the conflict is occurring?
2. What is the demographic profile of the area?
3. What type of characterizations best fit the local economy?
4. What are the key features of the local landscape?
5. What are the key points of human-environment contact?

Summary

Each of the three cases presented above represents in turn a conservancy, siting, and exposure dispute, and each one is driven by the logic of the forced option. People living in Scotia, California, could only sit passively by as anonymous junk bond traders trafficked with their futures. But they responded, indeed felt they must respond, to the efforts of "outside agitators" to save the trees that meant jobs and futures for them. Residents of Convent, Louisiana, were compelled to respond to the plans of a Japanese company to build the world's biggest PVC plant in their backyard. If they did nothing, the plant would be built. Similarly, many residents of Centralia, Pennsylvania, could not ignore the underground mine fire; they felt obliged to act. Those who did try to ignore the fire quickly found they could not ignore their activist neighbors. It is in these ways that environmental conflicts are often perceived as Manichean battles between right and wrong, good and evil, justice and injustice.

Framed in these terms, community residents are less likely to choose environmental strife and more likely to feel that the conflicts choose them. Once joined, however, local environmental controversies quickly become a cacophonous chorus of claims and counterclaims.

This book is a short, concise inquiry into the community dynamics of environmental conflicts, with particular attention to how and why these controversies are variously interpreted by local groups and associations, regulatory agencies, the media, politicians, and others with a stake in their outcomes. Its purpose is to help students think more carefully and critically about local environmental conflicts by proposing a strategy and set of key terms for understanding and, perhaps, investigating them. The portfolio approach distills the key questions, providing a set of conceptual tools for exploring local environmental controversies. Beginning with basic descriptive information about the conflict and about the local area in which the conflict occurs, subsequent chapters treat readers to considerably more analytic endeavors.

The Book as a Map

This book is a resource for students of communities and environmental conflicts. The discussions to follow delineate key dynamics or forces *which may* influence the origin, nature, processes, and outcomes of a particular conflict. Following are five chapters, each of which discusses in some detail a dynamic source of environmental conflict, providing case material throughout as illustrations. In the order of their appearance, these sources are *presence of the past, trust and betrayal, problems of uncertain knowledge, perceptions of fairness*, and *oppositional activity and social capital*. The goal of these chapters is to help readers develop richer, more complex understandings of conservancy, siting, and exposure disputes by following an inductive logic which moves from description to analysis. A final, concluding chapter takes this task one step further, by encouraging readers to analyze conflicts from the vantage point of the symbolic realist perspective. Below we present a brief summary of each of these chapters.

Chapter 2: The Presence of the Past

Local environmental conflicts do not occur in a social and historical vacuum. Local people always have some type of long-standing relationship with the environment they inhabit. This relationship may be one of relative indifference and neglect, but it may also be one characterized by extensive enjoyment of aesthetic vistas provided by the local landscape and/or by use of locally available environmental resources. In some cases these landscapes and resources are linked with long-standing community traditions and collective identity; to threaten the integrity of the local environment is to threaten the heart and soul of the people who inhabit that environment.

The past manages to make itself felt in other ways as well. Communities are patterns of social relationships, styles, manners, and so on, some of them long-standing. There are local norms for expressions of solidarity and conflict, traditions of group formation and collective action, common understandings of who is in and outside of the community. By no means do these norms, traditions, and understandings determine a community's response to crises, but they do fashion and guide both thought and action. In addition, sometimes conflict participants invent new histories in the heat of conflict which offer new interpretations of past events or make salient aspects of the past previously neglected or ignored. Such inventions are undertaken for strategic reasons: to mobilize support and justify particular courses of action. We introduce a historical dimension to the study of local environmental conflicts not to advocate historicism but rather to cultivate an appreciation for the indisputable presence of the past in personal and collective life.

Chapter 3: Trust and Betrayal

Local environmental conflicts bring community residents into extensive and protracted interaction with such powerful social organizations as corporations and government regulatory agencies, sometimes as adversaries and sometimes, at least initially, as potential sources of assistance. Residents may discover through this contact that the organizations do not behave as they expected: rather than move swiftly to protect residents from harm, they instead engage in evasiveness and foot dragging, appearing more concerned with protecting taxpayers' dollars, company profits, and the local economy than residents' welfare. Examples of such betrayals of trust are legion in environmental disputes. A U.S. Department of Public Health report concludes that several stillbirths in a small town do not constitute a statistical cluster linked to airborne contaminants from nearby factories, but are more likely the results of poor hygiene and lifestyle choices of pregnant women. A petroleum company claims it successfully cleaned up a catastrophic oil spill in pristine fishing waters, but local communities are advised to avoid eating the fish from these waters, and commercial markets won't buy them. The federal EPA claims it successfully cleaned up a hazardous waste site adjacent to a neighborhood, but residents continue to experience trouble breathing and children break out in rashes after playing in their backyards. The EPA suggests the complaints might be "psychosomatic." Faced with this kind of organizational bias against acknowledging the legitimacy of their troubles, residents are likely to define powerful institutional actors as, at the very least, unconcerned, if not downright hostile.

The sociological challenge is to unravel the complex array of factors that give rise to ostensibly craven actions. We argue for the need to take account of both the intentions of the powerful social actors engaged in troubling behavior as well as the perception of that behavior by local residents and other conflict participants. We reserve the term *premeditated betrayal* to cover those cases where powerful social actors are intentionally being duplicitous and misleading. We use conflict theory and political economy to illustrate how the impetus toward self-serving, deceitful, and miscreant acts are deeply embedded in existing social arrangements. At the same time, accusations of betrayal can occur in the absence of any intentionality. Indeed, government personnel may be branded as unresponsive or malfeasant even in situations where they are trying hard to be helpful. We refer to this as "structural betrayal" and use organizational theory to explain why bureaucracies, which are poorly equipped to deal with novel or unusual circumstances as well as interrelated community problems, may respond to environmental conflicts and crises in ineffectual ways, which are read by local residents as intentional betrayal. We also introduce the concept of "equivocal betrayal," which we apply to situations where the intentions of powerful social actors are difficult to empirically document and are equally amenable to organizational and politically motivated explanations.

Chapter 4: The Problem of Uncertain Knowledge

Disputes about knowledge are a perennial feature of local environmental conflicts. These disputes revolve around the ambiguity of these events. One source of ambiguity is the simple problem of trying to predict the future. Consider the case of siting disputes. In this case, projections or extrapolations must be made about the likely consequences of activities. How much of a danger will the facility pose to the local community? Will there be accidents, such as fires, explosions, or releases of gases? How many new jobs will the facility create? The future as-yet-to-be-decided nature of these questions ensures conjecture, opposing science, and endless debate.

Disputes over contested knowledge shape up along both vertical and horizontal dimensions. The vertical dimension pits local residents against credentialed experts. Epidemiologists, toxicologists, hydrologists, wildlife biologists, and a host of other trained scientists are permanent fixtures of local environmental conflicts. They are located in a wide array of organizational settings, including government agencies, private industry, environmental organizations, and universities. In the past, scientists were granted considerable authority to make declarative statements about the empirical world, but increasingly both the knowledge generated by scientists as well as their privileged position are being challenged by ordinary citizens who believe they too know things of value about the world. Indeed, local residents who have lived in a community for years may feel like they are more authoritative experts on local environmental conditions than trained scientists who breeze in for 2 weeks' worth of research.

The horizontal dimension, in contrast, is one which pits local residents against each other. Residents can have fierce disagreements about such things as whether or not chemical contaminants are in their drinking water and, if so, whether or not these pose any health risks. Shared perceptions about the safety of one's immediate environment may be a prerequisite for civil communal life; when a group in a community starts to question that apparent safety, they may be greeted with hostility and acrimony by other residents who do not share their concerns and who do not appreciate having their own feelings of security threatened.[47]

Chapter 5: Perceptions of Fairness

Fairness and its many allied terms, *impartiality, justness, equality*, and the list goes on, is much easier to talk about than actually achieve. But fairness is never far from people's minds and hearts in environmental controversies. At its most basic, fairness issues address the distribution of costs and benefits from environmental decision making. Who gets (or loses) jobs? Who gets the pollution? Who has to bear the burden of increased noise and traffic? Which property owners take a financial hit because a noxious facility is located in their neighborhood or because government efforts to preserve wetlands have rendered it impossible to pursue the most profitable uses of their land? Fairness forms central themes in such disparate forms of collective action as the environmental justice movement and the sagebrush rebellion. Claims about fairness are often not limited just to the outcomes of particular conflicts but linked to broader historic patterns of injustice.

What counts as a fair distribution of costs and benefits? To make this issue even more complex, sometimes it is not even clear what counts as a "cost" and as a "benefit." Fairness cannot be discussed apart from the values that inform the judgments about these issues. Indeed, fairness is a fundamentally contested issue because values themselves are contested. Value disputes and perceptions of unfairness often elicit surprisingly strong emotions. Sometimes, such emotions are intentionally inflamed as part of an oppositional mobilizing strategy.

Chapter 6: Oppositional Activity and Social Capital

By oppositional activity we mean the variety of ways residents combine into local groups, organize protests, use the media to carry their messages, establish ties with regional or national organizations, and engage in similar activities to voice their objections and agendas regarding contested local issues. Through oppositional activity, grassroots activists network with allies and contend with enemies. These activities have tremendous implications for social capital, that fund of goodwill which facilitates communal life.[48] In Chapter 6 we explore the ways oppositional activity both intentionally and unintentionally builds and erodes social capital.

Students of social capital draw a distinction between bonding and bridging capital.[49] Bonding capital operates on a local, horizontal plane, drawing together neighbors and residents. Bridging capital, in contrast, links local residents and external groups. There are many permutations of the ways in which oppositional activity might build and erode bonding and bridging capital; we address three. These include the simultaneous building of both bridging and bonding capital, the building of bonding capital in the absence of bridging capital, and the simultaneous building and eroding of bonding capital.

Chapter 7: Social Facts and Brute Facts: Confounding the Social and the Physical

There is a kind of third estate in environmental sociology. It is comprised of social scientists who think that the examination of social life need not preclude inquiry into organic and material conditions, resources, and constraints. Members of this third estate include those sociologists who study the body as a powerful presence in social and cultural affairs.[50] Also included among this group are a number of environmental sociologists who acknowledge the importance of the physical and organic to the study of people and biospheres.[51]

In this chapter, students are introduced to a style of inquiry that begins with the assumption that the physical and organic environment exists outside our languages and senses. Unlike a more conventional sociological topic, say, the family, the environment has a hard and obdurate reality—quite independent of us. It will not go away simply because we stop acting toward it or thinking about it. But the meanings of environment, what we think and feel about it, is dependent upon language or, more broadly, culture. In short, environment (unlike family) exists both outside and inside of human actions and meanings. Return to the two quotations that start this chapter. Read them again. What Catton and Bell are describing is the point of departure for this final chapter.

The term *symbolic realism* will assist us to make some sense of this dual nature of nature.[52] However much societies have tinkered with and changed nature, it nevertheless continues to be a brute presence in our lives, a thing outside of society and culture, a physical-organic world with its own rhythms, cycles, disasters, and other mutations. In short, it is *real,* it exists, whether or not we know it. But always modifying that realism is our capacity (indeed our compulsion) to symbol. The environment is always symbolic; in other words, insofar as how we act and what we know about this brute presence is dependent on our particular social and cultural practices. The following passage applies the idea of symbolic realism to a sociology of environmental hazards and disasters:

> [We are attempting here to] join environmental sociology's assumption that biospheres and social structures are interdependent with a key assumption of symbolic interaction that people act on the basis of the meanings they attribute to events and conditions. From this perspective, social responses to hazards and disasters are affected by both the nature of the disruption in human/ environmental relations and the appraisals people make of those disruptions.[53]

In this final chapter we fashion a way of looking at local environmental controversies from the vantage point of symbolic realism. It is arguably the most demanding chapter but one that will, hopefully, kindle your imaginations by suggesting new and provocative research questions.

A Concluding Word

One goal of this book is to get readers started on an investigative journey. In line with the metaphor of a journey, readers will frequently encounter our use of the imagery of "lenses" in the chapters to follow. Just as novice hikers will "see" much more along the Appalachian Trail if they go equipped with a guidebook, binoculars, a magnifying glass, and infrared night goggles, so the conceptual lenses we present in this book are meant to draw attention to facets and complexities of local environment conflicts easy to overlook by students new to their study.

Just like medical doctors need in-depth knowledge of the endocrine system, the cardiovascular system, and the central nervous system (among others) before they can begin to make diagnoses of disease in particular individuals, so social scientists and others need in-depth knowledge of the possible lay of the land before they can begin to analyze local conflicts. In our estimation, initial presentation of this material is best accomplished through an in-depth discussion of each key force or dynamics taken, to the maximum extent feasible, in isolation from the other factors. This conceptual separation is an artificial one, however. As we touch upon in the last chapter, what matters in terms of understanding the origin, nature, dynamics, and outcomes of any local environmental conflict is the particular mix of dynamic factors present and how these interact with each other over time.

STUDENT EXERCISES

1. Using one of the three cases of local environmental conflicts presented in this chapter, answer as many questions as you can from Boxes 1.2, 1.3, and 1.4. What additional information would one need to know to adequately answer all of the questions presented in these three boxes?

2. Create a hypothetical conservancy dispute over efforts to preserve habitat for the lesser three-toed red-eyed lizard by making up defensible answers to the questions listed in Box 1.2. In what ways, if any, do you think the answers to these questions might have been different if you had done a siting or exposure dispute instead?

3. Follow a local dispute in the local broadcast news and/or local paper for a week (this does not have to be an environmental conflict). At the end of that week, create a time line for the conflict, using the questions presented in Box 1.3.

4. Using the questions presented in Box 1.4, describe the context of a rural area, town, suburb, or urban area you lived in at some point in your life. In what ways do you think knowing these contextual elements would help you explain any environmental conflict which might develop there?

5. Provide three to five examples of ways in which communities are affected by technological, political, economic, and/or cultural developments which originate beyond their borders.

Notes

1. Catton (1980), 104.
2. Bell (2004), 2.
3. We want to emphasize that we are talking about textbooks here, because there is an extensive history of research on communities and their environments in rural sociology and disaster studies. For one example, see Barton (1969). Bell also

pursued an in-depth examination of environments and communities in his 1994 book on Childerly, England.

4. For example, see Gould (1994); Hannigan (1995); Harper (2003); Frey (2001).

5. A more extensive discussion of this case is provided in Chapter 3.

6. Fowlkes and Miller (1982).

7. James (1956), 68.

8. Giddens (2000).

9. Beck (1999).

10. McKibben (1999), 18.

11. Olson and Cameron (1995), 20.

12. Stanley (1989).

13. Glanz (2002), A14.

14. McKibben (1999).

15. Giddens (1991).

16. Giddens (2000), 45.

17. Carmean (2002); Copps (1995).

18. Shirley (1994); Gobster and Hull (2000); Lowry (2003); Tidwell (2003). This final book is primarily about the loss of wetlands in coastal Louisiana, but it does provide a brief discussion of restoration efforts and the tremendous challenges confronting those efforts.

19. Picou, Gill, and Cohen (1997).

20. Glaser and Strauss (1967).

21. Fine (2004).

22. Of necessity, the vignettes we present in this book do not present the complete richness of these cases, many of which would require a book-length treatment to do full justice. Rather, we have highlighted particular portions of the cases as a means of illustrating analytic themes of interest to us. We encourage readers to spend time examining the original sources from which our vignettes are drawn or to spend time exploring the Web or other relevant resource material if they are interested in seeing "what eventually happened" in particular cases.

23. Case material from Harris (1996).

24. Harris (1996), 19.

25. Harris (1996).

26. The descriptive questions outlined in this section are derived from the social constructionist approach to social problems. For a general introduction to this approach, see Best (1995) and Loseke (2003). For a specific application to environmental conflicts (though not local conflicts), see Hannigan (1995).

27. Gottlieb (2001).

28. Bryan and Wondolleck (2003).

29. Dizard (1999).

30. Loseke (2003).

31. Wheeler (1998), 180–181.

32. Case material from Roberts and Toffolon-Weiss (2001).

33. Roberts and Toffolon-Weiss (2001).

34. Ibid.

35. Walsh (1988); Walsh and Warland (1983).

36. Beamish (2002).

37. Espeland (1998); Walton (1992).

38. Cable and Cable (1995).

39. The same can be said of beginnings, a topic we pursue in some depth in Chapter 2.

40. Allen (2003).

41. Kroll-Smith and Couch (1990).

42. Couch and Kroll-Smith (1985).

43. Picou, Marshall, and Gill (2004); Picou and Gill (1998).

44. Lewicki, Gray, and Elliott (2003).

45. Case material from Kroll-Smith and Couch (1990).

46. Kroll-Smith and Couch (1990).

47. Kroll-Smith (1995).

48. Putnam (2000).

49. Ibid.

50. Bourdieu (1979); Kroll-Smith and Floyd (1997).

51. Catton (1982); Couch and Kroll-Smith (1997); Kroll-Smith, Gunter, and Laska (2001); Irwin (2001).

52. Kroll-Smith, Gunter, and Laska (2001).

53. Couch and Kroll-Smith (1994), 28.

2

The Presence of the Past

*[Every environmental] disaster is . . . a unique private tragedy,
inflicting its own special wounds, its own peculiar species of
pain; and in order to understand fully what an event like this
means to the people who survived it, one needs to know something about who they were and where they came from, how they
organized their lives and what they asked of the future. . . . [W]e
need to locate the people . . . in the larger sweep of history and
on the wider social and cultural map.*

Kai Erikson[1]

Local environmental conflicts always occur someplace, in a rural township, village, suburb, or perhaps a city. Places like these are always
freighted with a past. Whatever is going on at the moment, in other words,
is not independent of a local history. "It is the past," Kroll-Smith and Couch
remark, "that shapes the patterns in which a community responds to crises,
the resources available for response, and the culture that interprets the crises
and channels reactions."[2] The salience of history, it appears, is proportion-
ate to the gravity of the moment. A clinical analogy is appropriate here.
Psychotherapists frequently comment on the significance of a particular
family's history in interpreting how parents and siblings respond to a contemporary crisis. While a rural township or suburb is not a family, like a
family it is made up of people, most of whom have a shared past, if only, as
in the case of some suburbs, a history of casual acquaintances. Similarly to

a family in crisis whose particular history provides a framework for response, a local environmental conflict is likely to be defined and acted toward, in part, through the peculiar history of that locale. History, in short, loads the dice in favor of a particular pattern of social and cultural responses to collective stress.

History, of course, is a complicated idea. It appears all-inclusive. To know the history of something is to know "all there is to know" about it, to grasp it inclusively, in its totality. From this vantage point, the idea of history is daunting indeed. Students of environmental conflicts are right to ask us, "Hey, do you mean I have to know the whole history of this village or town to make sense of the environmental conflict I intend to examine?" Well, yes, but not from the totalizing perspective of an inclusive history.

We propose, rather, to narrow the big idea of history to three more focused and, hopefully, more useful conceptions of the past. In this chapter we explore the utility of the past in the study of contemporary environmental conflicts by considering *history as tradition, history as harbinger,* and last, *history as invention.* These variants of history, of course, are not all-inclusive. Other variants could (and should) be considered. But they do assist us in accounting for the significance of the past in conservancy, siting, and exposure disputes. Consider each idea briefly.

Tradition is derived from the Latin term *tradere,* which means to transmit or to pass on something important or useful to another person for safekeeping.[3] Traditions are always properties of communities or other collectivities and play an important role in defining group identity and maintaining group cohesion. In this chapter we examine how the past enters the present in the form of traditions intricately linked to particular locations and/or particular environmental resources. This approach to history is relevant in cases where groups oppose actions which threaten access to, and/or continued integrity of, these places and resources. Since these conflicts may go to the very heart of group survival, they have the potential to become very poignant and bitter affairs.

A *harbinger* was originally a person, one who heralds or announces what is to come. Over time the word was separated from the person and came to mean foreshadowing or presaging. History as harbinger suggests how what preceded the present prefigures, or anticipates, or shapes it. *Harbinger* is a particularly apt word for our purposes because it alludes to the probable or likely role of history in interpreting the present, while eschewing the more deterministic, almost fatalistic, assumption that the past must be relived. This assumption, more properly called historicism, turns a blind eye to the serendipitous, contingent, protean character of life in the present. History as harbinger focuses on the intersection between the past and the varying, mutating circumstances of the present.

Finally, we intend by the word *invention* a particular version of the past crafted for a specific purpose. This purpose might be to guide or legitimate a present course of action or to interpret or evaluate existing circumstances. Here, the past makes itself felt in the present through intentional and deliberate acts; we can observe the process of history being actively *worked up* and *worked on* by conflict participants. Invented histories, we will argue, burnish competing claims to authenticity and truthfulness, rooting them in the sanctity of the past. We are interested in how local people and groups contrive a history to persuade others that their particular version of the landscape, toxic risk, or endangered species is corroborated by the past.

Think of these three versions of history in ocular terms, as lenses for seeing the varied ways the present is joined to the past. Each lens refracts the light of the past at a particular angle to the present, allowing us to see the complicated role of history in contemporary environmental controversies. Not surprisingly, these three versions of history are often discernible in the same community or neighborhood struggling with environmental controversy. Examples of the ways in which these three approaches to history connect with material presented in Chapter 1 is provided in Box 2.1.

Box 2.1   Making Connections With Previous Chapters

In Chapter 2 we begin to make the transition from description to analysis. As discussed in Chapter 1, the descriptive time line of a conservancy, siting, or exposure dispute begins with some event that precipitates the conflict (see Box 1.3). When we turn our attention to explaining *why* the conflict happened where and when and how it did, it is often useful to extend our focus back beyond the start of a particular conflict. To understand what is going on in the present, we need to delve for clues in the local area's past.

Examining history as tradition allows us to build on the material presented in Chapter 1. In Box 1.2, we instructed students to sort conflict participants out as to whether they were local or extra-local in origin. By examining the role of tradition in local environmental conflicts, readers will get a better sense of why this distinction matters. The demise of traditional practices of immense value to local people will likely be of no concern to outsiders. Indeed, extra-local individuals and organizations are likely to be ignorant of these practices, as well as their importance to the lives and identities of community residents.

The section on the harbinger role of history allows us to further pursue the importance of the distinction between "locals" and "outsiders," as well as develop analytic insights into the importance of local context. What we explicate here is that the contextual factors identified in Box 1.4 should not be taken as given but rather understood as the result of long-standing historical processes, including complex relationships between the local area and extra-local technological, economic, political, and cultural developments. Finally, "history as invention" illustrates one way in which conflict participants may create new claims and frames in the heat of battle, through the use of novel interpretations of the past (see Box 1.2).

History as Tradition

The Yavapai and the Orme Dam

For three days in September 1981, in temperatures which sometimes reached as high as 110 degrees, nearly 100 members of the Yavapai tribe walked along a busy stretch of highway leading from their reservation home at Fort McDowell, Arizona, to the state capitol in Phoenix.[4] Included among the marchers making the 32-mile trek were frail and arthritic elders and youngsters pulled in wagons. "Those who were too sick or weak to march drove alongside in cars and pickup trucks, offering support and water to the marchers."[5] A protest rally was held once the marchers reached the state capitol. At the rally, tribal leaders presented a handwritten bark scroll to one of the governor's top aides. This scroll recorded the Yavapai's opposition to long-standing plans to construct what would be called the Orme Dam at the confluence of the Salt and Verde Rivers; the resulting reservoir would inundate much of the Fort McDowell Reservation. Tribal members chose to present their views on a bark scroll "to make it hard for bureaucrats to file away and forget."[6] While the march through the desert and the political rally were particularly dramatic forms of protest, they had been preceded by over a decade's worth of organized resistance by the tribe, environmentalists, and other allies.

Orme Dam was proposed as part of the Central Arizona Project (CAP), a massive water management program authorized by the U.S. Congress in 1968. The main purpose of CAP was to bring Colorado River water to the Phoenix area. The original proposal was ambitious: seven new dams, the enlargement of one existing dam, nearly 400 miles of aqueducts, four new pumping stations, and a series of smaller canals. Among the seven new dams was the Orme, which had been on the drawing board since the 1940s. This dam would provide a reservoir for water taken from the Colorado, as well as offer flood protection for the Phoenix area.[7]

The CAP was itself part of a broader history of massive hydrological restructuring of the American West. Euro-American settlement of this arid region required access to quantities of water far greater than nature provided. Urban development in Los Angeles, Las Vegas, and Phoenix, ranch and farm growth, and suburban sprawl required the desert to, literally, bloom. Powerful interests supported these projects. In the case of Orme Dam, these interests included the Federal Bureau of Reclamation, farmers and ranchers, important area businesses such as copper mines and major utilities, business leaders, municipal governments, leading state newspapers, and "nearly every politician ever elected to anything in Arizona."[8]

Opposing the construction of Orme Dam was the tiny Yavapai tribe, about 400 members of whom resided at Fort McDowell at the height of the controversy, and their allies.

The fact that the reservoir created by Orme Dam would destroy most of the Fort McDowell Reservation was not viewed as sufficiently important to mention in the first two official reports on the project written in 1947 and 1963 respectively. Nor was it mentioned in the first Environmental Impact Statement written in 1972. Nor were the Yavapai themselves kept well informed of the project's developments or its full implications for their land. When organized resistance developed, government officials and supporters of the dam naively thought it was simply a ploy to drive up the price of the land. It was an assumption that made perfect sense, given the cultural perspective of the dam's supporters. The relationship of most Americans to their homes is at least as much instrumental as sentimental. By this we mean home ownership is looked upon as a financial investment; we expect that over time our houses will appreciate in value. We generally do not have qualms about buying and selling property and indeed consider ourselves either lucky or savvy when we are able to turn a profit in such transactions.

To outsiders the Yavapai seemed to be in special need of such a cash influx. The tribe suffered from both high unemployment and chronic poverty. From the perspective of the dam's supporters, the Yavapai should have welcomed the government's buyout and relocation money as a chance to be more financially secure and perhaps start afresh. That the Yavapai would seek to secure the highest dollar amount possible for their land made sense to the dam supporters; that is rational behavior in a capitalist economy. That the Yavapai would oppose a government buyout regardless of the compensation offered was beyond imagining.

The dam supporters failed to appreciate the true depth of the Yavapai's opposition because they were unable to perceive the Yavapai as having any interests and motives other than their own. To understand the Yavapai, we must look not to capitalist markets but to history. We need to know how the past reverberates in the Yavapais' relation to their land.

Prior to the arrival of Euro-American settlers, the Yavapai occupied a large section of present-day western and central Arizona. The Fort McDowell Reservation constitutes 0.03% of this traditional homeland.[9] As is common among Native American tribes, cultural identity is intimately linked to particular places. "Land is central to how the Yavapai understand themselves. . . . They believe that their capacity to be Yavapai depends on their having a relationship with *this* land, the same land that sustained their ancestors."[10] "Land is their bridge to the ancestors who came before and descendants who will come after."[11] This linkage with the past occurs through traditional religious ceremonies conducted at sacred sites and shrines. There is more than just a symbolic dimension involved here; the land also records and retains the past. In some cases, such as the tribal cemetery at Fort McDowell, the land literally contains the past. Interred in this cemetery are the remains of the victims of the Bloody Salt River Massacre of 1873 and tribal members killed in the major wars of the 20th century (World War I, World War II, Korean, and Vietnam). The building of Orme Dam would have presented two options for the cemetery—either inundating it or relocating it—both of which the Yavapai considered sacrilege.

The Yavapais' opposition to the Orme Dam hardly constitutes their first struggle against efforts to remove them from their land. Indeed, such struggles have been ongoing since white settlers first arrived in the region. In the 1860s, the federal government built several forts in the central part of what would become the state of Arizona and undertook a concerted effort to force the Native American tribes in the area onto reservations. The Yavapai resisted and tried to live away from the reservations. Facing starvation and barely surviving the Bloody Salt River Massacre by federal troops, the bedraggled group finally agreed to relocate to the San Carlos Reservation, located 200 miles away. The Fort McDowell Reservation was created by an executive order of President Theodore Roosevelt in 1903. By the early 20th century most of the Yavapai had returned to that small part of their traditional homelands now made available to them, either to Fort McDowell or a smaller reservation at Camp Verde.

The returning tribal members had to contend with white farmers who sought to homestead their land while denying them access to the area's limited water supplies. Shortly after returning home, representatives of the Bureau of Indian Affairs (BIA) recommended that the Yavapai be relocated to the Salt River Reservation. Salt River was already home to the Pima and Maricopa tribes, traditional enemies of the Yavapai. Government officials tried numerous tactics to get the tribe to relocate, including refusing aid and condemning the dams and ditches needed for irrigation. Despite the fact that Roosevelt's executive order creating the Fort McDowell Reservation promised the tribe would never again be forced to leave their land, "[s]ince the reservation was established in 1903, there has virtually never been a time when some group was not trying to take their land or use their water."[12]

The resistance of the Yavapai to Orme Dam can only be understood against the backdrop of this broader struggle. This resistance paid off in 1986, when the federal government abandoned plans for the Orme Dam in favor of an alternative water control project. For some people what the Yavapai accomplished was nothing short of miraculous. A small tribe of

Native Americans and their allies defended their land against powerful western water interests. Examining the battle from the long sweep of history, however, suggests that maybe we should not be so surprised by this outcome. "In threatening their land, Orme Dam threatened them, and its loss represented cultural extinction. In trying to derive a price for their land the bureau [of reclamation] was, in effect, creating a market for their cultural 'selves.'"[13]

❖

"Tradition refers to customs and ceremonials by means of which the past speaks to the present."[14] Traditions allow us to transcend the brevity of our individual lives, connecting personal triumphs and tribulations with a broader story that began before our birth, and will continue after our death.[15] Due to their transcendent nature, traditions reinforce membership in social groups, reminding us of the identities we share with others. The importance of tradition in the life of one Inuit man is shown in the following quotation.

> When I go whaling . . . there's a lot of things that go through my mind, not about the world today, but about the world where we were before, where my ancestors were coming from. Yeah, you can almost hear echoes [from the past] when you are whaling.[16]

As this quotation illustrates, customs and ceremonials may implicate environmental resources in centrally constitutive ways. When traditions are integrally melded with particular locations and/or particular utilizations of the natural world, we can speak of places and resources as being *tradition bound*. Once a pervasive feature of human societies, modernization has severely eroded the people-place nexus. Secularization, rationalization, geographic mobility, the integration into national (and increasingly international) markets, rapid social change, high levels of individualism, and a youth-obsessed culture—all of these have served to undermine traditional society, as well as sever our connections to local environments. (For a more focused discussion of one of these trends, see Box 2.2.) This is not to argue that modern societies are completely devoid of tradition-bound resources and places, a point we will return to shortly. It is just that the articulation of tradition-bound resources and places is most strongly expressed, and most clearly demonstrated, in premodern societies with strong ties to particular locales. Consider the case of the Navajo.

Box 2.2   Globalization

In at least one respect, the reality of globalization stands in marked contrast to the troubling predictions of George Orwell. Orwell wrote about a future society organized around a immutable center of authority that reaches deep into our psyches, shaping our thoughts and feelings. Reflect a moment on today's world, and the Orwellian idea of Big Brother is not likely to come to mind. Far from one cardinal point of authority controlling our lives, there are, it seems, a plethora of points each vying for our attention, loyalty, resources, and so on. The idea of globalization is often used to help us make sense of this extraordinary fragmentation of social and cultural life. Take the idea of space, for example. At one time, not too long ago, we could locate ourselves and others in a relatively fixed piece of geography. Space or territory mattered in terms of knowing ourselves and others. Today, however—in a global world—space is far less salient as a predictor of who we are or what we might become. Nor does it limit the number and kinds of people we can meet and come to know. With digital communication, the world is no longer bound by geography; we can roam (at least virtually) everywhere on earth—right from our couch.

But globalization is more than connectivity and the absence of centralized control; it is also a harbinger of risks. As global travel and trade become normal economic practices, our personal lives, our health, our life chances are increasingly tied to events, trends, and circumstances in far-flung places whose names we might not even be able to pronounce. As we write, authorities in the eastern Chinese province of Anhui reported an outbreak of avian influenza at a poultry farm in Chaohu City. Several dozens of birds were recently shipped from this farm to a poultry distribution center in the Netherlands. Risk is no longer a local matter; it is now a global concern.

Suggested in this example is the evocative idea that in a global world, national boundaries and national identities become increasingly eclipsed by international and multinational business arrangements, organizations, and corporations. In 1984, 40 tons of methyl isocyanate leaked from a plant in Bhopal, India. The plant was co-owned by a consortium of Indian investors and Union Carbide, a U.S.-based corporation. More than 15,000 people died and close to 200,000 were injured. The accident was, in part, the result of poorly designed equipment owned by the U.S. corporation.

Globalization is changing each of us; it is changing our societies, our politics, our cultures, and our environments. Far from subsiding, its effects are accelerating. Recall the recent and compelling evidence of global environmental change.

NOTE: For a good overview of the sociological implications of globalization, see Beck (1999).

For the Navajo, life is special within the space created by the Four Sacred Mountains. These mountains are known today as Blanca Peak, Mt. Taylor, the San Francisco Peaks, and Hesperus Peak. The First Man and Woman created the four sacred mountains with soil brought from the lower worlds into the current earth's surface world. Many medicine men carry soil from these four mountains in their medicine bundles. These mountains serve as the principal source of Navajo strength, and prosperity. . . . Only within the space created by these mountains—the symbolic Navajo homeland—can curing rituals work.[17]

Tradition-bound places and resources often hold not just value for local people but what Espeland has referred to as incommensurable value.[18] By this, Espeland means there is *nothing* that can serve as a substitute or replacement for these resources and places. The Yavapai of central Arizona expressed the incommensurable value of their land to a negotiator trying to secure it for a dam and reservoir site, by asking, "[H]ow much would he charge for his children, or whether he would be willing to accept a 'similar' child in exchange for his own."[19] Places and resources are especially likely to hold incommensurable value when they are connected with the sacred or are in other ways central to the cultural identity of local peoples. Among the Inuit, whales relate to both of these dimensions.

> Whaling does not only provide food. There is a wealth of tradition. . . . The whale festival is well known, which among the Naukan Yup'iit [Siberian Inuit] lasts about a month. Very much in the spiritual life of our people is determined by whaling. . . . Without whaling, there is no Yup'iit.[20]

The connection between threats to group identity and conflict intensity and intractability has been recently elaborated by Gray.[21] While her focus is not on the relation between identity and traditional places and resources, her general observations are still quite pertinent. "Conflict almost inevitably arises when people's identities are threatened. . . . Identity challenges call into question the legitimacy of how a group has defined itself and even its very right to exist."[22] We would predict, furthermore, that conflict that develops over threats to tradition-bound places and resources will be especially fierce if the group is already engaged in what it perceives to be a rearguard fight for its very survival. While groups do not willingly relinquish places and resources that hold incommensurable value, the actual or potential loss of such places and resources is even more tragic when it is among the last of a rapidly diminishing supply.

The contamination of Prince William Sound, Alaska, by an Exxon oil tanker allows an empirical encapsulation of the points raised thus far. In addition to a thriving commercial fishing industry, the waters of Prince William Sound and the surrounding shore land also supported subsistence hunting and fishing activities of Native Alaskans living in the area, activities which comprised important cultural traditions and which were considered central to tribal welfare.

It is during the cycle of subsistence that bonding is strengthened and expanded. The sense of worth is solidified and new skills are learned. It is during the bonding times that our individual value is placed within our community, as we are able to understand what we must do to preserve our lives and to live in harmony.[23]

These traditional subsistence practices were threatened on March 24, 1989, when the supertanker *Exxon Valdez* hit an outcropping of rock and leaked 11 million gallons of heavy crude oil into the fecund waters of Prince William Sound.[24] Chief Walter Meganack, of Port Graham, Alaska, captures the event:

The excitement of the season had just begun, and then, we heard the news, oil on the water, lots of oil killing lots of water. It is too shocking to understand. Never in the millennium of our tradition have we thought it possible for the water to die, but it is true.[25]

Thousands of marine mammals and hundreds of thousands of seabirds died as a result of the spill.[26] Because crude oil is toxic to humans, areas of the sound where fish, shellfish, and marine mammals were contaminated were closed to extractive activities. Ecosystem damage resulting from the spill has slowed or prevented long-term population recovery for some species. Two species important to Native Americans' subsistence activities, harbor seals and Pacific herring, have not recovered. A third species important to the Alaskan Natives in the area, the pink salmon, has shown signs of recovery, but has not returned to prespill levels.[27] The following indicators demonstrate the impact of this spill on traditional subsistence hunting and fishing activities in one Alaskan Native community: "The village of Tatitlek harvested 644 pounds of wild resources per capita in 1988 and saw harvests decline to 258 pounds in 1989 and 153 pounds in 1990."[28] The following two quotations by Alaskan Natives illustrate, first, the incommensurable value of subsistence resources, and second, the importance of these tradition-bound resources for maintaining one of the few links with the past left to Alaskan Natives.

I still hunger for clams, shrimp, crab, octopus, and gumboots. Nothing in this world will replace them. To be finally living in my ancestors' area and be able to teach my kids, but now it is all gone. We still try, but you can't replace them.[29]

When we worry about losing our subsistence way of life, we worry about losing our identity. . . . It's that spirit that makes you who you are, makes you think the way you do and act the way you do and how you perceive the world and relate to the land. Ninety-five percent of our cultural tradition now is subsistence. . . . [I]t's what we have left of our tradition.[30]

While tradition-bound places and resources are far more common in preindustrial societies, they do exist in industrial and postindustrial societies. Preservation disputes are often waged in the language of tradition. "Preserving the countryside," for example, "can . . . be motivated by a desire to maintain the continuity with previous generations, to preserve a particular way of life, and a particular sense of collective identity."[31] The mountain folk of Appalachia or the Cajuns of southern Louisiana have unique cultural heritages reflected in language, food, stories, and song, some of which are linked to or dependent on tradition-bound places and resources (such as the harvesting of wild ginseng in southern Appalachia).[32]

By bringing to bear questions about tradition-bound places and resources, we have created a lens which brings into clear focus aspects of local environmental conflicts which otherwise remain half hidden or invisible. A brief summary of the key questions students need to ask when considering the role of history as tradition is provided in Box 2.3. We now turn to another consideration of the way in which the past makes itself felt in contemporary conflicts: the harbinger role of history.

Box 2.3   Adding to the Portfolio: History as Tradition

1. Are there traditional cultural practices (customs, ceremonials) linked to specific local places and/or particular locally available resources?

2. In what ways will actual or proposed environmental actions threaten the integrity of and/or access to tradition-bound places and resources?

3. To what extent do tradition-bound places and resources hold incommensurable value for local peoples?

4. Is the present conflict the latest effort in a long-standing struggle by local peoples to preserve tradition-bound places and resources?

5. Are the threatened places and resources among the last remnants of the local environment still available for traditional uses?

History as Harbinger

Owens Valley

Located 240 miles east-northeast of Los Angeles, cradled between the White and Sierra Nevada Mountains just north of the Mojave Desert, Owens Valley might at first glance appear an unlikely site for what has become known as "California's Little Civil War."[33] The label "war" is, however, an accurate description of the battles that occurred here during the 1920s, battles which included not only traditional protest activities such as forming citizens' committees, circulating petitions, and writing letters to public officials but also notable violence as well. Sabotage—destruction of property—was a lively pastime in the valley during those turbulent years, with dynamite the weapon of choice.

Like the Orme Dam case, Owens Valley was a water war. The basic components of the conflict are simple enough. Owens Valley had water in abundance, a situation unusual for Southern California. By the early 20th century the City of Los Angeles had set its sights on that water. In subsequent years the city would become notorious for its rapacious thirst for water. Aggressive, ruthless, Los Angeles pursued water as if its very survival depended on it; and indeed it did. It was in the Owens Valley case, however, that the city acted in a most deplorable manner.

Following the development of plans to construct an aqueduct from the valley to Los Angeles, the city used a variety of tactics to secure the valley's water. These included buying up land, water rights, and ditch companies, filing lawsuits, and obtaining the backing of the federal government. Not all the city's tactics were aboveboard. Valley residents mobilized, fighting the city with both legal and illegal means. Examples of the latter are portrayed in Table 2.1. Despite their efforts, valley residents were unable to stop a powerful adversary like Los Angeles. "By the end of 1926, Los Angeles controlled 90 percent of the Valley's land and water."[34] Defeated, the resistance movement had largely petered out by the late 1920s.

The small communities of the valley fell on hard times during the 1930s but eventually did revive, built on a new economic base of tourism, a few large cattle ranches, and an extensive federal presence. Yet Los Angeles' expropriation of the valley's water left significant long-term costs. "The Owens Valley was an early victim of environmental degradation, the elimination of farms and natural waters destroyed vegetation, deprived wildlife, and converted large portions of Owens Lake into a dust bowl."[35]

California's Little Civil War might have remained an isolated incident had the City of Los Angeles not begun planning a second aqueduct (or barrel) from the region in 1959. The Department of Water and Power (DPW) initially estimated a groundwater pumping rate in the valley of 89 cubic feet per second to meet the needs of this second barrel, a modest enough withdrawal that the construction of the pipeline between 1963 and 1970 met with little resistance from valley residents. Estimates of the quantity of water needed crept upward, however. When the second barrel came online in 1970, Los Angeles was actually pumping out groundwater at a rate slightly double the original estimate.[36] The environmental impact of this

Table 2.1   Incidents of Sabotage Against the Los Angeles Water Works in
Owens Valley, California, 1924–1931 and 1975–1984

Date and Source	Location	Description of Report	Source
May 21, 1924	Alabama Gates	Concrete wall of aqueduct rent by large explosion	*Inyo Independent*
April 4, 1926	Bishop Ranch	City of Los Angeles well-feeding aqueduct destroyed by dynamite	*Inyo Independent*
May 21, 1926	Alabama Gates	Ten-foot hole blasted in concrete aqueduct wall at site of May 1924 explosion	*Inyo Independent*
May 26, 1927	No Name Siphon	Large-diameter iron pipe carrying aqueduct water destroyed near Little Lake in most costly blast	*Inyo Independent*
May 27, 1927	Big Pine	Intake to City of Los Angeles power plant destroyed	*Inyo Independent*
June 5, 1927	Cottonwood Creek	Concrete aqueduct wall damaged 12 miles below Lone Pine	*Inyo Independent*
June 19, 1927	Turtle Creek	Sixteen-foot hole dynamited in aqueduct 2 miles below Lone Pine	*Inyo Independent*
June 25, 1927	Alabama Hills	Bomb exploded on hillside in attempt to block aqueduct with landslide	*Inyo Independent*

(Continued)

Table 2.1   (Continued)

Date and Source	Location	Description of Report	Source
July 16, 1927	Alabama Hills	Fourteen feet of aqueduct wall damaged at site of June 25, 1927, attack	*Inyo Independent*
July 16, 1927	Tebo Gates	Control gates and 40-foot length of aqueduct destroyed	*Inyo Independent*
Nov. 7, 1931	Grapevine Canyon	Ten-foot section of aqueduct blown out where pipeline forms a siphon	*Inyo Independent*
May 8, 1975	Owens River north	Locks and control devices broken on Bishop Department of Water and Power (DWP) control gate	*Inyo Independent*
Sept. 11, 1975	Not identified	Insulators on DWP electrical lines shot out, causing power failure	*Inyo Independent*
May 20, 1976	Near Diaz Lake	Aqueduct gate opened by blow torch to fill Diaz Lake for recreational use	*Inyo Independent*
Sept. 16, 1976	Alabama Gates	Alabama Gates spillway bombed	*Inyo Independent*
June 29, 1979	Between Big Pine and Independence	Shack and platform at DWP well fired	*Inyo County News-Letter*

Date and Source	Location	Description of Report	Source
June 29, 1979	Lone Pine	House, barns, and shop on DWP lease fired	*Inyo County News-Letter*
Nov. 15, 1979	Not identified	Two men in possession of explosives arrested for shooting out insulators on DWP high-voltage line	*Inyo Independent*
Mar. 13, 1980	Not identified	Bomb threat at DWP offices	*Inyo Independent*
July 30, 1981	Not identified	DWP skip loader parked near office destroyed by fire of suspicious origin	*Inyo Independent*
Aug. 8, 1984	Mono Lake	DWP power boat exploded in suspicious circumstances.	*Inyo Independent*

pumping became quickly visible. "As the water table went down, stately cottonwood trees began to die, spots of greenery shriveled, irrigated acreage shrank, and the dust thickened."[37]

In response to this new assault, a second wave of protest activity swept through the valley during the 1970s and the first half of the 1980s. This second round of protest took place within a changed national context that presented opportunities not available in the 1920s. Most notably, the recently passed National Environmental Policy Act (NEPA) and the California Environmental Quality Act (CEQA) created legal avenues for redress. This second protest movement took a decidedly environmental turn not present during the earlier movement.

Yet in many other respects the second wave of opposition drew upon the symbolic and tactical legacy of the Little Civil War. "The renewed protest mobilized in customary ways and defined its purpose in a language resonant with the lessons of experience."[38] This was not difficult to do, as the memory of mistreatment at the hands of outsiders—"the rape of Owens Valley"—was very much alive in the consciousness of local residents. "The 1920s protest movement and the subsequent urban domination became part of a living history."[39] Once this interpretive link to history was made, a path was cleared to employ the strategies and tactics of the past, which included more conventional activities, like forming citizens' committees and circulating petitions, but also a renewal of sabotage. A quick perusal of Table 2.1 demonstrates the way the past foreshadowed the present in this particular conflict.

In what ways, and for what reasons, may events that transpired in the past presage present response patterns? We want to be very careful to avoid any deterministic answer to this question; communities are never *doomed* to repeat the past. For this reason, the imagery we want to encourage readers to use is that of the cultural toolbox.[40] Our cultures provide us with a reservoir of resources that help us interpret our world and develop strategies of action.[41] The elements found in any group's cultural toolbox— beliefs, values, symbols, stories, myths, songs, folk wisdom, practical knowledge, technological know-how—accumulate over time and are in part shaped by past experiences. It is this set of cultural tools that a community will initially use to understand, and respond to, environmental conflicts and crises. One way to think about history as harbinger, then, is in terms of the following question: What went on in this community's past that resulted in an abundance, or an impoverishment, of cultural resources useful to meeting present challenges?

We illustrate the utility of this question through an exploration of three environmental controversies. In the small community of St. Louis, Michigan, an official investigation in the mid-1970s revealed severe contamination problems at the local chemical factory. The facility was shut down in 1978 and subsequently dismantled. Contamination problems also emerged at the county landfill located on the outskirts of the town, where tons of waste material from the chemical factory had been buried (for a time line of the conflict, see Table 1.1).[42] In the 1980s, in the small community of Centralia, Pennsylvania, an underground mine fire that had burned for several decades appeared to be moving toward the town, posing, at least for some residents, a substantial risk. Toxic gases vented from holes in the earth's crust. Subsidence, or sudden holes in the earth's surface, began to open in backyards and streets (see Chapter 1).[43] In Buffalo Creek, West Virginia, a makeshift dam located at the high end of a narrow Appalachian valley gave way just before 8:00 a.m., February 26, 1972, sending some 132 million gallons of water mixed with coal mining debris on a deadly and destructive path through the unsuspecting communities below. One hundred and twenty-five people died in the flood, and 4,000 of the valley's 5,000 inhabitants were left homeless.[44]

Each of these tragic events shares a number of important similarities. First, all of these disasters occurred in small towns, or, in the case of Buffalo Creek, a number of geographically close small towns. Both St. Louis and the Buffalo Creek valley had populations of approximately 5,000, while Centralia had a population of roughly 1,000. Second, these disasters are marked by hazard agents which posed physical threats to the towns' inhabitants. Third, they created economic hardships. Fourth, they threatened the future viability of these communities. Fifth, they placed tremendous stresses and strains on individuals and families. Sixth, all of these disasters ultimately stemmed from human activities and negligence.

In spite of these commonalities, each of these communities responded to their environmental catastrophe in markedly different ways. St. Louis officials joined with other leaders in the county to work for redress through governmental channels, seeking and eventually obtaining "financial and logistical assistance from a wide range of agencies."[45] No grassroots groups emerged in response to this contamination crisis. One state official told several sociologists investigating this disaster that the St. Louis case was "a pretty quiet affair."[46] In contrast, the considerably smaller community of Centralia, Pennsylvania (about one fifth the size of St. Louis), gave birth to no less than seven grassroots groups pushing for various resolutions to problems stemming from the underground mine fire. This community's response to a local environmental hazard was a factionalized, noisy affair. Despite the tremendous amounts of energy devoted to the problem, residents' efforts were largely ineffective. At Buffalo Creek, survivors of the disaster passively sat by while recovery and compensation efforts were spearheaded by outsiders. Like the St. Louis/Gratiot County case, the Buffalo Creek flood gave rise to no grassroots groups, no noisy protests. Like the Centralia case, the residents of Buffalo Creek seemed incapable of acting effectively on their own behalf. Apart from a lawsuit, which required minimal participation by survivors, the Buffalo Creek case is best classified as a "nonresponse."

What sorts of insights can we gain about these three very different kinds of responses by considering the harbinger role of history? How did the past equip officials and residents of St. Louis to respond to their local troubles? With an economy characterized by a mix of agriculture and industry, Gratiot County had its share of past experiences with such weather-related disasters as droughts, floods, and blizzards, as well as economic recession connected with the downturn in the state's auto industry and the closure of several mobile home factories.[47] These past challenges encouraged residents to see themselves as people who faced adversity head on. This does not mean that they relied solely on their own resources to redress local problems, but that they did not wait for others to solve these problems for them. They understood that no outsider was going to care about the local area in the way they did, and therefore they needed to take a proactive role in the recovery process, leading where possible, pushing and prodding others when needed. Local identity, in other words, was that of a resilient community capable of facing, and eventually overcoming, tough times.

Local leaders were accustomed to accessing whatever opportunities and resources were available to respond to local problems. With the emergence of the contamination crisis, leaders behaved as they typically did in a volatile moment: they worked through official channels to attain some technical and financial assistance from responsible parties. Past successes had also provided local officials with a sense of efficacy that their efforts would have some kind of tangible payoff. As part of their general pragmatism, officials and residents were also willing to compromise and "make do" with whatever assistance they were able to secure, rather than holding out for politically difficult solutions to their misery.

Centralia confronted a challenge any community would have found daunting. Tragically, the community's past had insinuated itself into the very fabric of local personal and political life, leaving the village without the kinds of resources needed to effectively cope with calamity. Its origins as a company town completely dependent upon the largess of coal barons figured prominently in shaping its response to the fire. While the legacy of this past is sometimes obvious, its influence also works in subtle ways and leaves its mark in unexpected places. We provide examples of all of these, beginning with the latter.

The settlement history of an area can shape long-term consequences for local residents. In Centralia the settlement patterns were tied to the boom-bust cycles common to extractive economies like coal mining and characterized by successive waves of in- and out-migration. To put it bluntly, people moved into the area in good times and left when times got hard. This substantial transient element meant the local population had far fewer people interested in putting down roots and working toward a vibrant local community than would otherwise have been the case. This situation was further compounded by the fact that successive waves of immigrants were made up of people from different ethnic backgrounds. Early settlers to the area included English, Welsh, and German Protestants; these were followed in the mid-19th century by Irish Catholics. Between roughly 1875 and 1925 immigrants were comprised of Catholics from Eastern and southern Europe. These groups could not be readily absorbed into the existing community. As a result, these successive waves of immigrants produced permanent fissures in the local social fabric.

During the 19th century the coal barons also worked to disempower local residents. They believed firmly that extraction of wealth required a passive, dependent workforce. Labor unrest was a particular source of concern. This reached a heightened flurry of activity during the 1860s and 1870s with the acts of arson and violence associated with the near mythical Molly Maguires. Strikes and other forms of protest and activism plagued the area for a good part of the 19th century. The coal barons responded by pressuring "the [state] government to allow the formation of a quasi-public police force."[48] Pennsylvania's "coal and iron police" existed from 1866 to as late as 1935. Hired and paid by the coal companies, the coal and iron police were granted the full powers of regular, state-sponsored forces. Usurping the town's capacity to determine its own affairs, this privately funded but publicly deployed police force enforced a rigid social control. "In Centralia what passed for legal violations and punishments of the rule breakers was dictated by authorities remote from the community, thus denying residents access to a major source of civic consciousness."[49]

With this brief social history in mind we can begin to see how and why the residents of this small village encountered the mine fire disaster with a poorly developed civil society. As if it consciously sought to challenge the commonsense view that small towns are tightly woven social fabrics, whatever passed for group affiliation in Centralia did not occur at the community level. At best, it was family, church, or ethnic group that represented meaningful social ties. Residents could not call on a collective memory of a unified, efficacious community from which they could draw inspiration and guidance. One ramification of this can be seen in the divisiveness that wracked public meetings, where participants spent their time reinforcing their own groups' beliefs and belittling and blaming others in the community who disagreed with them. Residents' lack of experience in civic involvement resulted in repeated instances where political actions produced the exact opposite of the outcomes intended. Centralians seemed incapable of undertaking effective actions even within the narrow confines of grassroots organizations, where they only had to deal with a small number of like-minded people. "Participants interrupted one another at [organization] meetings, which had no agendas; issues debated were left unresolved; [and] leadership was a shifting, competitive proposition."[50]

Kai Erikson's study of the Buffalo Creek flood illustrates yet another way in which the past presages the present. Erikson sought clues to the valley residents' passive and dependent response to the flood in the mountain ethos of the Euro-Americans who settled the region in the 19th century. Early mountain people eked out a living on small homesteads in remote mountain hollows. Reliance on the family was high, while more inclusive, community-based organizations were sparse and underdeveloped. Individuals were thus inordinately dependent on their families, making it difficult for them to develop strong, distinctive, autonomous identities. At the same time, social isolation and economic hardship encouraged a fatalistic outlook.

The next generation of mountain people shifted from subsistence farming to mining coal. Small coal camps gathered the disparate mountain people together into close geographic proximity and hence fostered the development of community, that is, social connections that extended beyond one's own family. Similar to Centralia, however, the coal camps greatly decreased the control people had over their own lives. A man worked for the coal company, lived in a house owned by the coal company located in a town built by the coal company, and shopped in the company store. Miners and their families soon became dependent on remote others for their everyday well-being. Dependence joined the capricious, danger-prone life of mining to amplify an already troubling culture of fatalism that worked to make misery unavoidable and, in the end, acceptable.

The elements of fatalism, passivity, dependency, and an underdeveloped civil society did not comprise the totality of the culture of mountain people in West Virginia. Indeed, prior to the flood, the percentage of residents in the valley on welfare was low, and people's sense of control over their lives and positive outlook toward the future were reflected in well-maintained homes, many of which had seen add-ons and other forms of renovations. But these elements were nevertheless buried deep in people's personal and collective lives, creating a predisposition—a cultural potential—to respond to calamity in a certain manner. Faced with catastrophe, old habits emerged and shaped human responses.

> When [the residents of] Buffalo Creek report that they no longer feel in charge of their own destinies, they are warning us of a turn back to the fatalism of the old Appalachian ethos. When they report an increasing concern with illness and compensation, they are warning us of a return to the world of dependency.[51]

This section illustrates how communities respond to present conflicts and crises armed with cultural habits often formed decades or more in the past. History, from this vantage point, is harbinger; it foretells without necessarily determining. As shown in Box 2.4, it points to questions which direct attention to the meaningful connections between past and present. Although a tricky maneuver, when done well, this can be a convincing argument.

Box 2.4   Adding to the Portfolio: History as Harbinger

1. What types of crises, calamities, challenges, and conflicts has the local community confronted in the past?

2. Does the cultural toolbox of local peoples include a living history of resistance against exploitation and injustice from which they can draw symbolic and strategic resources to use in a present conflict?

3. Does the cultural toolbox of local peoples include a history of resilient, proactive, and pragmatic response to crises?

4. Is the cultural toolbox of local peoples characterized by an impoverishment of past experiences with civic involvement and political action?

5. Does the cultural toolbox of local peoples include a history of dependence on outsiders to redress pressing community needs?

There is yet another way in which the past may influence contemporary conflicts. While the harbinger role of history may be subtle, with residents displaying little awareness of how past experiences shape their options and choices, "history as invention" is an active and intentional use of the past to persuade, cajole, and argue for a certain outcome.

History as Invention: Oil Spill at the Guadalupe Dunes

"Underneath the Guadalupe Dunes—a windswept piece of wilderness 170 miles north of Los Angeles and 250 miles south of San Francisco—sits the largest petroleum spill in U.S. history."[52] While estimates of the size of the spill vary, the figure most often quoted by government officials is that of 20 million gallons, a quantity almost double the amount of oil lost in the much better known 1989 *Exxon Valdez* disaster in Prince William Sound, Alaska.

The Guadalupe Dunes spill failed to capture media attention in the same way the *Exxon Valdez* calamity did, in part, because the California spill did not result from a single, dramatic event. Indeed, in some respects this oil did not spill so much as it leaked, slowly, over the course of almost four decades. It was the accumulated outcome of innumerable routine actions and unintentional releases that occurred at the Unocal pumping and storage facility.

Like the Owens Valley case, the spill underneath the Guadalupe Dunes was located in a region with a history of political activism. Residents of San Luis Obispo, the county home of the Unocal facility, were experienced in the politics of "siting controversies, industrial crises, and environmental disasters."[53] In spite of their "nascent distrust of industrial enterprises as well as the intentions of federal and state governments,"[54] local residents did not view the Unocal Corporation as a rapacious and unscrupulous outsider. Indeed, for over three decades the oil spill underneath the Guadalupe Dunes was a "nonissue." It was only in the mid-1980s that the spill finally reached a size and severity that its impacts became increasingly difficult to ignore. As the oil began to seep into public consciousness, the significance of the site as an environmental and health hazard emerged. But it would take another decade before "the spill provoke[d] a concerted effort on the part of activists to protest the dunes contamination."[55]

Years of local indifference toward the spill site created a particular problem for activists. Before they could convince a disinterested public to mobilize against the company and the oil, activists had to successfully promote a new interpretation of the facility as worthy of protest. To accomplish this reinterpretation, activists started to tell new stories about the past. Unocal was reinvented as a bad corporate neighbor, and the Guadalupe spill was placed within a broader pattern of environmentally degrading projects foisted upon the county by both public and private interests.

As part of the new past created for this case, "locals retrospectively ascribed to Unocal a 'history of negligence.'"[56] Past events previously ignored, if not largely forgotten, were suddenly imbued with new and ominous meanings. The local press, for example, ran stories about a fire that had occurred at a Unocal tank farm in 1926, a conflagration that consumed 128 million gallons of oil. While the immediate cause of the fire was a lightning strike, activists argued for another interpretation: Unocal had failed to install grounding wires at the tank farm. Another indicator of long-standing corporate negligence was the 1969 blowout of an offshore oil platform near Santa Barbara owned by the company that would become Unocal. Santa Barbara is located just 65 miles south of San Louis Obispo County. Pictures of oiled beaches, dead and dying birds, and the loss of aquatic life were widely disseminated in the national media. More recent problems were also singled out for public display. These include a 1992 spill of 6,000 gallons of crude oil into the ocean at Pirate's Cove and revelations of a "400,000 gallon petroleum plume floating on top of the groundwater"[57] under the community of Avila Beach.

Local activists thus created a new frame: "Unocal cannot be trusted." They supported the veracity of this frame by digging up past misdeeds of the corporation. Activists also connected the Guadalupe oil spill with an older frame: "Our communities are under threat from outsiders." This frame was bolstered by pointing to the untrustworthy nature of similar types of extra-local organizations also active in the area. In the 1970s the Abalone Alliance emerged to protest the construction of the Diablo Canyon nuclear power plant. By the early 1980s, activist efforts shifted to oppose a proposal by Reagan's Secretary of the Interior James Watt to sell leases off the southern coast of the county for oil exploration and extraction. Whether they were fighting against nuclear power or offshore oil development, county activists regarded it all as the same battle. By telling new stories of the past, local residents were able to see the spill in a new light, connecting it with "their larger struggle to ensure the health and well-being of their home."[58]

It is in situations where the telling of new stories about the past is an integral feature of local environmental conflicts that we want to employ the lens "history as invention." Our use of the term *invention* is not meant to discount these new stories as sheer fabrication (though in some cases they may be). Rather, this term is used to capture those instances where history becomes something that is consciously and purposively *worked up*. Consider the case of the 112-member Skull Valley Band of Goshute Indians, 25 members of which reside on a small reservation about 80 miles outside of Salt Lake City, Utah. The tribal chairman, Leon Bear, is seeking to lease reservation lands for storage of spent radioactive fuel from the nation's nuclear power plants. While this action would bring tens of millions of dollars into an impoverished tribe, it would also place at risk all of Utah's 2.3 million residents. Bear's efforts have thus been controversial, with opposition from some members of his own tribe. Bear, however, defends locating the storage facility on tribal lands not just with economic rationales but also by invoking Native American traditions.

> Beyond the money the tribe could gain, Bear says, the nuclear deal has an Indian spiritual rationale. "Much of the uranium was mined by Navajos on their reservation, and now it's returning to a reservation," he says. "It was

taken out of Mother Earth, and now it's looking for a place to rest. We're
stewards of the Earth, and who's better to take care of this than Native
Americans?"[59]

Note how a particular version of the past is creatively reworked and
offered as a moral appeal. Stewardship of radioactive waste hardly falls
within the traditional practice of this tribe. Nuclear power plants have only
been in existence for about a half century; they are a uniquely Anglo industry. Furthermore, waste from nuclear power plants is a product of human
activity, a substantial reworking of the uranium originally taken out of
Mother Earth. The linkage between nuclear waste storage and tribal traditions is not readily apparent. But by tinkering with history, Bear makes a
case for the tribe's capacity and responsibility for watching over nuclear
waste.

History is also invented when the past becomes the focus of active exploration, when groups or individuals examine archives (diaries, letters, bills of
sales, and similar documents), conduct oral histories, and undertake archae-
ological digs to determine what things really were like "back then" (when-
ever "back then" may happen to be). It is, of course, always possible to
discover new information about the past, because our existing knowledge
about the history of anything will inevitably be incomplete and selective. It
is in those situations where aspects of the past previously downplayed,
ignored, or even forgotten suddenly become the subject of intense scrutiny
that we can talk about history being invented and can examine the process
by which never before seen versions of yesteryear are crafted to meet
present-day needs and circumstances.

Understanding not only *how* but *why* history is invented in vitro in a
particular conflict requires identifying the opportunities a dispute provides
for making use of the past. For starters, we can expect history will be
actively *worked up* in those cases where the past is being used as a precedent to guide and legitimate present courses of action. The proposal for
locating a radioactive waste storage facility on the reservation of the Skull
Valley Band of Goshute Indians is one example where a present course of
action is being inventively linked with precedents set by past traditional
beliefs and practices.[60] In addition, new versions of the past may be crafted
as a resource to facilitate current mobilization efforts. This situation contrasts with the kind of harbinger scenario we saw in the Owens Valley case.
There, the memory of past events long perceived as unjust were already
present in the cultural toolbox of residents of the valley, a "living history"
available for use by later generations of protesters. Here, we are referring
to history invented in the course of a particular conflict, as was seen in the
case of the Guadalupe Dunes.

A conflict can also provide opportunities for inventing history in circumstances where local people perceive a need to identify, measure, and come to grips with loss. Conservancy, siting, and exposure disputes make people think about loss in new ways. Assumptions that people previously took for granted—that their drinking water was safe—may no longer hold. Aspects of their past existence that were once unremarkable may become singled out for special attention. People in a neighborhood may have never given much conscious thought to how much they enjoy seeing the ducks, egrets, and other waterbirds that reside in a nearby marshy area until someone proposes draining and developing it.

There can be therapeutic value to this process, as people work through a collective sense of loss. There can also be strategic value, either in terms of gaining compensation for loss that has already occurred or in terms of heading off proposed activity that would result in loss. At the same time, we need to recognize that people often romanticize the past and thus may come to believe they have lost something that in fact never really existed. In both the Owens Valley and Centralia cases discussed above, residents used the symbol of a lost, halcyon world characterized by social harmony and mutual support to motivate present protest activities. While environmental disruptions and hazards did produce intense conflict in both locations, it was hardly the case that either of these communities was a portrait of tranquility before their ecological miseries began. Indeed, the past of both these areas is marked by a great deal of internal divisiveness along ethnic, religious, and (especially in the case of Owens Valley) class lines.

Like all claims made in environmental conflicts, new stories about the past are open to scrutiny. Since histories are invented as a resource to advance some agenda—to influence particular courses of action, to facilitate protest efforts, to provide a yardstick for measuring loss—they have the potential to result in very real consequences. It is therefore not surprising that participants in a conflict would question the veracity of particular versions or interpretations of the past which threaten their interests.

For example, in situations where the past is used as a precedent for current courses of action, or to measure loss, the question of *where* in the past we look for guidance and comparison becomes paramount. Consider the case of ecological restoration (a type of conservancy dispute). The goal of such projects is to return particular ecosystems to a more "natural" state.[61] Does this mean prior to the arrival of European colonizers? Certainly the Europeans introduced many exotic plants and animals to this continent and in the process significantly altered a myriad of local ecosystems.[62] However, Native Americans were physically altering the landscape for millennia before the "white man" ever set foot on these shores. Intentional burns, for example, were used by many tribes to clear land for agriculture and to improve hunting.[63] How far back in the past must we go to achieve something that we all can agree is "more natural"?

This points to another complication: ecosystems change naturally over time. Old species die out; new species arrive and establish themselves. At what point does a new species, introduced into an ecosystem, cease to be an "exotic"? Consider the case of wild horses in the West. Horses are not native to the Americas; they were introduced in the West by European explorers and conquerors yet have now been established in this ecosystem for about six centuries. Should a restoration project here include, or exclude, wild horses?

History as invention thus presents many opportunities for disputes over knowledge, a topic we consider in Chapter 4. At this juncture, however, students should be persuaded that the past, however it might be construed, is often a significant factor in making sense of local environmental controversies. Examples of key questions that students of local environmental conflicts need to ask in cases which give rise to invented histories are listed in Box 2.5.

Box 2.5   Adding to the Portfolio: History as Invention

1. Are there new stories about the past being crafted in response to a conflict?

2. Does the nature of the conflict present opportunities to use history in a precedent-setting manner, that is, using the past to guide or legitimate present courses of action?

3. Is the past being used to identify, measure, and come to grips with loss? Does any romanticization of the past occur in conjunction with this process?

4. Are new stories being told about the past in order to facilitate mobilization and protest, for example, by inspiring or enraging local people?

5. Are invented histories the focus of dispute and contention?

A Concluding Word

In this chapter we have discussed ways in which the past makes its presence felt in contemporary environmental conflicts. From history as tradition, harbinger, or invention, the past is never far from real-time controversies. Our counsel: add the idea of history to your portfolio. Keep it at the forefront of your inquiries into local environmental disputes. Be prepared to see more than one of these variations of the past acting simultaneously to fashion a contemporary conflict. And most important, don't limit yourself to our threefold idea of history. Look closely; perhaps you'll see another.

One thing we know for sure: whatever variation of history is fashioning a local environmental dispute, it is working in tandem with several other cultural, social, and organizational dynamics. The activities of powerful extra-local organizations play a role in all of the local histories recounted in this chapter, often a prominent one. Sometimes this role takes the shape of outside exploiter and oppressor, as we saw in the Orme Dam and Owens Valley cases, and sometimes as celebrated provider of local employment opportunities, as we saw in the St. Louis, Michigan, case as well as in the Scotia, California, case presented in Chapter 1. Frequently, however, conservancy, siting, and exposure disputes alter the relationship between community residents and powerful outside organizations. These conflicts might, for example, bring residents into protracted contact with a government agency with whom they have not had previous dealings or alter their perceptions of the trustworthiness of a corporate owner of a local factory. All too often, these encounters leave residents feeling betrayed by the very organizations they thought would serve their interests and protect them from harm. We explore this problem of disenchantment and alienation in the next chapter.

STUDENT EXERCISES

1. Consider the case of a rural area, town, suburb, or urban neighborhood you have lived in at some point in your life. Are there any places and/or environmental resources in or near this community which are linked to traditional uses? Use the questions in Box 2.3 to speculate how local residents might respond to threats to those places or resources.

2. Once again, consider the case of a rural area, town, suburb, or urban neighborhood you have lived in at some point in your life. What has gone on in the past of this community that might shape any present responses to conservancy, siting, or exposure disputes? Use the questions presented in Box 2.4 to speculate about the harbinger role of history in this rural area, town, suburb, or urban neighborhood.

3. In Chapter 1, Box 1.4, we presented a list of contextual factors which might be used for both descriptive and analytic tasks. Reexamine this list in light of the discussion of the role of history presented in this chapter. What new insights have you developed about the ways in which context might help you develop explanatory accounts of why local environmental conflicts happened when and where and how they did?

4. In Chapter 1, we discussed "the end of nature" as a broad social change sculpting local environmental conflicts. Illustrate the applicability of this term to the two California cases presented in this chapter (Owens Valley and Guadalupe Dunes).

5. In this chapter, we used the Orme Dam case to illustrate the lens of history as tradition. What types of additional insights might be gained by using the material presented in the other two sections (History as Harbinger and History as Invention) to analyze this case?

Notes

1. Erikson (1976), 48.
2. Kroll-Smith and Couch (1990), 10.
3. Giddens (2000).
4. Case material from Espeland (1998).
5. Espeland (1998), 185.
6. Ibid.
7. Ibid., 99.
8. Ibid., 3.
9. Ibid., 215.
10. Ibid., 2; emphasis in original.
11. Ibid., 200.
12. Ibid., 199.
13. Ibid., 205.
14. Giddens (1994), 28.
15. Giddens (2000).
16. Johnny Mike, Inuit, quoted in Freeman et al. (1998), 19.
17. Carmean (2002), 59.
18. Espeland (1998).
19. Ibid., 208.
20. Tatyana Achigina, quoted in Freeman et al. (1998), 29.
21. Gray (2003).
22. Ibid., 21; see also Rothman (1997).
23. Alaska Native in the Prince William Sound community of Cordova, quoted in Ott (1994), 47; cited in Gill and Picou (1997), 173.
24. Picou, Gill, and Cohen (1997), 3.
25. Chief Walter Meganack, Port Graham (1989); cited in Gill and Picou (1997), 167.
26. Lord (1997).
27. Gill and Picou (1997).
28. Ibid., 176; see also Morrison (1993).

29. Chenega Bay resident, quoted in Fall, Stanek, and Utermohl (1995), iv; cited in Gill and Picou (1997), 179.

30. Alaska Native, quoted in Palinkas et al. (1993), 8; cited in Gill and Picou (1997), 173.

31. Barry (1999), 99–100.

32. Hufford (2002); for Cajun culture see Tidwell (2003).

33. Case material from Walton (1992).

34. Ibid., 189.

35. Ibid., 236.

36. Ibid., 244.

37. Ibid., 249.

38. Ibid., 242.

39. Ibid., 233.

40. Swidler (1986).

41. One important type of cultural resource is social capital, a concept we discuss in some depth in Chapter 6.

42. Aronoff and Gunter (1992a, 1992b); Gunter, Aronoff, and Joel (1999).

43. Kroll-Smith and Couch (1990).

44. Erikson (1976).

45. Gunter, Aronoff, and Joel (1999).

46. Ibid., 629.

47. Aronoff (1993); Michigan Agricultural Experiment Station (1988).

48. Kroll-Smith and Couch (1990), 19.

49. Ibid., 20.

50. Homrighaus, Couch, and Kroll-Smith (1985), 90.

51. Erikson (1976), 251.

52. Case material from Beamish (2002); quotation from pg. 1.

53. Beamish (2002), 111.

54. Ibid., 112.

55. Ibid., 111.

56. Ibid., 118.

57. Ibid., 118.

58. Ibid., 130.

59. Kasindorf (2002), 4A.

60. The dividing line between history as tradition and history as invention is a porous one, because ultimately all traditions are invented and may be reworked to meet present circumstances. Giddens (1994, 2000).

61. Gobster and Hull (2000).

62. Crosby (2003).

63. Vale (2002).

3

Trust and Betrayal

When Hurricane Katrina struck, it appears there was no one to tell President Bush the plain truth: that the state and local governments had been overwhelmed, that the Federal Emergency Management Agency (FEMA) was not up to the job and that the military, the only institution with the resources to cope, couldn't act without a declaration from the president overriding all other authority. . . . The government's response to Katrina . . . was a failure of imagination. On Tuesday, within 24 hours of the storm's arrival, Bush needed to be able to imagine the scenes of disorder and misery that would, two days later, shock him when he watched the evening news. He needed to be able to see that New Orleans would spin into violence and chaos very quickly if the U.S. government did not take charge—and, in effect, send in the cavalry. . . . The failure of the government's response to Hurricane Katrina worked like a power blackout. Problems cascaded and compounded: each mistake made the next mistake worse.

Evan Thomas[1]

In late August 2005 Hurricane Katrina blew ashore on the Mississippi-Louisiana Gulf Coast. The storm produced in its wake a second disaster as several breeches in the levee system that surrounds New Orleans allowed water from Lake Pontchartrain and the Industrial Canal to pour into the city. Tens of thousands of people were trapped by the floodwaters, over a thousand people lost their lives, and hundreds of thousands of people were left homeless, including one of the authors of this book. Heart-wrenching images filled our television screens of people stranded in the flooded city: infants and children, elderly, disabled individuals in wheel-chairs; people trapped on balconies and rooftops; thousands waiting for days in and around the New Orleans Convention Center without food, water, or adequate sanitation; thousands more at the Superdome under equally dire circumstances, waiting for buses to take them anywhere away from the ravaged city. People died in hospitals and nursing homes while waiting for rescue.

Within days of the disaster, the national news media were awash with criticisms of the federal government's response. For a number of days, it looked like the U.S. government was going to abandon tens of thousands of its citizens to a grim fate. Louisiana officials and African American leaders lambasted the tardy and ineffectual federal response. Reporters compared conditions in the flooded city to ones they had encountered in refugee camps in Somalia and Darfur. Ordinary people wondered why the U.S. government could get aid to victims of wars and disasters in distant countries but not to its own citizens. Why couldn't one of the richest countries in the world mobilize a speedy rescue of people trapped in such horrific conditions? Almost everyone, it seemed, agreed that the federal government, and in many cases state and city governments, had failed to do what needed to be done. One of the social consequences of this failure is reflected in the following comment made by a New Orleans college student to one of the authors of this book: "I will never trust the federal government again."

The New Orleans disaster captures on a large scale the downward spiral of disintegrating relations between residents and officials. A similar spiral is repeated on a much smaller scale in countless communities around the country. Government, it seems, often fails to respond to local environmen-tal controversies and catastrophes in the manner citizens expect. This obser-vation begs a more rudimentary question: What is it that residents expect from government in a time of acute or chronic stress? In a democratic system, it is reasonable for citizens to expect that government will provide assistance in times of collective crisis, protect the general welfare, be an impartial enforcer of the laws, and fairly arbitrate conflicts.[2] During routine, business-as-usual periods, most people's direct contact with government is limited to such mundane and circumscribed activities as voting, obtaining a driver's license, or filing for unemployment. In general, these occasions provide little opportunity to test expectations against reality. Conservancy, siting, and exposure disputes alter this routine pattern, bringing citizens into protracted and often volatile contact with government. Suddenly, ordinary citizens have the opportunity to observe government agencies and officials up close and in action, and all too often they do not like what they see.

Faced with a recalcitrant and worrisome environmental problem, people are likely to find government agencies unhelpful, perhaps hostile, or perhaps simply uninterested. Indeed, they might find—or perceive, as we argue below—that instead of protecting them from harm, government actions put them at greater risk. Instead of making decisions in a fair and impartial manner, public officials are apt to be viewed as siding with the wealthy and the politically connected. While our primary focus in this chapter is on government officials and oversight agencies, such feelings of disillusionment can extend to other powerful social actors, most notably corporations. Community residents, for example, may have long viewed a particular company as a "good corporate neighbor" until it is revealed that it has been engaging in illegal dumping of toxic wastes.[3]

It is time to clarify why we are qualifying the above statements with words like *perceive* and *viewed*. Powerful social actors respond to environmental controversies and crises in many ways that engender citizen frustration and anger. These run the gamut from lies and cover-ups to foot dragging, indecisiveness, and dodging responsibility. All of these responses may leave residents feeling like they have been betrayed. Disillusionment and loss of trust are apt to follow. Yet what we want to emphasize in this chapter is that governmental responses that are troubling to residents may or may not coincide with organizations' and officials' intention to be craven, treacherous, reckless, or unresponsive. Perception refers specifically to what citizens "see" and "hear" from the words and actions of organizational representatives. Intention, on the other hand, is akin to old ideas of "good faith" and "bad faith" and refers specifically to the aim or purpose of organizational actors.

Is it possible that officials could act in good faith yet still be accused of dereliction of duty and betrayal of residents' trust? Is it possible that powerful social actors with divergent intentions could respond to local environmental crises in remarkably similar ways? In the present chapter we turn to conflict and organizational theories to help us explain why the answer to both of these questions is yes. (See Box 3.1 for a related discussion on social theory.) In the process, we will take what might appear as a

---

Box 3.1   Social Theory

Sociology is a theoretical discipline. Though most sociologists study or examine some aspects of the empirical world, they do so using ideas, abstractions, or concepts.

Take the ubiquitous word *society*, for example. Now, it is true that sociologists study something we call society, but how many of us have actually seen one? Have you touched one? Sociologists are also fond of using the concept *social role*. But what is a role? Have you seen one? Think of concepts as the grammar of sociology. Think of theories as statements that connect concepts in ways that allow sociologists to bring some parts of the complex world into focus and allow for a certain kind of understanding.

What sociologists do, in one sense, is no different from what everyone does. Humans, as we know, must make some sense of the world they are in. If I'm in an airport, I should have an abstract idea of airport that helps orient me to the physical features of buildings, hangars, runways, towers, and so on. The idea of airport also signals a certain way of behaving, a certain orientation to time, and the list goes on. To be a human being means that I am able to describe a place, a person, an event, or a feeling with words that stand for or represent places, persons, events, and feelings. To be a sociologist means that I am able to engage in a similar process though for quite different ends. In short, dear readers, we all theorize. Indeed, what interests many sociologists is how, in fact, we abstract those bits and pieces of life from the overwhelming streams of human experiences, organize them into intelligible wholes, and recount them as life stories.

Environmental sociology, as we will see, borrows its concepts from a number of areas, including community sociology, political sociology, conflict sociology, and social movements. Most important, it also allows for a kind of border crossing, an invitation to consider the abstract relationships between the physical and organic on the one hand and the social and cultural on the other. We address this interdisciplinary promise of environmental sociology in Chapter 7.

NOTE: A good reading on the role of theory in sociology is Giddens (1987).

---

rather straightforward idea of betrayal and break it down into three distinct types: *premeditated, structural,* and *equivocal.*

Premeditated betrayal refers to cases where powerful individuals and organizations intentionally act in a craven, reckless, and self-serving manner. Other, equally appropriate, terms include *malfeasance* and *miscreance*; this is betrayal in its most stark, compelling, and ugly form. Here, organizations intentionally deceive communities and work to cover up those deceptions. This is the dark side of official organizational response to local environmental conflicts and crises. We tackle premeditated betrayal first, both because it is the most egregious example of the loss of collective trust and because it is the most straightforward of the three forms of betrayal we present in this chapter.

We situate explanations of premeditated betrayal within the conflict perspective. Conflict theorists maintain that while advanced capitalist societies such as the United States are good at keeping up the appearance of being democratic meritocracies, in actuality they are highly inequitable systems whose institutional arrangements serve the interests of privileged and powerful elites.[4] An individual's premeditated betrayal, in other words, is only part of the story; the impetus toward disregard for public welfare is deeply embedded in existing social arrangements.

Structural betrayal refers to situations where residents perceive serious failure on the part of powerful organizations, but this occurs in the absence of any intent on the part of government or corporations to behave in a negligent manner. We turn here to sociological insights from organizational theory to explicate the subtle, deeply embedded tensions between local ways of life and the culture and habits of bureaucracies.[5] Communities are historical, emotional, complex, and multifaceted social arrangements; bureaucracies, on the other hand, are narrow, focused, hierarchical, inflexible, rule-governed arrangements. These two disparate social configurations can coexist through the routine and mundane affairs of life, each encountering each other briefly, if at all. But at those crises points, where government or corporate organizations are forced to encounter and respond to local needs in a timely and efficient manner, these two different social configurations, communities and bureaucracies, are often in tension if not in open conflict with one another. Structural betrayal results from communities and bureaucracies responding in a normal, expected, and incompatible manner to stressful life events.

We reserve the term *equivocal betrayal* for cases where there is limited empirical evidence regarding corporate and official intentions, and both conflict and organizational theories provide plausible explanations of the ostensibly miscreant behavior. These are the hard calls, and the discussion presented in this section is intended to encourage students of local environmental conflicts to avoid rushing to judgment in employing these conceptual labels.

When reading the sections to follow, keep in mind that all conceptual labels are abstractions from the messiness of everyday life. The most likely scenario is that any particular local environmental controversy will display all three of these types of betrayal, though one may be markedly more prevalent than the other two. Examples of ways in which the causes and consequences of betrayal connect with material presented in previous chapters is provided in Box 3.2.

Box 3.2   Making Connections With Previous Chapters

There are obvious reasons for the predictable disputes between governments and communities. One obvious source of contention is the powerful voice of state and federal governments in legislating, regulating, and adjudicating environmental issues and disputes. In Chapter 1, Box 1.3, we directed students to document key government actions as an important part of the descriptive time line of local environmental conflicts for precisely this reason. A society governed by rule of law puts extraordinary authority in the hands of elected and appointed officials. Indeed, as we pointed out in Chapter 1, authoritative government actions end many environmental controversies.

Another obvious reason for the predictable disputes between governments and communities was presented in Chapter 2, where we discussed the City of Los Angeles' confiscation of water from the Owens Valley, as well as the Bureau of Reclamation's efforts to flood the Fort McDowell Reservation, home of the Yavapai Indians. Citizens and governments are often at odds over development and natural resource use. One of the questions we directed students to use to assess the harbinger role of history is the following: Does the cultural toolbox of local peoples include a living history of resistance against exploitation and injustice from which they can draw symbolic resources to use in a present conflict? (See Box 2.4.) As the above two examples indicate, such an outside exploiter may be a governmental body. In other words, as a result of past experiences, local people may be predisposed toward cynical views of government.

The Guadalupe Dunes case, also presented in Chapter 2, provides a different scenario. As this case illustrates, sometimes environmental controversies and crises make local residents aware of malfeasance that has been there all along. These situations are fertile ground for invented histories, as activists and residents reinterpret past actions through the new lens of intentionally craven, self-serving, and reckless acts. At the same time, when examining a case where an invented history raises such accusations, it is important to scrutinize these claims and not just to accept them at face value. Invented histories, after all, provide particular interpretations of events that may or may not be accurate.

"Outside exploiter" is hardly the only way government bodies interface with communities and indeed is probably not even the most typical. For example, as seen in the recent spate of hurricanes along the U.S. Gulf Coast, communities turn to the government for assistance in times of collective crises. These experiences shape the kinds of resources found in local cultural toolboxes, as illustrated by the St. Louis, Michigan, case presented in Chapter 2. Government actions can also foster local dependencies, which could include welfare assistance (see the Buffalo Creek case, Chapter 2) or such locally important sources of employment as prisons and military bases (see Box 1.4). Government laws on historic preservation or treaties granting Native American tribes access to particular places and resources create conditions under which precedents set in the past can be used to justify present courses of action (see Box 2.5).

Premeditated Betrayal

The Cornhusker Army Ammunition Plant

In 1942, operations began at the Cornhusker Army Ammunition Plant (CAPP).[6] Located outside the town of Grand Island, Nebraska (population 33,000), the facility covered 19 square miles of farmland in the Platte River Valley. "[T]he plant packed explosives into munitions ranging from 105-millimeter shells to 1,000-pound bombs."[7] During the peak of the Vietnam War buildup, the plant ran full time, six days a week, employing just over 5,000 workers. The plant was shut down one day a week so that the explosive dust that settled everywhere could be washed away.[8] Otherwise, the dust might ignite.

Substances used to make explosives include TNT, RDX, and aluminum flakes. The cleaning process produced vast quantities of wastewater contaminated with these toxins. Another source of wastewater at the plant was laundry. Workers typically came off shift with their clothes coated with dust. After every shift, each worker removed his or her clothes on-site and left them with the plant laundry.

> In 1970, during the height of production for the Vietnam War, the Army actually kept track of the laundry's wastewater, estimating that the procedure generated a daily outflow of approximately 473 cubic meters (roughly 100,000 gallons) of water contaminated with explosive residues.[9]

Workers referred to the wastewater as "red water." This designation came from the high concentrations of TNT, which gave the water a pinkish tint. The water was deposited on-site, in "a network of more than fifty cesspools and leaching pits."[10] Due to the types of contaminants in the water, it evaporated at a considerably slower rate than normal. This meant the primary route of water loss from the cesspools and leaching pits was percolation through the porous soils. Combined with rapid groundwater flow underneath the site, conditions were optimal for significant off-site migration of contaminants. Some Army officials recognized the potential for severe environmental problems as early as 1970.

Studies conducted at the facility in 1980 documented a number of alarming conditions. The explosive compound RDX was found in the base's groundwater in concentration levels which exceeded the Army's fairly lax proposed limits by a factor of 8. Toxic contaminants were believed to have already traveled off-site; at the rate they were estimated to be moving, they would reach the town of Grand Island in 4 years.

In 1982 a story ran in the local paper, the *Grand Island Daily Independent,* which reported some contamination problems had been discovered at the base. A Cornhusker official, however, reassured the public that there was "no evidence" that any domestic wells, including the base's own wells, had been contaminated. "At about that time, Army specialists also confidently told the public that it could take more than a century for the compounds to reach the town's outer limits."[11]

In a public meeting held in April 1984, the Army publicly acknowledged for the first time the extent of the contamination problems. Findings from studies conducted over the previous 2 years were finally released. The conclusions of these studies exposed the Army in an intentional act of prevarication.

> [M]ore than half of the 467 private wells the Army tested in the Le Heights and Capitol districts of Grand Island had extremely elevated levels of RDX. The Army's underground contamination, in other words, had already migrated more than three miles from the edge of the facility.[12]

What the Army would not release to the public was the information it already possessed on an array of disturbing health effects stemming from exposure to RDX. RDX is a neurotoxin; its effects on the human nervous system include seizures and loss of consciousness. At the time of the Army's revelation, RDX was also listed as a possible carcinogen by the U.S. Environmental Protection Agency (EPA). Neither the EPA nor the Nebraska Department of Health had established any safety standards for RDX in drinking water. Initially, the EPA accepted by default "the Army's contentions that levels of RDX below 35 parts per billion presented no danger to human health."[13] This would change in 1988, when the agency concluded that the Army's standard was 17 times too lenient, dropping the standard from 35 ppb (parts per billion) to 2 ppb.

A far more immediate response to the Army's revelations was undertaken by some residents of Grand Island, who organized into the grassroots group Good Neighbors Against Toxic Substances (GNATS). This group filed a lawsuit against the Army in 1984. Some GNATS members had their own wells tested and found other contaminants besides RDX, "including disturbing levels of the solvents dichloroethane and trichloroethane."[14] Some residents began to make connections between these contaminants and health problems such as recurrent headaches and skin rashes.

Throughout the 6-year legal battle that followed, the Army provided little information to the activists and haggled about such things as which residents were entitled to free bottled water. The defense the Army employed in the lawsuit was that the contaminants which had migrated off-site were from production for the Korean War and earlier periods. Since the disposal methods used at the facility during the 1940s and 1950s were perfectly legal at the time, the Army contended it could not be held liable for pollution problems stemming from those practices. Experts retained by the plaintiffs could not prove any of the contaminants that had migrated off-site were from more recent production at the facility. On the advice of their lawyer, GNATS members finally dropped the lawsuit in 1990, deciding it would be difficult to win and therefore not worth the risk given the costs involved. By the early 1990s, the contaminants had migrated 2 miles farther from the plant, threatening a new group of Grand Island residents.

The frustration of the grassroots activists is summed up by GNATS member Chuck Carpenter, who describes his battle with the Army as a "nightmare."

> Carpenter says that perhaps the worst part of the entire saga is the way the Army treated him and his neighbors. Years ago he told the local press that it felt like being a guinea pig, but today he puts it a little differently. "We were treated like mushrooms. The Army kept us totally in the dark."[15]

Perhaps nothing can more quickly lead to feelings of betrayal and loss of trust than discovering that one's own government has not only pursued actions which put you, your family, and your community in harm's way but also lied about it. Cover-ups and deception are intentional acts. Like the child who breaks the cookie jar or the spouse pursuing an illicit affair, falsehoods are told to avoid the negative repercussions which might follow if the truth is revealed. Certainly the U.S. military has an interest in deception; it oversees some of the most contaminated real estate in the world. After all, cleaning up sites contaminated with radioactive isotopes and toxic chemicals is exorbitantly expensive, costs which may be pushed even higher by substantial legal settlements.

We find the same dynamics at work in the private sector, as shown in the popular films *Erin Brockovich* and *A Civil Action*, both based on true stories. The events recounted in the second film were first portrayed in the book *A Civil Action*, by Jonathan Harr.[16] The subject matter of this book and subsequent film is a case of water contamination in Woburn, Massachusetts. During the 1970s a number of children in Woburn were diagnosed with childhood leukemia. Subsequent investigation revealed that the majority of these children lived in neighborhoods which received the highest percentage of domestic water from city Wells G and H. These wells had only been opened in the 1960s and were only used part of the year because residents complained about poor water quality.

Tests of water from Wells G and H begun in the late 1970s would reveal the presence of a number of contaminants, including the industrial solvent trichloroethylene (TCE). One of the possible sources of TCE was a tannery owned by the massive corporate conglomerate Beatrice Foods. Some residents filed a lawsuit against Beatrice and W. R. Grace, another likely source of contamination. Throughout the trial, the tannery operator (and former owner) and Beatrice representatives consistently maintained there had been limited use of TCE at the tannery. Furthermore, none of the substance was disposed of improperly. The lawyers for the plaintiffs were unable to produce evidence to contradict this claim, and the jury ruled that Beatrice was not the source of the TCE in Woburn Wells G and H. Following its acquittal from the civil suit, however, Beatrice became a target of an investigation by the EPA. This investigation would produce evidence of substantial use of TCE by the tannery, as well as illegal, on-site disposal. Workers at the tannery had destroyed incriminating evidence and lied through their teeth in order to protect themselves from the negative fallout of civil and criminal proceedings.

As this example illustrates, there are certainly personal motivations which drive lying, deception, and other forms of miscreant behavior. These include not only the desire to avoid punishment but also perhaps the lure of financial gain and advancing one's career. It is, after all, much cheaper and easier to just dump toxic chemicals somewhere on the sly rather than to have them hauled off-site and treated. We certainly do not want to discount these personal motivations, but our primary focus as sociologists is in understanding the systemic forces which influence individual and organizational choices. It is one thing if the rare company violates prevailing community standards by dumping toxic chemicals out back, and quite another if this is a widespread, common practice. Are acts of premeditated betrayal rare, isolated occurrences, or do they follow broad social patterns? If acts of premeditated betrayal are a recurrent feature of our society, then what are the institutional arrangements which produce them?

Conflict theorists would answer yes to this first question and answer the second by turning to the imperatives of the capitalist market system, the close connections between states and corporations, and the many obvious and subtle ways in which existing social arrangements promote and protect the interests of powerful and privileged elites.[17] Let's begin with the first of these. To survive in a competitive marketplace, firms must maximize profits.[18] A sure route to business success is given by the old adage, "Buy low, sell high." Keeping the costs of production as low as possible is simply an astute, an even essential, business practice. If the prevailing market rate for low-skill labor in an area is $8 an hour, a rate paid by existing fast-food outlets, would it make any sense for a new fast-food outlet to pay its low-skill workers $25 an hour?

This market imperative has important environmental implications, because the cheapest options are also often the most ecologically degrading options. Clear-cutting, strip mining, discarding of mine tailings in nearby streams, dumping toxic wastes in lagoons on the back lot of the factory, burning refuse in incinerators—these are all less costly options than more environmentally benign alternatives such as selective logging. Therefore, it is hardly surprising that prior to the implementation of more stringent environmental regulations in the 1970s, the above-mentioned practices were all common in this country. Yet all of these practices can put communities in harm's way, which is why engaging in these acts when the danger is known constitutes an example of premeditated betrayal.[19] There are probably few things that more quickly dis-illusion and outrage community residents than learning some company was willing to put their health and lives at risk in order to "make a buck."

Sometimes, the causal routes by which environmental perturbations trouble local residents are subtle and circuitous and hence become the subject of the kinds of knowledge disputes we discuss in the next chapter. Sometimes, however, the local consequences of corporate cost-cutting, profit-maximizing decisions manifest themselves in stark and tragic ways. Take the case of Bhopal, India. On the night of December 3, 1984, a gas leak of methyl isocyanate (MIC) from the Union Carbide plant located in this southern Indian city killed 15,000 people and injured 200,000 more.[20] The plant was experiencing financial difficulties prior to the leak, and as a result, a number of cost-cutting measures which compromised plant safety were implemented.

> Several months before the accident, a refrigeration unit designed to inhibit dangerous chemical reactions in the storage tanks at the Union Carbide facility was shut down, ostensibly for cost-cutting reasons. Other critical mechanical safety devices were also inoperative or failed at the time of the leak. . . . [S]ome of the instruments for detecting pressure and temperature levels of the chemicals produced at the plant prior to the accident were unreliable, and there was a conspicuous lack of redundancy measures—computer backups, automatic shutoffs and alarm systems—that might have detected and stopped the gas leak before it spread beyond the confines of the plant.[21]

Another factor conflict theorists use to account for broad patterns of premeditated betrayal is the close connections between states and corporations. This political-economic perspective examines the ways in which the government colludes with private industry to promote economic growth and capital accumulation.[22] In the United States, the points of contact and lines of influence between corporations and the state are extensive and deeply embedded.[23] Corporations make substantial contributions to the election campaigns of public officials and flood the U.S. and state capitols with well-paid lobbyists. Legislators use their control over agency budgets to encourage actions which promote business interests and economic benefits (such as timber extraction from national forests) and to discourage actions which cost companies money and contribute to a hostile economic climate (such as excessive environmental regulation). Corporate executives are appointed to key positions within the executive branches at both the state and national levels, bringing an "industry perspective" to such influential positions as secretary of the interior.

Industries, in other words, work hard to influence the legislatures that pass and rescind laws and the governmental agencies ostensibly created to regulate private economic activity. At times, industries are so successful at this latter endeavor that they are able to capture the agencies that were supposed to be overseeing and regulating them.[24] For example, the U.S. Department of Agriculture championed massive application of synthetic pesticides, and the U.S. Army Corps of Engineers and the Bureau of Reclamation championed the building of massive hydroelectric projects. Agency capture constitutes premeditated betrayal because the intent of the collusion is to create institutionalized patterns of favoritism. Of course, when local people encounter a government agency which consistently comes down on the side of industry, they may lose trust in any notion of an open, democratic, and responsive government.[25]

A primary analytic directive of conflict theory is to identify ways in which existing social arrangements promote and protect privilege; the notion of institutionalized favoritism provides one example of this. One place we see institutionalized favoritism is in rules and procedures which wealthy and powerful social actors are in a better position to exploit than adversaries with fewer resources at their disposal.[26] In pragmatic terms, this means when ordinary citizens become involved in environmental controversies, they may discover they are not competing on a level playing field. Such a revelation may leave residents feeling betrayed by a system of government they thought would be responsive and fair.

For example, corporations can afford top legal representation, and in fact may assemble teams of highly specialized attorneys which concentrate on particular aspects of a legal proceeding, such as filing motions or refuting the testimony of expert witnesses.[27] If corporations have sufficient resources to outlast their adversaries, they may work every legal angle they can to delay and drag out proceedings. Such a strategy is undertaken with the hope that the other side will exhaust its resources and be forced to withdraw from the lawsuit. The legal burden of proof may also work to aid corporations and hinder community residents. For example, for corporations it is preferable if chemicals "are assumed innocent (not hazardous) until proven guilty."

A final form of premeditated betrayal is expressed in threats and intimidation. If community residents feel betrayed when powerful social actors fail to protect them from harm, imagine the response if the same actors threaten to punish (harm) them. One form such threats can take is that of a local factory letting it be known that it will close down and relocate elsewhere if nearby residents start complaining too much about the amount of air pollution coming out of its smokestack. Sometimes, however, the threats and intimidation used by powerful social actors can take especially ugly and egregious forms. One notable example is the Nigerian government's persecution of Ogani people for protesting the pollution of their land by Shell Oil.[28] During the mid-1990s,

> Nigerian soldiers oversaw the ransacking of Ogoni villages, the killing of about 2,000 Ogoni people, and the torture and displacement of thousands more. . . . The army also sealed the borders of Ogoniland, and no one was let in or out without government permission. Ken Saro-Wiwa and other Ogoni leaders were repeatedly arrested and interrogated. Finally, the government trumped up a murder charge against Saro-Wiwa and eight others, and, despite a storm of objection from the rest of the world, executed them on November 10, 1995.[29]

Questions which will help students assess whether they are dealing with instances of premeditated betrayal are provided in Box 3.3. Anyone who spends time examining local environmental conflicts is likely to encounter at least some and maybe a lot of unscrupulous, ethically troublesome, and perhaps even illegal acts. Yet appearances of bad faith actions can be deceiving, and we would advise any ostensible act of betrayal to be viewed through all three of the lenses provided in this chapter before making a determination of the intentions involved. It is to the task of developing these additional forms of betrayal that we now turn our attention.

Structural Betrayal

Love Canal: Industrial Chemicals, Suburban Neighborhoods, and Citizen Anger

From 1942 to 1952, Hooker Chemical Company buried 21,800 tons of organic solvents, acids, and pesticides in a partially completed canal in

---

Box 3.3   Adding to the Portfolio: Premeditated Betrayal

1. Do powerful organizations pursue courses of action which put neighborhoods and communities in harm's way, then use lies, deception, and cover-ups to conceal the risks and/or their own culpability?

2. Do private companies compromise public safety in the pursuit of profits?

3. Is there collusion between government officials/agencies and private individuals/companies?

4. Do the rules which guide the decision-making process work to the advantage of the wealthy and powerful?

5. Do powerful social actors use threats and intimidation to influence decision-making outcomes favorable to their interests?

Niagara Falls, New York.[30] The chemicals were put in metal or fiber drums, an acceptable disposal method at the time. Unfortunately, many of the drums broke apart as they were being buried, releasing raw chemicals into the canal bed. In April 1945, only a few years into the dumping, an engineer who worked for Hooker wrote an internal memo describing the canal as a "[q]uagmire which will be a potential source of law suits."[31] A prescient memo, indeed. Once full, the canal was covered with clay to keep moisture from reaching the drums and eventually the chemical stew. Grass was planted over the clay seal.

In 1952 the Niagara Falls School Board approached Hooker Chemical and asked the company to donate this empty grassy field to the city for a new school. Hooker resisted, telling board members that it could not guarantee the safety of the area. The school board countered with a threat to assume ownership of the property through eminent domain. Hooker Chemical agreed to sell the grassy-covered canal full of volatile chemicals to the board for $1. Shortly thereafter, working-class and middle-class homes were built around the new school.

In the winter of 1976 a heavy snowfall melted, softening the soil. Chemical odors penetrated people's houses, a creek running through the neighborhood turned a reddish brown, and sump pumps in some homes overflowed with smelly, abrasive effluent. Rusty drums dripping with old chemicals began to surface in the playground of the school. Small but frightening explosions began to occur on the playground as once buried toxic chemicals worked their way to the surface and literally burst through at various places.

Citizens complained. Newspapers reported the story. Two years after the first evidence of a disaster in the making, the federal government responded. The EPA, the first agency at the scene, found 82 toxic chemicals in air, water, and soil samples near the dump. Moreover, the report linked area health problems, including miscarriages, to exposure to these toxins, some of which were carcinogenic.[32]

The New York Department of Health (DoH) and the New York Department of Environmental Conservation (DEC) learned of the problem in 1978 by reading the federal EPA report. On August 2, 1978, the DoH recommended temporary relocation of pregnant women and young children. Many residents wondered aloud about the financial burden of relocating. And what does "temporary" mean? How will families function when children are here and Dad is there? And what about the elderly or people with chronic health problems? Should they relocate too? The DoH could not answer these questions.

On August 9, Governor Hugh Carey signed an order for the permanent relocation of 239 families with documented birth defects and miscarriages. But his order was delayed as agencies disagreed over who was in charge of the relocation and how it would be funded. Eight months later, relocation began. Again, many of the questions following the recommendation to relocate were asked of this permanent relocation. And again, the government had no plausible answers.

In February 1979 the DoH approved the relocation of all pregnant women from the subdivision and provided limited relocation expenses. That order was delayed, however, while the state constructed a drainage system that was promised to rid the neighborhood of the chemicals. An engineering project, in short, replaced a relocation initiative, leaving residents wondering what was going on, who was in charge, and, most important, what should they do in response to this organizational and environmental calamity.

The confusion continued. In July 1979 the DEC began to move 120 families to motels. The relocated families did not know what was going to happen to their houses or themselves in the months to come. Families that remained wondered aloud how their houses and yards could be safe while their neighbors' properties were too dangerous to inhabit.

On May 16 the EPA reported chromosome damage in 36 residents living near the canal. On May 19 two EPA officials were kept hostage in the house of a local resident-activist. The White House was called, notified of the hostages, and given a deadline to act, or else. In hindsight, the EPA officials were not in any real danger. But the symbolic politics of this act leveraged the buyout residents were seeking. Five minutes after the deadline set by the group, the White House issued a press release announcing that it was authorizing the temporary relocation of all 810 families from the Love Canal area. On October 1, 1980, President Carter signed a bill to permanently relocate all families from the contaminated area. In 1981, the U.S. Senate authorized $15 million to purchase and relocate the families at Love Canal.

❖

It is not difficult to understand why people who suddenly find themselves embroiled in this kind of nightmare would turn to others for assistance. Indeed, the more wishful among them might imagine the calvary riding over the hill to their rescue. Initially, Love Canal residents were grateful for government involvement, especially New York state's DoH. Over time, however, residents' perceptions soured as many came to believe the government was not responsive to their needs, purposefully covering up the true extent of the danger, and more concerned about containing costs than protecting their welfare.[33]

Certainly the Love Canal residents felt betrayed by the government agencies they believed should be protecting them from harm. Yet, for all the ire directed against them, the rank-and-file DoH personnel assigned to the case were in fact working hard to come up with viable solutions to local contamination problems.[34] How, then, do we account for the escalating spiral of animosity and accusations that went on in this case? How does a government agency come to be vilified by people they are trying to help? How do local residents come to adhere to off-the-mark interpretations of bad faith government actions?

To answer these questions we need to view the Love Canal conflict through a particular lens, one that juxtaposes the widely varying structural character of communities and government bureaucracies.[35] Drawing on insights from organizational theory, this lens allows us to appreciate the ways in which local residents and agency personnel often end up speaking past each other, each viewing the conflict in a particular way, ignorant of the concerns and constraints facing the other party. As a consequence, local residents misinterpret the motives underlying agency actions, while agencies pursue policies which unintentionally harm local residents. To visualize the basic nature of this conflict dynamic examine Figure 3.1.

Communities are holistic fields of living where people own or rent homes and apartments; raise families; educate their children; shop; attend churches, synagogues, or mosques; engage in volunteer and civic activities; recreate; make a living; grow old; and die. People typically experience a community in an extended temporal line as past, as present, and as future. Moving

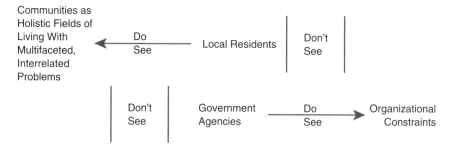

Figure 3.1   The Limited Vision of Local Residents and Government Agencies

between memories and plans, people experience community, neighborhood, and home as emotionally and culturally charged places.

Juxtaposed against communities as holistic fields of living is the narrow, instrumental, goal-oriented nature of the numerous formal, complex organizations we find operating in any modern town or city. These are

> large-scale, special purpose social units with explicit, impersonal goals in terms of which the activities of members are coordinated. In the interests of operational efficiency, the structure of these organizations is designed as a formal, hierarchical system known as a *bureaucracy*.[36]

Bureaucracies are often the source of dark humor. A political cartoon in Niagara Falls' local newspaper appearing during the height of the Love Canal controversy shows a family dressed in casual clothes sitting in their proper middle-class living room and two men in moon suits with giant oxygen tanks on their backs standing in front of them. The caption? "Everything is safe and under control."[37] Think about this cartoon for a moment from the analytic vantage point provided by Figure 3.1. The men in moon suits are doing the job dictated by the narrow, instrumental strictures of the government oversight agency they work for, to wit, determining whether the house has dangerous levels of contaminants. The aspects of the local context salient to them are the ones that pertain to this organizational mandate, their horizon of concern highly constricted.

The family living in this house does not have the luxury of such a narrow vantage point. They will remain in residence after the men in moon suits leave, and even if they are assured "everything is safe and under control," they may never feel as secure in the house as they once did. Indeed, when we factor in the temporal and emotion-laden aspects of residents' relationship to place, we see the capacity for all types of disruptions. The family projects back to the exhilarating time when purchasing the house was the fulfillment of a lifelong dream and recounts years of happy memories. The family also projects forward to an uncertain future where it seems unlikely they will ever be able to get the same type of enjoyment out of the house they once did.[38] They may recall persistent health problems among their children and worry that, regardless of the reassurances of the men in moon suits, their children have been exposed to contaminants and will experience health problems in the future.

Then, of course, there is the concern about property values. Even if given official clearance, the mere fact the men in moon suits were there is a stigma.[39] Indeed, if that stigmatization extends to an entire neighborhood or community, it will have widespread repercussions, for as property values go down, the tax base will also go down, perhaps resulting in fewer city services and underfunded public schools. Residents may lose the motivation and/or financial means to keep up their yards and houses, and as a consequence the overall quality of the neighborhood deteriorates, creating yet another damper on property values. The horizon of concern for community residents is simply far more expansive than that of the government bureaucrats. Residents incorporate past and future as well as present, and appreciate the ways in which problems, or even suspicions of problems, in one area reverberate throughout many facets of their lives.

Here, then, is one way in which government personnel, in the process of conscientiously performing their job, can inadvertently undertake actions which harm residents. Residents' lived experience is that of a complex entanglement of many interrelated problems, but an agency's narrow and instrumental focus on only a subset of those problems means that in the very act of ameliorating some problems, it may unintentionally exacerbate others. Consider again the case of Love Canal. Once the state DoH had amassed enough information on chemicals migrating from the canal through the neighborhoods to conclude a health hazard did exist, it did what it was supposed to do: inform the people and recommend relocation. However, this dire warning was not followed by any financial or logistical offers of assistance, even though the announcement itself had just rendered the residents' homes valueless.

To take another example, recall the case of the devastating flood that swept through Buffalo Creek, West Virginia, discussed in Chapter 2. That disaster left 4,000 people homeless. The Federal Emergency Management Agency (FEMA) responded by siting several trailer parks to house survivors. While this was a speedy response to a pressing need, the agency was narrowly focused on the problem of providing shelter, not on the broader problem of rebuilding an uprooted and fractured community. Concentrating on the efficient provision of living space, FEMA assigned people to trailer parks in a random fashion rather than making an effort to house former neighbors near each other. Ironically, the well-intended actions of this federal agency completed what the flood so tragically started: the destruction of community.[40] There is another way in which the procedures bureaucrats follow to "get the job done" can unintentionally create situations which leave residents feeling frustrated, angry, alienated, and betrayed. The source of this particular clash between bureaucratic and community structures relates to the very sine qua non of complex organizations: routinization, predictability, and standard operating procedures. Indeed, while it is common to poke fun at bureaucracies, it is precisely these features that render these organizations highly efficient and indispensable to a smooth-running modern society.

Yet when it comes to confronting local environmental crises and conflicts, bureaucracy's greatest strength can readily become its greatest weakness. Designed to anticipate and respond to a limited range of problems, a novel problem that demands innovation is likely to be avoided, redefined to make it fit a particular bureaucratic regime, or mismanaged by applying routinized procedures to no good effect.[41] Viewed from the perspective of organizational theory, bureaucratic inflexibility and its related problems are recurring and utterly expected phenomena. Viewed from the perspective of residents who may lack this particular vantage point, slow and inadequate agency response can easily be read as intentional dereliction of duty.

To take another example of the disparate perspectives portrayed in Figure 3.1, consider the bureaucratic imperatives of routinization and standard operating procedures. These imperatives encourage oversight agencies to approach local environmental conflicts and crises with an array of one-size-fits-all solutions. From an organizational perspective, there are sound reasons for wanting to make problems fit the existing solutions. It is time consuming and expensive to come up with new tools. Doing so requires establishing the necessary knowledge base (e.g., conducting studies), followed by trial-and-error efforts to figure out what alternatives work. The faster an agency can routinize responses, the lower the costs and the more readily they can get on with accomplishing *something*, even if that something is not really what needs to be done to correct the problem. This can be seen in the Love Canal case, where government officials "wanted the definition of harm to be narrow, to fit the resources they had available, so that some tasks could be successfully accomplished, accounted for, and pointed to."[42]

Viewed from a bureaucratic standpoint, this is rational agency action. But following the economist Herbert Simon, it is wise to remember that humans and their organizations operate within what he called "bounded rationality."[43] Human rationality is limited or bounded to the degree that the capacity of the human mind for formulating and solving problems is small compared with the size and complexity of the problems that need solving. Imagine the problems a complex organization must identify and solve as a deep lake that is clear for a few feet down and then becomes so dark and murky it is impossible to see any farther. The comparatively few problems at the surface are solved with routine competence. As problems occur in deeper, more obscure water, however, routine, customary actions are less likely to succeed adequate to the complicated tasks. Rationality, in short, works optimally on routinized tasks. The more fuzzy, vague, and unsettled the problem, the more likely new and innovative behaviors are needed. Innovation, of course, is not something bureaucracies do well.

The upshot may be government responses woefully inadequate to the problems at hand. Here we are talking about a different type of failure than the selective attention to only a subset of local problems, though this failure is likely to occur in concert with, and further compound, our present focus of concern. What happens when we add routinization, standard operating procedures, and bounded rationality to the mix is the potential for bureaucratic agencies to fumble even with problems that ostensibly fall under their legislative mandates. In many respects, environmental oversight agencies are perpetually trapped between a rock and a hard place: the bureaucratic imperative is to standardize procedures and minimize uncertainty, while the complexity of ecosystems (and related difficulties of foreseeing all consequences of intervention), combined with a steady stream of new technologies, almost guarantees these agencies will be forced to grapple with novel problems. All too often communities are caught in the gap between existing procedures and emergent needs. What this is likely to look like from the vantage point of residents is that no governmental entity is making any apparent effort to protect them from harm.

The oil spill underneath the Guadalupe Dunes presented in Chapter 2 provides a telling example of the problems that can stem from bounded rationality. This spill grew incrementally over a period of almost 40 years. The regulatory and response agencies responsible for oil spills were not on the lookout for a slowly emerging, ambiguously defined, and uncertain disaster. Their organizational competence and expertise was biased in favor of responding to sudden, immediate impact, and massive disasters like the *Exxon Valdez*, the proverbial "tanker on the rocks."[44]

Consider again the case of Love Canal. Residents viewed area contamination problems as an emergency in need of immediate remedial action. Given that particular interpretation of the situation, it made sense to turn to FEMA for assistance. The agency responded, however, by pointing out various criteria found in its charter and organizational mandate to argue that Love Canal did *not* conform to the kind of disaster situations it was mandated to assist.

> If the Love Canal situation were truly an *emergency,* traditional (FEMA) reasoning went, then essential cleanup and other remedial measures for the site and people should be accomplished within 60 days. If they are not done within that time, then, by definition, an emergency situation never existed. The Love Canal remedial work was not begun until some 70 days after the health commissioner's order—proof, under this reasoning, that the Love Canal situation, which had taken some 30 years to develop, simply did not qualify under the existing definition of an emergency. [45]

When public officials appear unresponsive to existing problems, or worse, create new problems and headaches for local residents, they are likely to be regarded, at the very least, as callous bureaucrats. Agency personnel may not have this self-perception, however. Indeed, they may be doing all they can to respond to a conflict or crisis and be caught off guard by residents' hostility. Again, the divergent perspectives portrayed in Figure 3.1 are crucial to understanding this conflict dynamic. Agency personnel may not understand that local residents have little knowledge or appreciation of the constraints they must work within. At the same time, lacking the holistic vision of local residents, agency personnel may not perceive how their own tunnel vision addresses only a subset of problems local residents face or how the solutions developed for these particular problems generate, or exacerbate, other problems. The feedback loop which creates an ever-deepening level of anger, frustration, and mistrust on both sides can be seen in the Love Canal case.

> State and city officials had conducted public meetings with the residents as early as May 1978 not only to describe the proposed epidemiological and environmental studies but also to tell residents about the remedial construction plans proposed by the Conestoga-Rovers firm. During the meetings, the residents criticized the plans and deplored the level of the information they received. The officials believed that they were offering tangible plans for help, and surprised at the anger expressed, they became somewhat shaken in conducting meetings where dozens of people asked probing questions that the officials were unprepared or seemed unwilling to answer.[46]

> The person who conducted [one public meeting] . . . mentioned later that he felt proud he had been able to remain cool, "to talk like a machine," despite the anger the Love Canal residents displayed. . . . Privately, the officials congratulated each other on not giving anything away, or not conceding anything

to the residents. Simply living through a heated meeting, getting it over and done without "losing cool" and without departing from an official position became one more mark of the professional.[47]

Examine Box 3.4. Included here are the kinds of questions which will help you assess whether particular government actions which produce angry and disillusioned responses from area residents are best classified as cases of structural betrayal.

Box 3.4   Adding to the Portfolio: Structural Betrayal

1. What is the full array of problems local people associate with, or see stemming from, an environmental conflict or crisis?

2. What are the narrow, instrumental foci government agencies bring to the conflict or crisis?

3. Do government efforts to ameliorate one problem inadvertently create other problems for local residents?

4. Do local environmental perturbations present novel problems that do not readily conform to an agency's standard operating procedures?

5. Is there a feedback loop which creates ever-deepening levels of distance and distrust between residents and agencies, as government personnel respond to the anger, frustration, and resentment directed toward them by becoming defensive, withdrawing emotionally, and closing ranks?

Equivocal Betrayal

The Conflict Over Turtle Exclusion Devices on the Louisiana-Texas Coast

On the weekend of July 22–23, 1989, shrimpers along the Louisiana and Texas coast participated in a blockade of passes and shipping lanes to protest a court order mandating the use of turtle exclusion devices (TEDs) on shrimp trawls.[48] Approximately 1,000 vessels participated in the blockade, with many more smaller vessels on hand to lend support to the shrimpers.

> Shrimp trawls maneuvered their vessels across the affected channels and anchored side by side to create a formidable physical barrier, three or four vessels deep. The shrimpers tried to hold formation against tidal changes and strong currents. At . . . Galveston [Texas] the Coast Guard used water cannons to disperse the shrimpers.[49]

Additional blockades continued through the summer and fall of that year. But these were just the latest—and most dramatic—forms of protest in a battle that had been simmering for a good decade. The precipitating event was a marked decline in the populations of a variety of species of sea turtles, most notably the Kemp Ripley turtle. By the end of the 1970s, several species of sea turtles had been listed as threatened or endangered.

A number of factors contributed to the decline in turtle populations, including pollution and loss of nesting beaches from coastal development. These are difficult problems to address, however, given they involve activities of millions of people spread across a number of local and state jurisdictions. In addition, coastal development is driven by powerful economic and political interests. Rather than try to take on these challenges, policy advocates early on focused on one contributing factor to sea turtle decline that seemed far more amenable to government action: incidental drowning of turtles in shrimp trawls. If this form of turtle mortality could be prevented, the official reasoning went, threatened and endangered species might have a chance to rebound.

For their part, shrimpers contested the notion that shrimp trawls were responsible for turtle deaths. Using local knowledge based on personal experience, Texas and Louisiana shrimpers maintained that they seldom caught turtles in their trawls, and on those rare occasions when it happened, the shrimpers made valiant efforts to try and save them. As shrimpers told it, sea turtles are far more prevalent off the Florida coast than in the western Gulf of Mexico. A universal regulation mandating TEDs throughout the entire Gulf region might fit the one-size-fits-all mentality of the bureaucrats, but it did not fit the unique environmental conditions found in different coastal regions.

Still, the drive to mandate TEDs marched on. During the 1980s, the U.S. Fish and Wildlife Service (USF&WS), located in the Department of the Interior, aggressively pushed the use of TEDs. As the federal agency which bore the primary responsibility for implementing the 1973 Endangered Species Act, the USF&WS came down strongly on the side of conservation. A second federal agency, the National Marine Fisheries Service (NMFS), located in the Department of Commerce, tried to walk a fine line between conflicting mandates of protecting sea turtles and promoting the interests of the shrimping industry. The marine agents employed by the Sea Grant Extension Service, a sister agency of NMFS, also located in the Department of Commerce, acted as a liaison between shrimpers and government regulators and also sought to educate shrimpers on the need for and proper use of TEDs.

At the beginning of the TEDs conflict, shrimpers in the western Gulf were represented by the Louisiana Shrimp Association and the Texas

Shrimp Association. Given the strict mandates of the Endangered Species Act, one possible route to protecting the turtles would be to prohibit trawling altogether. Initially hopeful that minor gear modification would pacify environmentalists while allowing commercial harvesting to continue, the shrimp industry worked with the Sea Grant Extension Service, using research monies provided by NMFS, to find an acceptable technological solution.

The result was the first TED prototype, which was introduced in 1980. Theoretically, TEDs prevent turtles from entering shrimping trawls. When initially introduced, their adoption by shrimpers was strictly voluntary. NMFS and Sea Grant personnel were hoping shrimpers would go that route, precluding the need for mandatory regulations. The NMFS and Sea Grant attempted to sell shrimpers on the use of TEDs by dubbing them "trawl efficiency devices." As presented to the shrimpers, using TEDs would reduce drag, thus lowering fuel costs and making shrimping more profitable. NMFS, Sea Grant, and the shrimping industry had, in other words, tried to come up with a win-win solution, one that would satisfy environmentalists concerned with protecting sea turtles while simultaneously advancing the economic interests of the shrimpers.

The TEDs only accomplished these miraculous outcomes, however, if they were properly installed, and as shrimpers soon discovered, it was difficult to install the TED prototype correctly. Improperly installed, TEDs created a number of problems for shrimpers, including increased drag and shrimp loss. Shrimpers rejected the prototype TED, claiming it was dangerous and did not work. "In 1983 a smaller, lighter, collapsible TED was introduced."[50] Despite optimism on the part of NMFS, Sea Grant, and environmentalists, and despite the fact that NMFS distributed TEDs free to any shrimper who voluntarily adopted it (thus saving shrimpers the $200–$300 purchase price), shrimpers also rejected this TED. By 1985 it was becoming increasingly clear that the strategy of voluntary compliance was not working.

This failure resulted in the hardening of positions on both the environmentalists' and shrimpers' side. While environmentalists were supportive of gear modification as a solution to turtle death and injuries in trawls, they became increasingly frustrated at the slow progress and low rates of shrimper compliance. By the mid-1980s, environmentalists had become more aggressive in their efforts to protect sea turtles. The National Wildlife Foundation and the Center for Marine Conservation took to the courts trying to force NMFS into compliance with the Endangered Species Act by making TEDs mandatory rather than voluntary. The July 22–23, 1989, blockade recounted above occurred in the aftermath of a July 21st court order which imposed the use of TEDs on recalcitrant shrimpers. This was only one moment in an ongoing tug-of-war, however. The Commerce Secretary quickly lifted the regulation, in part because of fear of violence from the shrimpers and in part because the secretary favored alternatives to TEDs, like tow-time limitations. This proved to be a short-lived respite for the shrimpers, however. "[B]y September of 1989 the reimposition of TEDs was inevitable."[51]

In a study conducted in the early 1990s, Margavio and Forsyth found that 99% of the 51 shrimpers they surveyed "agreed with the statement that 'TEDs are a threat to my way of life.'"[52] Even after TEDs were made mandatory in the fall of 1989, compliance rates among shrimpers only ran about 40%–50%. The growing dissatisfaction of shrimpers had gained organized expression several years prior to this, with the formation of the new grassroots group, Concerned Shrimpers of America (CSA). This development signaled growing rank-and-file dissatisfaction with the two organizations which had represented shrimpers at the start of the controversy, the Louisiana Shrimp Association and the Texas Shrimp Association. From the shrimpers' perspective, the threat of mandatory TEDs produced desperate times requiring desperate measures.

Unlike the two older organizations, the CSA was an advocate of desperate measures. It was the CSA which promoted and organized the blockades of shipping lanes. The CSA also provided shrimpers with a powerful unifying ideology. At the heart of this ideology was the increasingly vocalized contention that, at least in the western Gulf, incidental drowning of turtles in shrimp trawls was exceedingly rare.

Surrounding that assertion of "fact" was a contending explanation of TEDs. The real motivation underlying TEDs was not the protection of sea turtles but rather the promotion of a hidden agenda to punish shrimpers for past political activism and to rid the gulf of commercial harvesters. This hidden agenda, furthermore, was being pursued by powerful opponents sporting the kinds of political connections which allowed them to work effectively behind the scenes. For shrimpers aligned with the CSA, pursuit of TEDs in a context where the shrimpers believed they were clearly not needed constituted evidence they were being persecuted by a conspiracy which included large corporations, national environmental organizations, wealthy and influential individuals, and the USF&WS.

As the shrimpers saw it, one major player promoting this hidden agenda was the giant corporation Waste Management Inc. "Shrimpers believe that the TEDs regulations are payment for their past grassroots resistance to waste disposal plans in the Gulf."[53] Shrimpers cite as evidence supporting this contention Waste Management Inc.'s financial contributions to the Center for Marine Conservation, the leading advocate of TEDs.

Another powerful enemy was the Gulf Coast Conservation Association (GCAA), which represents recreational fishers along the southern United States from Virginia to Texas. Many offshore species, such as speckled trout and red drum, are targeted by both commercial and recreational fishers. As the populations of these species decline, the competition between these two groups increases. The trend over the last three decades is toward much greater governmental restrictions on commercial harvesting. The elite base and political connections of the GCCA is seen in the following quotation:

> The GCCA had its beginnings in 1977 in Texas when fourteen sportfishing entrepreneurs met in a Houston sporting goods store to launch a sportfishing organization. Among them were Walter Fondren, Jr. and Perry Bass. Fondren's father had founded Humble Oil Company. Fondren served as chairman of the Gulf of Mexico Fisheries Management Council. Perry Bass, a member of the Fort Worth, Texas, Bass family whose fortune is based in oil and banking, served as director of Texas Department of Natural Resources.[54]

For the shrimpers, the majority of government actions undertaken in the case did not feel democratic and protective but rather autocratic and threatening. Not only their economic livelihood but a valued way of life was at stake. The USF&WS and the courts were all too ready to hammer the final nails in the coffin by making TEDs mandatory. Shrimpers' own local knowledge about turtle mortality was excluded from the decision-making process. As ordinary working folk in a modest-sized occupation, shrimpers knew they lacked the political clout of their adversaries. The very system of government decision making, it seemed, had been designed to work against them.

❖

The shrimpers involved in the TED conflict recount experiences and offer analyses that certainly make the actions of the powerful individuals and organizations involved in this case sound like premeditated betrayal. While we suspect this is an accurate accounting of part of what was going on in this case, careful scrutiny leads us to question whether premeditated betrayal was as extensive as the shrimpers' claim. We cannot definitively debunk the shrimpers' version of events, but we have no cause to simply accept it out of hand either. The problem is a lack of sufficient empirical evidence regarding the intentions of the powerful organizations and individuals involved in the TED controversy. What we do have are shrimpers' accusations, which are fine, so long as we treat them as claims, but become problematic if, in the absence of corroboration, we present them as hard evidence of malfeasance.

We can turn to our preceding discussions on premeditated and structural betrayal to gain insights into the problem here. Powerful social actors are not going to advertise their bad faith actions; indeed, we can expect lies, deceptions, and cover-ups to be the norm when individuals and organizations are engaged in unethical, unscrupulous, or criminal activity. This does not mean that corroborating evidence is never going to be available. Indeed, revelations of official and organizational intention might come through a variety of sources, including public admission of guilt, investigative journalism, whistle-blowing, civil or criminal legal proceedings, and Freedom of Information Act (FOIA) requests. Our concern in this section is with cases where this kind of information is not available; the challenge is in trying to determine whether that absence signals a successful cover-up or the lack of any intentional malfeasance from the start.

In this section, we present several strategies for dealing with situations where there is little or no empirical evidence to corroborate residents' claims of premeditated betrayal. First, critically scrutinize the plausibility and reasonableness of residents' and activists' claims. What evidence do they put forth to support their contention that powerful individuals or organizations acted in bad faith? Is it extensive or limited? Is it circumstantial or hearsay? Is it selective, omitting other evidence that might contradict their claims? Is it open to alternative explanations?

Let's return to the conflict over the use of TEDs. The shrimpers' account of bad faith actions went further than collusion between wealthy private sector interests and government; they pointed to a vast behind-the-scenes conspiracy to rid the Gulf of Mexico of commercial harvesters. From their view, the real reason TEDs were mandated had nothing to do with saving sea turtles, which the shrimpers maintained were not endangered by their trawls anyway. No, there was a darker, more sinister purpose at work: TEDs were mandated for the sole reason that they furthered the hidden agenda of "doing in" the shrimpers.

In order to help readers recognize conspiracy theories when they hear them, consider the following account, taken from a fictionalized conservancy dispute portrayed in the novel *The Buffalo Commons*:

> You sit down with any bunch of Fish and Wildlife or Park Service people, and most Forest Service and BLM people, and you'll hear it [the hidden agenda for the Western U.S.]. . . . What they want is to change the face of the West, restore it to wilderness and habitat for all sorts of species from grizzlies to

wolves and buffalo. And how would they do that? By systematically driving out ranching in particular, and agriculture in general. Since Congress won't give them money to purchase land, they're doing it by other means, mainly regulation calculated to undermine ranching.[55]

It is difficult to definitively disprove conspiracy theories because, after all, by their very nature conspiracies are carried out behind the scenes, in secret. A successful conspiracy would leave no evidence for others to find. Yet even if we cannot definitively disprove conspiracies, we can certainly raise questions about their plausibility. For starters, the social conditions necessary for conspiracies—coordination among a geographically dispersed group of individuals and organizations able to pursue a secret agenda for an extended period of time—are a bit difficult to pull off. An additional problem is that once individuals believe a conspiracy is afoot, they come to interpret all kinds of action, inactions, and utterances through that framework. What believers take as convincing evidence of shadowy machinations and hidden agendas may appear quite dubious to those outside the fold.

In the TEDs case we can raise further concerns about plausibility by juxtaposing accusations of conspiracy against what may be a far more straightforward explanation for government regulatory action: shrimp trawls really do kill sea turtles. This does not mean that they are the *only* cause of population decline; indeed, it is likely they are not even the most important cause. Nor does this mean that there were no bad faith actions that went on in this conflict—the CCA no doubt saw TEDs as a window of opportunity for their far-from-hidden agenda of promoting sports over commercial fishing—but this is a far cry from saying TEDs were just a smokescreen for the real purpose of putting the shrimpers out of business.

Not that we want to leave the impression that critical scrutiny of accusations of premeditated betrayal will always punch holes in residents' claims. Indeed, we suspect the conclusions reached by such an examination will often find residents' accounts plausible. While they may be able to offer little in the way of hard evidence, they may be able to muster a considerable amount of circumstantial evidence. A Department of Environmental Quality official accepting a lucrative job with a private sector waste management company not long after approving a controversial solid waste landfill operating permit for the company hardly constitutes conclusive evidence that something fishy was going on, but it certainly is suspicious.

In some conflicts there may be political contention about the intentionality of ostensibly mean-spirited acts. Finger pointing becomes part of the conflict dynamic, with different participants offering different interpretations of the situation. Let's return to the case of Hurricane Katrina. In the aftermath of the flooding of New Orleans, FEMA was lambasted for its slow response time and general ineffectiveness in handling the disaster. Some public figures called for an immediate firing of all FEMA employees. Yet not everyone was willing to paint in such broad brushstrokes; for example, one elected official from Mississippi contended most of the rank-and-file FEMA employees were decent folks who simply wanted to do their jobs. The problems which existed originated at the highest organizational levels: an unqualified director appointed for political reasons, the transference of FEMA to the Department of Homeland Security, and the gutting of FEMA's budget to provide money for fighting terrorism. In time, sufficient evidence may surface to allow us to sort out how much of FEMA's woefully inadequate response to the New Orleans' disaster should be attributed to premeditated betrayal and how much to structural betrayal. In the interim, arraying participant claims provides a means for conveying the different interpretations that might be given to a particular set of governmental actions. Undertaking such an exercise helps to avoid too hasty a condemnation of all agency actions and personnel once it becomes apparent the agency is guilty of at least some bad faith actions.

An additional strategy which can be used when confronted with scanty evidence of intentionality is to determine how readily ostensible acts of pre-meditated betrayal can be explained using conflict and organizational theories. In other words, is it possible that troubling government and corporate actions are actually structural rather than premeditated betrayal? In the absence of sufficient evidence, we probably won't be able to determine which conceptual label is the appropriate one, but what we can do is present both sides of the argument.

Let's consider an issue that can become a lightning rod of contention in local environmental conflicts: citizen participation in the decision-making process. There are many types of government actions for which agencies are legally mandated to offer participation opportunities. At a minimum, there must be a public comment period when interested parties can submit written statements about some proposed action, such as the promulgation of a new regulation or the issuance of a permit, and perhaps public hearings as well. There are also many decision points where agencies have the discretion of opening the process to public input. Participation opportunities are most broadly governed under the 1946 Administrative Procedures Act, but particular environmental statutes may provide additional mandates and guidelines as well. For example, the 1986 Superfund Amendments and Reauthorization Act (SARA) mandates a 2-month public comment period following the announcement of preliminary cleanup plans for abandoned hazardous waste sites.[56]

When residents believe timing and location of public participation venues hinder their involvement in decision making, they may come to believe such obstruction was intentional, the result of bad faith actions on the part of government agencies and officials and perhaps other powerful individuals and organizations.[57] For example, a public hearing on a water discharge permit may be held on a Wednesday afternoon from 1:00 to 3:30 and may be held in the state capitol rather than in the community where the facility requesting the permit is located. For local residents, attending the hearing is likely to be inconvenient and under certain circumstances may entail a significant burden. This would be the case, for example, if the state capitol was located a considerable distance from the community, so that residents had to make a day's commitment to simply attend the hearing. The burden would be compounded if at least some residents had to take off work to attend, and compounded further if the residents were low-income individuals for whom a lost day of wages presented a significant financial hardship. Added to this could be the cost of additional day care for children, as well as road expenses for gas and food. How much more convenient it would be for residents if the hearing had simply been held in their own community in the evening!

As it is, the decision to hold the hearing far away, and during regular working hours, might very well make residents feel like they are being intentionally excluded from the process. It is quite possible that assessment is the correct one. Certainly conflict theory posits such a pattern of intentional exclusion as a pervasive feature in environmental decision making. Conflict theorists contend that, appearances aside, our system of government is not set up to be highly democratic or overly concerned with the trials and tribulations of ordinary folks. Rather, the driving force underlying policy and action is the promotion of profitability in the private capitalist sector and the protection of elite privilege. Citizen input about unacceptable technological risks and environmental costs of economic development projects is not conducive to that goal.

This seems straightforward enough, and we suspect there are many instances where conflict theory provides a valid account of the participatory venues being offered in a particular controversy. Yet conflict theory is not the only plausible explanation available. We can use organizational theory to argue that an agency's scheduling of participation venues at inconvenient times and places may be a case of structural rather than premeditated betrayal.

As we illustrate in Figure 3.1, residents and bureaucrats often fail to see the world from the other's vantage point. A particular government decision, such as whether or not to issue a water discharge permit, may be a very big deal for community residents living near the facility seeking the permit. It may not, however, be a big deal for the agency handling the permit application. Indeed, the agency may receive hundreds of permit applications each year, which in true bureaucratic fashion get processed in a routine manner. If controversy is the exception rather than the norm, this will be reflected in procedures. Hearings will be held in the state capitol, as this is the location most accessible to the organizational representatives who normally attend. Hearings will be held during the day, because agency personnel would rather keep their evenings free for nonwork activities, such as spending time with their families. There is no intentional obstruction going on here, just civil servants carrying out routine procedures in a routine way.

In an ideal situation, students of local environmental conflicts would have access to the kinds of empirical evidence which would allow them to determine the intentionality underlying ostensibly craven, reckless, self-serving, unresponsive, and deceitful acts. This section has presented students with strategies they may use when such evidence is simply not available. A list of the kinds of questions which can be posed in such circumstances is presented in Box 3.5. Because these questions address issues of evidence and plausibility, scrutinizing any apparent act of betrayal through the lens presented here can help students of local environmental conflicts ensure they are employing the labels of premeditated and structural betrayal in a sensible and defensible manner.

Box 3.5   Adding to the Portfolio: Equivocal Betrayal

1. What sort of evidence is there to corroborate activists' and community residents' claims that powerful organizations acted in bad faith?

2. How plausible are activists' and local residents' accounts of bad faith actions on the part of corporations, government agencies, and other powerful organizations and individuals?

3. Is there political contention about the intentionality underlying ostensibly craven acts?

4. Can particular actions read by residents as examples of bad faith actions on the part of powerful individuals and organizations be explained using conflict theory?

5. Can the same set of actions read by residents as examples of bad actions on the part of powerful individuals and organizations be explained using organizational theory?

A Concluding Word

A person does not have to examine very many local environmental conflicts for it to become apparent that oversight agencies, elected officials, corporations, and other powerful social actors are frequent targets of resident anger and oppositional activity. While in some communities these hostilities are long standing, in many others such strained relations are a direct outgrowth of conflict and may well have been preceded by trust and goodwill.[58] When residents become involved in environmental controversies, they come into more direct and extensive contact with powerful organizations than would be the case had they remained apolitical. All too often, residents are dismayed by what that contact reveals. Expecting sympathy, assistance, and protection from harm, they instead encounter organizations which appear either indifferent or downright hostile. Obstructionism and evasion, unresponsiveness and favoritism, recklessness and craven disregard for public welfare—these are hardly the behaviors one would expect from organizations in a democratic society.

In this chapter we presented two explanations for such troubling organizational responses. On the one hand, such acts could be intentional, resulting in what we referred to as premeditated betrayal. On the other hand, they could be the unintentional consequences of bureaucratic constraints and procedures, producing what we referred to as structural betrayal. We used conflict theory to illustrate how the impetus toward miscreance is deeply embedded within existing social arrangements, and organizational theory to identify the inherent dissonance between the widely varying structural character of communities and government bureaucracies. We also argued that the challenge of acquiring sufficient empirical evidence can sometimes make it difficult to determine which explanatory account is applicable to particular cases of ostensible malfeasance. We called these situations equivocal betrayal.

Correct identification of the factors underlying troubling organizational responses is important not only for analytic reasons but for applied, pragmatic reasons as well. Residents' perception that corporations and government agencies have undertaken actions which put them at risk, or have taken a dismissive attitude toward local problems, results in anger and outrage. Such powerful emotions fuel the conflict, leading to escalation and intractability.[59] If the miscreance is intentional, there may be no intervention that can dilute this dynamic. Indeed, in such situations, confrontational tactics (which will also further fuel the conflict) may be the only route by which community residents can hope to achieve redress. Yet if the root cause of spiraling animosity lies in miscommunication and misinterpretations between residents and powerful organizations, as shown in Figure 3.1, then conflict resolution mechanisms stand some chance of succeeding.

Compounding the problems of organizational betrayal are the uncertainties which surround environmental initiatives and troubles. We alluded to this complicating factor in this chapter, where we talked about the difficulties bureaucracies experience when confronting novel circumstances or the anger shrimpers felt at official dismissal of their local knowledge. In the following chapter we undertake an in-depth examination of the role of knowledge disputes in local environmental conflicts, examining not only sources of tension between residents and experts but among residents as well.

STUDENT EXERCISES

1. Exercise 4 in Chapter 1 asked you to use the questions presented in Box 1.4 to describe the local context of a rural area, town, suburb, or urban neighborhood you lived in at some point in your life. Looking back over that description, indicate how this area might be vulnerable to one or more environmental disasters. Choose one of the disasters on this list and write a brief disaster scenario. What would residents in this area expect from the government if this disaster were to actually strike? Speculate how residents might interpret the situation if the government did not respond in the expected manner.

2. Imagine that a number of people in your neighborhood are suffering from a persistent skin rash. Doctors have not been able to diagnose the cause of the rash, and it does not respond to any known treatment. Suspecting something in the water, neighbors turn to the state health department for assistance. The health department takes water samples, then months pass before residents receive a letter from the health department telling them very low concentrations of a certain chemical have been found in their water which *may* be causing their skin problems. No suggestions of "the next step" is provided in the letter. Your neighbors are incensed and begin to make vocal demands that "something be done about the problem." They also begin to attribute the health department's slow and inadequate response to the fact that the likely source of contamination is a massive chemical factory located on the edge of town. What sorts of evidence would you need to determine whether the health department's response in this case constitutes an example of premeditated or structural betrayal?

3. Exercise 2 in Chapter 1 asked you to create a hypothetical conservancy dispute involving the lesser three-toed, red-eyed lizard. Imagine now that you are a recent hire of the U.S. Fish and Wildlife Service and have been put to work developing a habitat protection plan for the lizard, which has just been added to the endangered species list. Write up a memo for your superiors outlining a strategy for developing and implementing a species/habitat protection plan which would reduce the likelihood of agency actions unintentionally angering and alienating residents living near the lizard's natural habitat.

4. Shrimpers in the TEDs case used a type of conspiracy theory to explain what they perceived as threatening and unnecessary government regulatory action. Pick one of the case vignettes presented in Chapters 1 and 2 and speculate whether or not it provides fertile soil for a conspiracy theory to flourish. Defend your answer.

5. As part of the descriptive detail of the case, you were directed in Chapter 1 to summarize the major strategies nongovernmental participants use to influence the course and outcome of controversy. What types of strategies do you think local activists are likely to adopt if they come to believe government agencies, corporations, and other powerful organizations are intentionally acting in a craven, reckless, self-serving, and deceitful manner?

Notes

1. Thomas (2005), 32–33.

2. This is an ideal portrayal, from which there will be considerable personal and community deviation. For a discussion of the latter, see Box 3.2.

3. Sociologist Bill Freudenburg (1993) revived Max Weber's idea of recreancy to capture the anger and frustration people experience when they lose trust in government or other responsible authorities. While most dictionaries define *recreancy* as disloyalty to a belief or duty, Weber added the important dimension of perception, making it a more sociologically interesting idea. A concept that points to citizens' perceptions of the resistance or unwillingness of organizations and officials to act on their behalf, recreancy signals a loss of trust and confidence in powerful social actors. We do not use this term in the present chapter, as it has not gained widespread currency in the literature.

4. Domhoff (1988); Mills (1956).

5. Mott (1974).

6. Case material from Shulman (1992).

7. Shulman (1992), 75.

8. Information from Charles Fisher, plant director during the Vietnam War era, as reported in Shulman (1992).

9. Shulman (1992), 76.

10. Ibid.

11. Ibid., 77.

12. Ibid., 78.

13. Ibid.

14. Ibid., 79.

15. Quoted in Shulman (1992), 75.

16. Harr (1995). Harr's book focuses on the legal intrigue of the Woburn case. For a sociological analysis of the case, see Brown and Mikkelson (1990).

17. Cable and Cable (1995).

18. Bell (2004).

19. One way in which clear-cutting can put a community in harm's way is by increased vulnerability to flooding.

20. Bell (2004), 106.

21. Bogard (1989), 3; see also *New York Times*, January 28, 1985.

22. Schnaiberg (1980); Schnaiberg and Gould (1994); Gould, Schnaiberg, and Weinberg (1996).

23. Domhoff (1998); Mills (1956).

24. Variations on this theme are captured in the concepts of iron triangles, cozy triangles, and subgovernment systems. For applications pertinent to environmental conflicts and decision making, see Bosso (1987) and Culhane (1981).

25. Cable and Cable (1995).

26. Coles and Foster (2001).

27. Harr (1995).

28. Other forms of intimidation include job blackmail and strategic lawsuits against public participation, or SLAPPS. For discussions, see Kazis and Grossman (1982) and Pring and Canan (1996).

29. Bell (2004), 17; see also Sachs (1996).

30. Case material taken from Gibbs (1982), Levine (1982), and Mazur (1998).

31. Levine (1982), 112.

32. Environmental Protection Agency (1978).

33. Levine (1982).

34. Ibid.

35. Mott (1974).

36. *Encyclopedia of Sociology* (1974), 111; emphasis in original.

37. *Buffalo Evening News* (1978).

38. Edelstein (1988).

39. Ibid.

40. Erikson (1976).

41. Beamish (2002); Clarke (1989).

42. Levine (1982), 42.

43. Simon (1997).

44. Beamish (2002).

45. Levine (1982), 118.

46. Ibid., 50.

47. Ibid., 98.

48. Case material taken from Margavio and Forsyth (1996).

49. Margavio and Forsyth (1996), 33.

50. Ibid., 6.

51. Ibid., 11.

52. Ibid., 37.

53. Ibid., xvi.

54. Ibid., 80.

55. Wheeler (1998), 77.

56. Mazmanian and Morell (1992).

57. For an overview of the kinds of problems discussed in this section see Zwart (2003), Futrell (1999), and Kuehn (1991).

58. For an example, see Dizard (1999).

59. Lewicki, Gray, and Elliot (2003).

4

The Problem of
Uncertain Knowledge

*If we knew all the laws of nature, we should need only one fact,
or the description of one actual phenomenon, to infer all the
particular results at that point. Now we know only a few laws,
and our result is vitiated, not, of course, by any confusion or
irregularity in nature, but by our ignorance of essential elements
in this calculation.*

Henry David Thoreau[1]

D ebating the merits of cutting old-growth forests, siting a hazardous
waste facility in a small town, and cleaning up toxins in the biosphere
are quite different controversies, though they share at least one important
feature: the problem of environments and communities is inevitably linked
to languages of expertise. Experts, however, rarely speak with a unified
voice. On the contrary, biologists, chemists, ecologists, epidemiologists, toxicologists, and engineers, to name a few types of experts, are apt to see the
environment and its problems in different, often contrasting, ways. Indeed,
within a single culture of expertise, clashing voices are frequently heard.
Two geological assays, for example, reach opposing conclusions regarding
the probability of earthquakes in a specific geographic area sited to bury

nuclear waste. The cacophonous chorus of science belies the promise of a world ordered by the rational, stepwise accumulation of knowledge.

Environmental conflicts are more often than not controversies over knowledge. They are disputes about knowing, about who can know, and what will count as valid and reliable knowledge in resolving differences. While there is always a visceral ingredient in any conflict, environmental conflicts are also noticeably cerebral.

This chapter examines the intersection of environmental problems, uncertain knowledge, and community conflict. It is a brief inquiry into the complicated relationships between individual knowledge and its role in configuring local environmental hostilities. It opens with a consideration of the uncertainty that plagues medical, ecological, and other rational inquiries into local environmental conditions. Next, borrowing from the language of lines and angles, we identify two key dimensions along which conflict develops: *vertical* and *horizontal*. Vertical disputes occur when local citizens and extra-local governmental or corporate experts reach opposing conclusions on the validity and reliability of tests, measurements, or experiments. Horizontal arguments are likely to occur *within* a community between competing citizens' groups with divergent claims to know something rational or scientific about local environmental troubles.

Both the vertical and horizontal axes of conflict over what will count as credible and dependable knowledge can occur simultaneously, and often do. But it is worth taking a look at each one separately for what it can tell us about the relationships between environmental troubles, uncertain knowledge, and community conflicts. Examples of the ways in which scientific uncertainty and the vertical and horizontal axes of knowledge disputes connect with material presented in previous chapters is provided in Box 4.1.

Sources of Uncertainty

The Northern Spotted Owl Controversy of the Pacific Northwest

In the late 1970s a battle erupted in the Pacific Northwest which would rage over the course of several decades, generate intense levels of acrimony and divisiveness, and become one of the best-known environmental controversies of the latter 20th century.[2] The conflict was over efforts to protect the northern spotted owl, and it pitted timber workers against environmentalists in a classic jobs-versus-environmental-protection standoff.

Box 4.1   Making Connections With Previous Chapters

The perplexing practical and political problems created by "the end of nature as we know it" are also the source of vexing knowledge problems. Combined with the scientific and technical basis of official environmental decision making (see Chapter 3), it is not surprising to find that scientists of all kinds figure prominently among conflict participants and that scientific statements of "fact" are a pervasive feature of environmental claims making (see Chapter 1, Box 1.2). Some frames may reflect scientific themes as well. In particular, frames which seek to cast some action as an "acceptable" or "unacceptable" risk are typically cloaked in the aura of science, as are efforts to label some claims "objective" and others "subjective" or "biased." Due to their central role in decision outcomes, scientific investigations are likely to figure prominently in the time line of a controversy (see Box 1.3 and Table 1.1.).

The vertical axis of knowledge disputes further develops the distinction between local versus extra-local conflict participants first seen in Chapter 1 (see Box 1.2) and more extensively developed in Chapter 3. Indeed, there is considerable spillover between this chapter and the previous one on trust and betrayal. The "official science" we talk about in this chapter refers to studies conducted by the many toxicologists, hydrologists, wildlife biologists, and other scientists employed by such government agencies as the U.S. Environmental Protection Agency. Battle lines in vertical knowledge disputes are frequently drawn between government scientists and local residents. Sources of uncertainty which plague all kinds of scientific endeavors can be a significant factor underlying what citizens perceive as intentionally slow and inadequate official response to local environmental problems. Uncertainty, in other words, can be a major contributor to structural betrayal, though it can also be used as a convenient excuse for premeditated betrayal.

In Chapter 1 (Box 1.4) we directed students to identify key points of human-environment contact, suggesting the potential of these to give rise to local knowledge claims. In the TEDs case in Chapter 3 we illustrated how such knowledge claims could clash with official scientific accounts, leading to accusations of intentional malfeasance. In the present chapter we undertake a more in-depth examination of local knowledge, allowing us to further unpack the complex relationship between uncertainty and premeditated, structural, and equivocal betrayal.

Knowledge disputes are inextricably linked to ambiguity, which has come up at several points in previous chapters. In the History as Invention section in Chapter 2, we discussed the inherent difficulty of determining which point in the past should provide the standard for ecosystem restoration projects, a theme explored again in this chapter in the Chicago Wilderness case. In Chapter 3, we discussed the ambiguity that can surround the intentionality underlying ostensibly craven, reckless, and self-serving acts (see Box 3.5). Ambiguity of all kinds can generate horizontal knowledge disputes; such disputes may manifest through the formation of contending grassroots groups (see Box 1.3).

Situating this conflict in broader historical developments is useful. Two of the accomplishments of the conservation movement of the late 19th– early 20th centuries were the creation of resource agencies like the U.S. Forest Service and the implementation of scientific management of natural resources. (For a brief history of the U.S. environmental movement, see Box 4.2.) The two primary goals guiding management decisions on public lands were to maximize extraction (though in a more sustainable way than the private sector) and to nourish game species for hunters. These two goals came together in the systematic war against predators waged by such resource agencies as the U.S. Department of the Interior, which protected both domestic livestock and the wild species targeted by hunters. Then, the conservation movement was almost exclusively focused on rural and wild areas and dominated by privileged, white sportsmen.[3]

Economic prosperity and the triumph of the "automobile culture" in the post–World War II era brought increasing numbers of individuals to national parks and other public lands. As a result, increased demands were made for nonhunting recreational uses of these spaces. These changing demands gained official recognition in the 1960 passage of the Multiple Use-Sustained Yield Act, which addresses the renewable surface resources of national forests. This act states, in part, "It is the policy of the Congress that the national forests are established and shall be administered for outdoor recreation, range, timber, watershed, and wildlife and fish purposes."[4] The act goes on to state that "some land will be used for less than all of these resources . . . and not necessarily the combination of uses that will give the greatest dollar return or the greatest unit output."[5] The 1976 Forest Land Policy and Management Act extended this multiple-use mandate to land managed by the Bureau of Land Management (BLM), also emphasizing wildlife (noncommodity) values.

The 1960s saw an upswing in public concern about environmental issues, as reflected in the growing popularity of the contemporary environmental movement. Books like Rachel Carson's *Silent Spring* helped to usher in a far more holistic understanding of ecosystems; the natural environment came to be seen as incredibly complex and interdependent, with apparently minor changes having the potential to reverberate into significant, unanticipated consequences. The contemporary environmental movement also championed the shift away from the exceedingly anthropocentric worldview of Western society; nonhuman species had intrinsic value, apart from any pragmatic uses they presented to humans.

These changing beliefs and values worked together to produce a new focus on nongame species. New appreciation was developed for the ecological role played by predators, and there was greater recognition that

Box 4.2   A Brief Look at the U.S. Environmental Movement

The dominant social paradigm of U.S. society is firmly rooted in Western cultural ideals about the relationship between humans and the natural environment. Humans are seen to stand outside of, and in a superior relationship to, nature. This separation, we contend, is based on our intelligence. Humans, we argue, are creative problem solvers who use technology to overcome ecological limitations. It is, furthermore, desirable that we humans bend nature to our will and utilize environmental resources to serve our needs. Through use of our intelligence, we can rest assured that the natural world will deliver up an endless supply of raw materials and waste disposal capabilities.

The U.S. environmental movement has challenged all of these core cultural beliefs. The first phase of significant environmental activity in this country occurred during the Progressive era of the late 19th and early 20th centuries and is typically referred to as the conservation movement. This movement was spurred by the closing of the western frontier, which challenged the popular belief that there would always be more land to farm, more forests to cut down, and more rivers to fish just over the hill and round the bend. As the "endless frontier" mentality hit up against the hard reality of a continent rapidly filling up, a few visionaries such as John Muir began championing wilderness preservation. The belief that the natural world might have an intrinsic value apart from the ways in which it served human uses began to gain a tenuous foothold.

Two world wars and the Great Depression in between reduced public interest in environmental issues, and it was not until the 1960s that a second upsurge in concern would transpire. Playing a crucial role in changing attitudes was the 1962 publication of Rachel Carson's *Silent Spring*. In this book Carson, a marine biologist and noted nature writer, condemned the widespread use of synthetic chemicals in the post–World War II era. A major focus of her critique was the popular pesticide DDT. *Silent Spring* helped to shift public environmental beliefs by drawing attention to the complexity, interdependency, and fragility of natural ecosystems. It also set the tone for the contemporary environmental movement by joining earlier conservationist issues with a new focus on the risks that advanced technologies pose to human welfare.

Over the four decades since Rachel Carson published *Silent Spring*, Americans consistently register moderate to strong commitments to environmental beliefs and values. Cultural change is occurring, but it has not yet taken the form of a wholehearted embrace of an environmental agenda. Indeed, Americans are the most prodigious resource users on the planet; we display a deep-seated commitment to a kind of hyperconsumerism where prosperity is measured by the amount and kinds of "things" we own. What Americans want, it appears, is both economic prosperity *and* environmental protection, tensions which have enormous implications for local environmental conflicts.

SOURCE: Cable and Cable (1995); Catton and Dunlap (1980); Dunlap (1992, 2002); Kline (2000); Mauss (1975); Milbrath (1984); Nash (1967).

species which had no immediate economic or recreational value for humans were still integral parts of ecosystems. Growing recognition of the need to protect all kinds of species of flora and fauna was codified in the 1973 Endangered Species Act (ESA).[6] The purposes of the act are to "provide a means whereby the ecosystems upon which endangered species and threatened species depend may be conserved, [and] to provide a program for the conservation of such endangered and threatened species."[7] As Yaffee explains,

> The 1973 law went far beyond earlier efforts at endangered species protection. While previous laws recognized educational, historical, recreational, and scientific values in endangered species, the 1973 act added aesthetic and ecological values, and listed ecosystem conservation as the first of several purposes of the statute. It offered protection to endangered species, subspecies, or isolated populations of animals or plants in imminent danger of extinctions. . . . Decisions as to what species warranted being stamped federally "endangered" were to be based solely on biological grounds, and species could be added to the federal list if they were threatened by almost anything, including "the present or threatened destruction, modification, or curtailment" of necessary habitat.[8]

Into this historical milieu walked Eric Forsman, a graduate student at Oregon State University (OSU). Forsman followed the trend of increased attention to nongame species by choosing to conduct his master's thesis research on the northern spotted owl. At the time Forsman began his research, very little was known about this particular bird, including its population size and habitat needs. That the reproductive pairs studied by Forsman always nested in old-growth forest suggested early during the research process that the birds might be in trouble. Indeed, Forsman's research suggested the birds not only had very specific habitat needs but were also highly sensitive to any alteration to their environment. The owls responded to disruption in their habitat by relocating to another section of old-growth forests and usually did not reproduce the year following relocation. As more and more old-growth forests were cut down, it would make it harder and harder for the owls to find a new home. The suppression of fertility linked to relocation spelled additional troubles for the future of the species.

Old-growth forests in the Pacific Northwest contain trees that are centuries old (what the Forest Service, or FS, refers to as "overmature"), as well as much dead and decaying wood. Because of this, the FS at the time regarded the old-growth forests as fire hazards and as a harbinger of insects which could spread from there to infest surrounding forests. They were too inaccessible to be of recreational value and did not contain species of interest to hunters (indeed, they were looked upon as "biological deserts"). From the FS's view, the best strategy was to cut down the old-growth forests and replace them with stands of managed Douglas fir. Most of the owl pairs studied by Forsman lived in habitat already marked off for timber sales.

Forsman and his faculty adviser Howard Wight began lobbying for the owl's protection. The Oregon Endangered Species Task Force (OESTF) began looking into the issue, pressing Forsman to specify the minimum amount of old-growth forest owls needed to reproduce and survive. Forsman's best guess at this time was 300 acres. "At 300 acres per site, protecting known sites would involve some 21,000 acres of public land scattered across a BLM and FS land base of 31 million acres in Oregon."[9] After 4 years of work the OESTF came up with a management plan which would protect 400 pairs of spotted owls, 290 on FS lands, 90 on BLM lands, and 20 on land with other ownerships.

By 1980, researchers had expanded their original estimates of the amount of land needed for owl habitat. Studies showed the average amount of old-growth forest used by each owl pair was 740 acres, with a minimal home range (combined old-growth and newer-growth forest) of 1,009 acres. In the Coast Range, mean home range per owl pair was found to be 4,728 acres.[10]

As the size of the estimated owl habitat grew, so did the amount of forest which would have to be removed from timber production to protect the owl's environment. Eventually, it came to look like protecting the northern spotted owl "could require the elimination of timber harvest activities over 11.6 million acres of land."[11] Boxed in by legislative mandates, a battle of competing knowledge claims emerged: Just how was the species endangered and what is the accurate composition and range of its home range? The scientific facts put forth by owl defenders were countered by other participants, and throughout the controversy basic information about the owl was marked by much uncertainty. Consider the basic problem of even counting the number of owls out there.

> [T]he wide ranging nature of the owl made information collection difficult. To count owls, researchers go into the woods and call to them. The fact that this is best done at night (in the dark) at regular intervals through often-steep, old growth forests makes this research labor-intense, demanding and dangerous. Moreover, the owl could potentially live in millions of acres of such forest adding to the difficulties in creating an accurate count. As a result of these inherent difficulties, estimates of the size of known owl populations varied considerably.[12]

❖

Look at the seemingly endless array of facts we now possess about biospheres, atmospheres, ecosystems, and pollution levels. It seems we possess a wealth of knowledge about our environment and that science is the place to turn for answers when we have questions about conservancy, siting, and exposure issues. Take a closer look, however, and we notice both expansive gaps in scientific knowledge and a remarkable absence of consensus among scientists over what, in fact, is a definitive account of this or that aspect of nature. The Enlightenment dream of a science capable of providing once-and-for-all answers to life's incessant puzzles is proving to be incorrigibly elusive.

The first problem is with the seemingly simple "fact" itself. Consider the following quotation from the now infamous contamination of Love Canal:

> That there are chemicals with known toxic effects to humans present in the landfill is undeniable. That they had made their way to the surface of the land-fill . . . is undeniable. That the presence of toxic chemicals was confirmed in and/or on the property . . . of landowners is undeniable as well. [W]hether the conditions at Love Canal had physically harmed or injured residents . . . was uncertain from the beginning.[13]

Students of environmental conflicts are wise to remember that facts are not incontrovertible statements of what is true. They do not exist like shells on the beach waiting for someone to pick them up. Although it might be of some comfort to assume that facts are simply obvious, it is a species of faulty reasoning. A fact is not *evident*. It is not self-evidently valuable or conclusive. A fact, rather, is more reasonably thought of as *evidence*. It is a fact because it supports some version of the world, the environment, people, events, and so on. A fact never speaks for itself; it always speaks for a scientific, theoretical, political, religious, or perhaps personal agenda. The modern fact, in short, is less a singular, concrete bit of information and more a part of an abstract version of the truth.

One study reports that creating a viable solution to old-growth harvesting and the protection of the spotted owl will result in the loss of 12,000 jobs; another study reports that 147,000 jobs will be lost. Move from these two quite different numbers back to the research methodologies that produced them, to the institutional affiliations of the investigators that created them, and to the funding source that paid for them. Viewed from this more abstract, inclusive vantage point, the 12,000 and 147,000 jobs lost represent two competing versions of the truth about employment opportunities and species protection. The idea that facts are evidence of some larger, more abstract set of assumptions, prejudices, and beliefs is of considerable assistance in understanding many local environmental controversies.

Experts can disagree among themselves because both the production and interpretation of "facts" rest on models and background assumptions that are open to dispute. Take the following statement, presented as an assertion of a fact: there are no significant human health risks from drinking water containing less than 17 ppb (parts per billion) polychlorinatedbyphenols (PCBs). Sounds authoritative. No fudging or hedging here. But, where does a fact like this originate? Probably from a leap of faith—scientists call it extrapolation—that begins with a few "data points."

Data points come from epidemiological field studies of exposed populations and toxicological laboratory experiments. Workers in factories producing chemical compounds are a prime target for studies on exposed populations. While such studies are needed for occupational safety reasons, workers are not representative of the broader population. Workers in hazardous facilities are adults, typically in the prime of life, and often male. Yet we know fetuses, infants, and children are more vulnerable to toxic chemicals and that there are sex differences in responses to medication, thus suggesting the potential for sex differences in chemical exposures.[14] Such studies do not take account of possible differences in exposure routes between workers and community residents (for example, inhalation and absorption through skin for workers versus ingestion for residents, if the substance is in their drinking water), nor do they address the problems of synergism (the interactive effects of a compound like PCBs with the multitude of other substances people are exposed to in their everyday lives).

There are, of course, ethical problems with conducting laboratory experiments which intentionally expose humans to a potentially harmful substance. Animals are used instead, but this also requires two important forms of extrapolation. First, because animal experiments are expensive, tests are not run on a wide range of exposure levels. Typically, tests are run at fairly high exposure levels, then dose-response curves are used to extrapolate health effects at lower exposure levels. The problem is that different dose-response curves yield quite different responses. One important difference is whether or not researchers use a threshold or nonthreshold model. The former assumes that health effects occur only after some threshold of exposure has been reached, while the latter model assumes *any* exposure will have health effects.[15]

These kinds of laboratory experiments also require extrapolating from animal species to humans. This requires the assumption that there are no species-specific responses to the substance. A study by Busch, Tanaka, and Gunter documented the fallacy of this assumption in one case. Beginning in the latter 1950s, researchers in Canada became concerned that erucic acid, a long-chain fatty acid naturally occurring in rapeseed (the oil-bearing crop that would eventually become known by the name canola) posed human health risks. Subsequent laboratory experiments on rats showed a compelling pattern of heart problems with animals who ate a diet high in rapeseed oil, and a plant breeding program was undertaken to eliminate erucic acid from rapeseed. It was only after this plant breeding program was completed that metabolic differences in how rats and humans break down long-chain fatty acids was discovered, indicating that humans would not have experienced the same heart problems. In this case, extrapolation from animal species to human was unwarranted.[16]

To provide one more example, extrapolation also occurs in fishery scientists' estimation of the population size of aquatic species. Think of the difficulty of counting fish stocks. Fishery scientists estimate populations of aquatic species by collecting the species present in a given location at a particular time, then extrapolating from that to develop a general picture of what the fish stocks of a given body of water looks like. The models on which such extrapolations are based incorporate assumptions, such as population movements of various species, which are open to questioning and dispute.[17]

One area in which extrapolation is necessary and inevitable is in efforts to predict the future. Such predictions present ample opportunity for contention. Consider the case of siting disputes. In this case, projections or extrapolations must be made about the likely consequences of activities. How much of a danger will the facility pose to the local community? Will there be accidents, such as fires, explosions, or releases of gases? How many new jobs will the facility create? The future—as-yet-to-be-decided—nature of these questions ensures conjectures, opposing science, and endless debate.

Future uncertainty is often couched in the language of risk. The idea of risk is inseparable from the idea of uncertainty.[18] If I am 100% certain of the outcome of a card game because I stacked the deck, I can't be said to be taking a risk by playing cards. In contemporary history, however, the "stacked deck" is conspicuously absent. We are far more uncertain than certain about things that matter to us. Pervasive uncertainty encourages us to think in the calculus of risk. Chance, fortuity, and contingency are ordinary modes of mental and social life. Risky foods, security risks, medical contingencies and dangers, environmental hazards, and the probability of loss are some of the more prominent areas governed by uncertainties.

In local environmental conflicts the uncertainty of novel risks is often mitigated by comparing that class of risks to far more familiar risks. Thus one side of a conflict might say, "You have more risk of being hit by lightning than developing lung cancer from breathing the particulate matter released by our smokestack." The other side might counter with, "Breathing the filthy, polluted air from this factory is just like smoking five packs of cigarettes a day for 20 years." Clarke describes the strategy whereby risks of hazardous technologies are minimized by creating apparent affinities with mundane events. Thus, evacuating a major metropolitan area in response to a meltdown at a nuclear power plant can be treated as analogous to the emptying out of the city, which occurs 5 days a week as commuters head home.[19]

It is important to remember that our focus here is on the process by which scientific facts are produced and translated into forms readily available for official use and public consumption. Scientists are trained to recognize, and report, the limitations of their study designs and sampling strategy. When publishing in scholarly venues, scientists use language which is cautious and circumspect in nature, such as "the research findings suggest that . . ." rather than "the research findings prove that . . ." Yet once entered into official and public forums, facts are more likely to be presented as self-evident and certain, a practice which obfuscates the investigative process by which the facts were produced, including the employment of background assumptions, limitations, qualifications, and hedging. In their public presentations of "the facts" of a conservancy, siting, or exposure dispute, conflict participants seeking to clothe their claims in the legitimation of science (which includes but is not necessarily limited to scientists) employ instruments, measurements, statistical charts, and other abstract representations of nature that affect precision and promise certainty. The problem, however, is that it is far easier to *appear* precise than it is *to be* certain.

Box 4.3 summarizes the types of questions students of local environmental conflicts might want to raise about the sources of uncertain knowledge in local environmental conflicts. We turn now to a consideration of how ambiguity and uncertainty can contribute to conflicts between local residents and outside experts.

Box 4.3   Adding to the Portfolio: Sources of Uncertainty

1. What is the existing state of scientific knowledge in areas relevant to the conservancy, siting, or exposure dispute? What are the institutional affiliations of the investigators generating relevant scientific knowledge?

2. What models and background assumptions underlie the "scientific facts" proffered in the case? Are these models the subject of criticism and questioning?

3. Are extrapolations about the future a source of controversy?

4. How is future uncertainty conveyed in the language of risk? What comparative (or analogous) risk profiles are offered, and do these serve to heighten or lessen the sense of impending danger?

5. Are instruments, measures, statistics, charts, and similar mechanisms used to couch "facts" in an aura of certainty and precision?

The Vertical Axis of Knowledge Disputes

Sheep, Radioactivity, and Contested Knowledge

Chernobyl is a small town in the Ukraine, 105 kilometers north of Kiev. A few kilometers from Chernobyl, the former Soviet Union operated four powerful nuclear reactors. On April 26, 1986, at 1:23 a.m., an accident occurred during a safety test in the fourth unit of the Chernobyl Nuclear Plant. An unexpected power surge caused a sudden burst of heat that destroyed the top half of the reactor, starting a nuclear fire that lasted 10 days.[20] The explosion and fire released an amount of radioactivity "equal to that from all the atomic bombs ever tested above ground."[21] Radioactive clouds, pushed by the winds, traveled east to Japan and west to Britain. Indeed, Chernobyl's radioactive debris fell on the United States. But our story occurs in the United Kingdom, specifically in the sheep farming district of Cumbria in the far northwest.[22]

Cumbria is a traditional farming culture. Its inhabitants labor at the difficult and taxing work of highland husbandry. Bound by a common history, long-standing traditions, and ancient dialects, residents of this rural district are among the last remnants of a pastoral way of life in increasingly industrialized England. But their provincial isolation was not enough to spare them the fallout of one of the world's worst industrial accidents.[23]

Less than a month after the nuclear fire at Chernobyl, thunderstorms carried radioactive caesium isotopes from contaminated clouds to the fertile soils of the Cumbrian hills. Two types of caesium isotopes fell to the earth during the storms: caesium 134 with a half-life of approximately 2.4 years and caesium 137 with a half-life of 28 years.[24] The raining caesium was a source of considerable concern for both the farmers and the British government.

> [A] sudden blanket ban on the movement and sale of sheep from defined areas [of contamination] in hill regions such as the Lake District of northern England . . . [would be] potentially ruinous to what was a marginal and economically fragile sector of British farming, because these farmers depended for almost all of their annual income on being able to sell a large crop of surplus lambs from midsummer onwards.[25]

At first, farmers heard reassuring accounts from scientists working for the Ministry of Agriculture, Fisheries, and Food (MAFF) who responded to the fallout by placing a 3-week ban on the movement and sale of sheep. Shortly after the 3-week restriction, however, the MAFF unexpectedly imposed an indefinite prohibition on movement to alternative pastures and the sale of all allegedly contaminated sheep. This confusing and frustrating change in directives initiated a cycle of conflict between the farmers and scientists over what would count as valid and reliable knowledge about sheep and contamination that continues today.

The source of the conflict is a melange of factors combining in unexpected ways to create intractable differences between farmers on the one side and government scientists on the other. The first error committed by government scientists was a miscalculation of the type of soil common to the Cumbrian hill country. Their initial 3-week ban was based on the belief that soil in the hills was alkaline based and would therefore trap the radioactivity, preventing it from reaching the grass. While some soil is alkaline based, a good deal of the hill soil is acid peaty based. Acid soil is porous, ensuring that radiocaesium remains mobile and accessible to uptake by plant roots.[26] Rather than admitting their error, however, the government scientists simply recalibrated their conclusions, and the MAFF switched its original 3-week ban to an indefinite ban.

The second error was the unwillingness of government scientists to listen to and accommodate the hard-won expertise of sheep farmers whose local knowledge was essential to the successful management of the problem. The sheep farmers quickly determined that the risk posed by fallout from Chernobyl was compounded by the preexisting problem of a nuclear processing plant operating a few kilometers from the hill country and itself a notorious polluter.[27] In 1957, the Sellafield nuclear reprocessing plant caught fire and released radiocaesium and other radioactive materials, contaminating the surrounding countryside. Farmers believed that fugitive emissions, announced by Sellafield, continued to escape the plant, and wondered aloud whether this might be an additional source of the caesium isotopes contaminating their sheep. Initially, however, the MAFF scientists vigorously defended their assertion that the contaminating isotopes were from the Chernobyl fire, not Sellafield. Local experience caused one farmer to question this assertion, his skepticism based on his observation that the crescent-shaped radioactive hotspot was located at the same altitude where steam clouds rising from the Sellafield cooling towers hit the mountains.[28]

The sheep farmers' implication of the Sellafield plant in the total load of radioactive isotopes contaminating the hill country sheep was at least partially validated by an important datum that emerged over a year after the Chernobyl fire. The MAFF scientists were forced to admit that other sources, including Sellafield, accounted for roughly half of the radioactive caesium found in the area.[29] Using commonsense knowledge derived from visual observation and simple reasoning, the hill farmers constructed a more complicated and, in the end, more accurate account of the origins of radioactive fallout in the Cumbrian hills.

———————————— ❖ ————————————

Evaluation and assessment are typically occasions for lively debate: What should be measured? How should it be measured? Who should conduct the measurement? What does a specific measurement mean? Suggested in the controversy over the origins of radiocaesium is the fault line between community ways of knowing and scientific ways of knowing. Experts see risks in the narrow grammar of probabilities and numerical coefficients. Communities, on the other hand, see risks embedded in their ways of life, woven into the cloth of day-to-day routines.[30] Scientists, in other words, think and talk about an environmental problem in one fashion, local community residents think and talk about that same problem in a quite different fashion. Communities identify issues and raise questions that are not part of the scientific approach to the problem, while scientists survey, measure, and calculate what is either irrelevant or unimportant to communities, or worse, perceived as error-ridden and wrong.[31]

Yet over the last several decades, ordinary people have become increasingly vocal about having their own experiences treated as a credible source of knowledge in the decision-making process.[32] Moreover, the National Research Council recently advised against decision-making approaches which treat members of the lay public as simple recipients of scientific knowledge, advocating instead for an approach to knowledge production that brings citizen experiences and knowledge in at the ground floor of problem definition and study design.[33] Community residents are uniquely placed to generate several types of knowledge about local environmental troubles. As outlined by Allan, these include

- Direct observation of a working practice, e.g., of smoke plumes emanating from disposal sites. . . . It is also commonly observed that emissions are more severe at night when formal inspection tends to be limited—the local community is well placed to make such observations.
- [Local observations] that health has been directly affected—as when workers at a neighboring site claimed they are suffering from incinerator emissions or members of a community noted unusual patterns of illness. . . .
- Comparisons with other sites . . . run by the same company or where similar industrial processes are in operation. This can involve the establishment of community networks where groups build upon the experience of others elsewhere.

- Systematic data collection—in one case, through a round-the-clock "toxic watch" recording activities and pollution levels.[34]

This grounded, experiential knowledge is typically viewed by residents as useful in mitigating at least some of the uncertainty surrounding environmental troubles, and indeed, as we saw above in the Cumbria case, may be used as a basis to counter scientific knowledge claims. To provide another example, let's consider the case of 2,4,5-T.[35]

During the 1980s, the herbicide 2,4,5-T was a source of controversy between British regulatory authorities and British farmers. Produced since the 1940s, 2,4,5-T (under its wartime name Agent Orange) acquired a notorious reputation from its use as a defoliant in the Vietnam War. The herbicide is suspected of causing, among other things, chloracne, birth defects, spontaneous abortions, and several types of cancer.

In spite of its less than wholesome reputation, 2,4,5-T was commonly used in Britain. Homeowners used it to control weeds in their gardens. Railway employees sprayed it on tracks to kill troublesome vegetation. Farmers and forestry workers regularly used it to protect crops and clear underbrush.

The British government took the position that the herbicide was safe to use if applied correctly. Its Advisory Committee on Pesticides concluded a review of the scientific literature on 2,4,5-T, proclaiming that it "can safely be used in the UK in the recommended way and for the recommended purposes."[36] The committee acknowledged that the public was concerned, but also pointed out that the public was not informed about the science of the issue.

The committee approached its task as if it were operating in a laboratory, free from outside noise and interferences. Deliberating on the fate of the herbicide as if it existed in a vacuum, the personal experiences of people who really worked with the substance could be safely ignored. The committee claimed that "its own knowledge and experience is backed up by a valuable body of medical and scientific expertise" far more legitimate than ordinary people can discover on their own.[37]

The position of the National Union of Agricultural and Allied Workers (NUAAW), however, approached the herbicide from a quite different epistemic vantage point. For those nonexperts, laboratory studies and literature surveys were inadequate sources of knowledge about their personal experiences with 2,4,5-T. In its report to Britain's Minister of Agriculture, Fisheries and Food, the NUAAW concluded that the personal experiences of people who use 2,4,5-T could not be replicated in the laboratory. "It is the Union's conviction, distilled from the experiences of thousands of members working in forests and on farms, that the conditions envisaged by the Advisory Committee are impossible to reproduce in the field."[38]

In other words, experimental data generated in laboratories cannot reliably predict the seemingly endless personal habits, experiences, serendipitous events, and so on of the seemingly endless number of people who come into contact with this caustic chemical agent. The NUAAW questioned the idea that government and industrial regulators could foresee all the particularities, unusual circumstances, or chance occurrences typically encountered in a normal work environment. Normal or routine from the vantage point of the worker in the field is best captured in Murphy's infamous law. Perhaps the most reliable approach to recommended use instructions is to base an application protocol on the assumption that what can go wrong probably will.

Reflected in this controversy is a more complicated conflict between two quite different ways of knowing, each claiming to be based on instrumental, rational knowledge. Blurring the traditional distinction between layperson and expert, farm and forestry workers are claiming to know something about the use of an industrial chemical that should be the basis for government regulation of the substance. The basis of their knowledge claims is the subjective human experience. For the scientific committee, on the other hand, valid and reliable knowledge in the modern world is the product of experimental science and pointedly not subjective experiences. Laypeople, of course, can trust their senses as sources of knowing. It is simply that when they do so, they cannot claim to know something scientific or medical about themselves or their world. Or so the advisory committee argued.

For the farm and forestry workers, however, professional scientific knowledge is incoherent, unable to account for their personal experiences. The conflict, it seems, is between a local, concrete knowledge based on systematic observation and analysis and a remote abstract knowledge based on experimental design and statistical coefficients. Such local, practical knowledge has always existed, of course; what is new is the public's role in challenging the validity and reliability claims of institutional science.

The problem between community knowledge and scientific knowledge is more than the different stances each takes toward what should count as important to know about an environmental problem. It is also the problem of *power*. The fact is that corporate or government scientists typically exercise jurisdiction over environmental questions. This jurisdiction is expressed in the capacity of institutional science to both set the agenda of research, deciding what variables will and will not be included in analysis, the size of the study population, and so on, and to control the expressive arena for the dissemination and discussion of the data.[39] Despite the call for changes from the National Research Council and similar groups, official science almost always enjoys both the first and the last word. Community ways of knowing might receive a hearing but are unlikely to be incorporated into the scientists' methods, studies, or reports. Indeed, knowledge claims by local people are more likely to be viewed by government or corporate researchers as "spurious" or "anecdotal," as seen in the following example.

As readers may recall from previous chapters, Centralia is a small town in northeast Pennsylvania plagued by a fire burning out of control in the mazeway of underground shafts and passageways constructed to mine anthracite coal. At a meeting between community residents and mine engineers, experts observed that a significant problem in abating the fire was the absence of good maps showing the exact locations of the shafts and passageways underneath the town. At this juncture a middle-aged man in the audience stood up and offered the following counsel: "Of course those maps are worthless, they were made to get mining permits not map the real ground below. You had to have them. But I'll tell you, I have walked under this town for fifteen years. I know where the air is getting in to feed the fire and the location of the tunnels carrying the fire. I'll work with you if you want." The mining engineer in charge of the meeting thanked the man and noted that "it was getting late. I wonder if there are any more questions."[40]

Illustrated in this brief exchange is the voice of power silencing an alternative, and presumably rational, approach to acquiring sorely needed information. In this exercise in power, two ways of knowing the world fail to collaborate on a solution to a complex environmental hazard. Mining engineers remain puzzled and the mine fire a riddle with no apparent solution. The retired miner knew something about the fire and offered to join his local expertise with the expertise of the scientists. Together, perhaps, a solution could be found. It is true, of course, that community expertise without mining engineering is not sufficient to mount a successful project to extinguish or abate the fire. But common sense suggests that mining engineering without the assistance of local knowledge would continue to propose solutions that prove both expensive and unworkable. Exercising their institutional authority to pick and choose what knowledge would count as useful in solving the riddle of the mine fire, the engineers chose to ignore the retired miner. The Centralia mine fire has burned for over 30 years with no end in sight.

As the several cases presented in this section illustrate, sometimes residents advance their own local knowledge, couched in fairly mundane terms, to counter the scientific claims of powerful social actors such as corporations and government agencies. Activists have learned, however, that their efforts are likely to be more successful if their claims are cloaked in the technocratic language of expertise. As a result, groups and organizations are unhinging the languages of expertise from expert systems, taking them into their communal worlds, tinkering with them sufficiently to make rational sense of their miseries, and appealing to significant institutional others based on a rhetoric of community rationality.

Ordinary people are fusing a moral appeal to safe or healthy environments with a popular appropriation of expert knowledge to make a particularly pervasive claim on institutions to change or modify behaviors and policies. It is one thing for a young woman cradling an infant to appeal to a government hearing board in the language of home, hearth, and children, for example; it is quite another when this same woman clutches her child to her breast and talks in the complicated language of toxicology, discussing the neurotoxic or teratagenic effects of boron or dichlorotetrafluoroethane on her child's cognitive development.

In such cases, people are doing more than relying on a rhetoric of civil rights or environmental justice, as important as these appeals are; citizens are also arming themselves with the lingual resources of toxicology, environmental impact assessment, biomedicine, risk inventories, nuclear engineering, and other instruments of reason. The emergence of citizen science to challenge the assertions of a corporate- or government-sponsored science is a key flash point in local environmental controversies.[41] One type of citizen science sometimes found in exposure disputes is that of popular epidemiology.

Defined as a "process by which laypersons gather scientific data and other information and also direct and marshal the knowledge and resources of experts," popular epidemiology challenges the paradigm of conventional epidemiology, accusing it of failing to identify anything but the most gross environmental origins of disease.[42] Emotionally and technically charged questions about environments and health are often beyond the purview of conventional epidemiology. "Are we in an environment in which invisible contamination is present? Is this contamination actually being absorbed by body tissue? Is the absorbed dose dangerous?"[43] Increasingly, communities are resisting state- and corporate-sponsored epidemiology, arguing for the validity and reliability of their own, homegrown version. Let's return to the case of 2,4,5-T.

For the NUAAW, statistical rates of such health problems as chloracne and miscarriages were unable to account for why a neighbor was inflicted with painful skin rashes after using the herbicide or why a woman whose husband carried chemical residue home on his clothes spontaneously aborted what appeared to be a healthy fetus. The frequency of these personal, nonstatistical experiences prompted the NUAAW to sponsor a survey among its membership to discern what laypeople knew about how to apply the herbicide and how to avoid physical contact with it or its gaseous vapors. Additional questions included frequency of use and symptoms after use. A total of 40 questions were asked.

In addition to the survey results, the report, which was submitted to Britain's Minister of Agriculture, Fisheries and Food, also included 14 case studies of people who suffered from medical problems after being exposed to the herbicide. In developing its case studies, the NUAAW relied on medical records, family histories, and employment records documenting contact with the herbicide. The intention was to "establish the level of exposure involved and the scale of alleged effects" for each case.[44]

The NUAAW constructed its own standard of validity to oppose the tests of significance clusters relied upon by the committee's experts. Based on its survey and case study data, the NUAAW proposed a principle for assessing the particular danger associated with the use of potentially risky substances. The concept, "balance of probabilities," was introduced as a reasonable approach to the inherent difficulties in foreseeing all of the ways in which 2,4,5-T would be used in mundane, uncontrollable situations.

The balance of probabilities test asked the British government to consider how the herbicide is used in local settings and to make a reasonable determination whether or not it is possible to control for all the contingencies and unexpected, chance events in applying the chemical. Note their reasoning:

> In our view the decision to ban the herbicide has to be made on the balance of probabilities. . . . [W]here lives are at stake a responsible body cannot wait, as was the case with asbestos, until there is a sufficiently impressive death toll.[45]

The NUAAW's appeal to the British government for the right to work in a safe environment is based on an accounting of personal experience, mundane or practical knowledge, and its own sociomedical study. Making epidemiological knowledge is often critical to forging a timely and medically judicious approach to environmental contamination. But making this knowledge is not the straightforward process it seems. Citizens whose health and well-being are at stake in these cases are rarely passive when faced with epidemiological studies that seem to be asking the "wrong" questions, attending to "insignificant" facts, and harping on unsound "standards of proof." More important, as this case illustrates, their responses might include conducting their own epidemiological studies.

Box 4.4 is a summary of the key issues identified in the study of uncertain knowledge, environmental troubles and community conflict viewed from the vertical axis. We turn our attention now to the other axis along which knowledge disputes develop.

Box 4.4   Adding to the Portfolio: The Vertical Axis of Knowledge Disputes

---

1. Are local residents questioning the veracity of expert (scientific) claims?

2. Do community residents advance their own local knowledge about environmental conditions?

3. Are experts willing to consider the potential validity of local knowledge, or do they summarily dismiss it as "anecdotal" and "spurious"?

4. Are residents appropriating the language of expertise to incorporate into their own local claims?

5. Do local residents conduct any popular epidemiological investigations?

The Horizontal Axis of Knowledge Disputes

The Chicago Wilderness Controversy

The words *Chicago* and *wilderness* might at first glance appear unsuited for one another. Chicago, after all, is the third largest city in the United States. What on earth could it have to do with wilderness? A good deal actually, as we will see, and much of it contentious.[46]

In the early 1900s, reflecting the progressive politics of the time, Illinois set aside 98,000 acres of municipal Chicago land as legally protected forest preserve. More important, "these preserves were not conceived as city parks, but as wild land preserves with a conservation mission."[47] In 1996 a new initiative was launched in Chicago. Dubbed "Chicago Wilderness," this project seeks to restore more than 200,000 acres in and around the city to its pre-European historical state of tall grass prairie. Dozens of local citizens were "trained" to recognize the flora and fauna from different historical periods and to work to enhance their growth while limiting and eliminating the growth of other species. The project met with considerable opposition from other citizens who placed a high value on the aesthetic and environmental utility of the contemporary landscape.

Ecological restoration, as the name implies, seeks to reclaim deteriorated or extinct ecosystems, re-creating what once was, or at least thought to be. Preservation, on the other hand, signals a quite different stance toward the environment. To preserve is to protect an existing ecosystem, to shield it from alteration and change. The restorationists assumed their vision of the future Chicago was a landscape reminiscent of a time long past and one worth reconstituting. More important, they made their arguments using both ecological and emotional appeals. The other faction, the preservationists, argued to the contrary that ecologies are not so much historical as they are contemporary, evolving systems that require nurturing, not wholesale reversion to some arbitrary point in the past. They too made their arguments in both the languages of ecology and emotions. The Chicago Wilderness Project quickly became an emotional dispute among the citizens of Cook County over the definition of "nature and science."[48]

By 1996 most of the flora and fauna present during the pre-European settlement history of this region was extinct or near extinction. Only in a few archipelagoes spared from the plow and the backhoe were found the original prairie and tall grass savannahs characteristic of the 18th-century Midwest. The Chicago Region Biodiversity Council (CRBC) announced in April of 1996 that it was sponsoring a major restoration initiative to reconstruct the ecosystem the early settlers encountered more than 200 years ago. The CRBC is an umbrella organization representing more than 90 local groups interested in restoring and protecting Chicago's wilderness. Two of its member groups, the Nature Conservancy and the Volunteer Stewardship Network (VSN), trained citizen volunteers in the science of restoration ecology. These trainees thought of themselves as citizen experts experienced in identifying flora and fauna and their appropriate ecological niches.

Ecosystem restoration, however benign and nurturing it might sound, is often a source of local conflict. For some of Chicago's residents, restoration meant clear-cutting woodlands they had lived beside for years. Restoration and destruction, in other words, go hand-in-hand; before the past can be re-created, the present must first be eradicated. For people who enjoyed the existing landscape, protecting the "natural areas" of woods and parks from restoration efforts made sense. By the fall of 1996 at least three citizen opposition groups had emerged: the Association of Let Nature Take its Course, Trees for Life, and the Voice for Wilderness.[49]

Among the tactics of the preservationists in their struggle with the restorationists was calling the claims of the citizen experts into question. A leaflet distributed by members of Trees for Life, for example, exclaims: "How are these amateurs experts?! They have no formal training or credentials!"[50] But more than questioning the legitimacy of credentials fueled this conflict. Preservationists questioned the science of the restorationists. A student of this controversy writes:

> During the painful growth period, when VSN [Volunteer Stewardship Network] attempted to establish themselves as expert "knowers" of the land, criticism was focused on just what made these lay volunteers favored members of the public who could create privileged stories about the local landscape's condition and needs.[51]

"Data wars" broke out between Chicago's preservationists and restorationists.[52] Restorationists claimed a specialist knowledge, won by hands-on training, of the area's contemporary and pre-European flora and fauna. From the perspective of the restorationists, area residents who did not educate themselves in the science of restoration "could not be expert knowers of the land or be in a position to justifiably pass judgement on restorationists."[53] For many preservationists, on the other hand, restoration science is at best misleading, and at worst, a risk to humans and wildlife. As one critic noted:

> [I]t sounds wonderful to say, "We're going to restore those woodlands . . ." Restoration doesn't sound like "We are going to cut down 158 black cherry trees . . ." [Restoration] includes girdling trees . . . burns that create pollution . . . and loss of some wildlife.[54]

Restorationists and preservationists in Chicago still cannot agree on a scientific definition of ecosystem, on what are truly "native" and "foreign" flora, what is a true "forest canopy," and so on. "Neither side can step outside the limits of its commitment to differing concepts of appropriate science."[55]

❖

The boundary disputes between citizens and experts over what will count as valid and reliable knowledge of local environmental troubles is often a source of marked and obdurate conflict. But this vertical pattern often occurs in tandem with another, more problematic, pattern of conflict. Residents of a town or neighborhood can find *themselves* in disagreement over the appropriate rational or scientific response to an environmental puzzle or danger. To understand the reasons for this, we need to examine both the useful distinction between Arcadian and historical communities and the continuation of ambiguity into the local level. Let's begin with the first of these tasks.

There are at least two meanings of the word *community*, and they are often confused. One meaning is grounded in the romantic, sentimental notion of the Arcadian community. Tranquility, peace, and harmony prevail here. We find the Arcadian community in film and literature (see, for example, Wordsworth's *Evangeline*). A second meaning is grounded in the blunt, enduring politics of everyday life where understanding is countered by misunderstanding, giving by taking, solidarity by alienation; in short, the historical community. As we specified in Chapter 2, communities do not enter into local environmental controversies as blank slates, but rather bring with them tools and liabilities from the past. It is useful here to extend this discussion. Historical communities may aspire to be more Arcadian, or they may romanticize a past they thought was more Arcadian. Actual historical communities, however, do not conform to the romantic notions of peace, harmony, and fellowship (though, of course, communities do differ in terms of how close or how far they fall from this ideal). Dissent, difference, opposition, and objection are among the prosaic realities of life lived in the company of others.

The idea of the historical, political community prepares us to expect to find differences *within* communities regarding how, in fact, environmental issues should be considered, indeed thought about. Combine the real politic of historical communities with the often confusing, perplexing character of environmental troubles, and it is not difficult to imagine a local public unable to reach consensus on the scope and degree of their troubles and what should be done about them, if anything.

There is one moment or event, however, in which the historical community does become something akin to the Arcadian ideal: the immediate aftermath of an acute natural disaster. Students of natural disasters point to the emergence of "therapeutic communities" in the wake of hurricanes, floods, and other "acts of God."[56] These communities, albeit short lived, are remarkable for their solidarity, cooperativeness, and expressions of empathy. So predictable are the emergence of therapeutic communities following natural disasters that sociologists refer to these types of calamities as "consensus-type" crises.[57] Reason suggests that a consensus is easier to achieve when the evidence of destruction is visible, unavoidable, and incontestable. A tornado touches down and ravages a street, leaving little doubt about damage.[58]

If the strong consensus immediately following a natural disaster is based in part on irrefutable evidence of destruction, perhaps the strong dissensus accompanying many local environmental troubles is based, at least in part, on the equivocal, ambiguous, contentious quality of much environmental evidence. People share a sensorial connection to visible, tangible physical destruction. Most environmental questions and issues, however, require cerebral, abstract, deductive connections that invite different points of view and opposing conclusions. Several studies of local environmental controversies point to the role of uncertain knowledge in creating community divisiveness.

The equivocal evidence of chemical contamination at Love Canal, for example, encouraged the emergence of three grassroots groups, each organized around a different "scientific" perception of the amount and kind of risks posed by the contaminants.[59] Similarly, seven local protest groups emerged in the wake of the radiation accident at Three Mile Island, each lobbying for a different assessment of the problems posed by the contamination.[60] Asbestos contamination in Globe, Arizona, split a community. "The nonvictimized" evaluated the evidence of risk far differently from their neighbors whose houses and yards were registering high rates of fiber exposure.[61]

As we saw in the Chicago Wilderness controversy, citizens in these cases differed over the validity and reliability of their respective claims to expertise. Complicating the vertical conflicts between citizen experts and corporate or government experts, horizontal disputes are waged between citizen groups who argue for the truth value of their specific expertise. Neighbors face one another as competing "experts."

Horizontal axis conflict can occur in tandem with vertical axis conflict. Citizen groups organized around varying explanations of an environmental issue or trouble are likely to find allies in extra-local organizations who are promoting an interpretation similar to their own. This occurred in the controversy between the restorationists and the preservationists in the Chicago Wilderness Project. The two contentious positions on the development of Chicago's open spaces found support in a variety of state and national organizations promoting either restoration or preservation. Ambiguity, uncertainty, and disagreements among the experts can spill over into the local arena.

At the horizontal level, disputes over what are valid ways of knowing local environmental problems can quickly slide into personal invective. In their study of Love Canal, for example, Fowlkes and Miller report:

> For the most part . . . families that believe that chemical migration was of limited seriousness do not so much marshal a body of evidence in support of their position as they discredit any and all claims that migration [was] widespread. They discredit those claims by categorically discrediting the people who make them. [62]

Indeed, we suspect the emotional intensity of horizontal axis conflicts is higher than those typically found in vertical axis disputes. Perhaps this is because the varying stakes in these disputes are experienced as threatening the preservation of the historic community and perhaps ripping apart any pretense to Arcadian tranquility. If my mundane reasoning leads me to conclude that the local water is potable, my neighbor who concludes it is contaminated might be seen as a threat to my way of life.

Readers can find a summary of the major highlights raised in this section in Box 4.5.

Box 4.5   Adding to the Portfolio: The Horizontal Axis of Knowledge Disputes

1. How ambiguous are the signals about environmental initiatives or troubles?
2. Do some residents join forces (form grassroots groups) to launch organized attacks on other residents' knowledge claims?
3. Do local residents disagree over who among them can authoritatively speak on (claim to be an expert on) knowledge issues?
4. Are disagreements among outside experts carried over into disagreements among contending factions of local residents?
5. Do local residents use personal attacks to discredit contending knowledge claims made by other residents?

A Concluding Word

Students of local environmental conflicts will almost inevitably encounter the complex problem of uncertain knowledge and dissension. Look for this conflict in both its vertical and horizontal expressions. A local citizen-based knowledge is likely to differ in significant ways from the knowledge of corporate and government scientists. Combining observation and experience with a calculating reasoning, citizens "know" their local environment in a quite different manner than the hydrologist, biologist, or epidemiologist sent to study their backyards. Local conflicts which incorporate both horizontal and vertical struggles over the certainty of competing knowledge claims are especially complicated and dynamic, and worthy of serious investigation.

Knowledge claims represent the cerebral side of environmental conflicts, though they may sometimes be joined with emotional appeals or become conflated with other issues. Especially along the vertical axis, science brings to disputes the language of rationality and the belief in an obdurate external reality which (at least from the scientific worldview) is theoretically capable of being studied, measured, and ultimately known. These underlying assumptions provide the milieu in which discussions about knowledge claims occur, and at least provide an impetus toward objectivity and emotional distance even in situations characterized by extreme ambiguity.

In the following chapter we shift our attention from the cerebral to the emotional side of local environmental conflicts. Disputes over justice, fairness, and values cannot be settled by even the pretense of an appeal to empirical conditions; the burning issues here deal not with questions of *what is* but rather *what should be.* While there are many aspects of local environmental conflicts which fuel anger, hostility, frustration, and outrage, there is probably nothing that can more quickly lead to volatile emotional responses than local residents' perceptions that they are being treated in an unjust manner.

STUDENT EXERCISES

1. Go back to one of the case vignettes presented in previous chapters. Imagine you are employed by a government regulatory agency charged with making key decisions in the case (for example, whether or not to allow timber to be harvested, how to clean up a contaminated site, whether or not to grant discharge permits, or whether or not to proceed with the construction of a dam). Write a report for your supervisor about what type of scientific investigations need to be conducted in this case. In other words, what kinds of information does the agency need to know before rendering its decision? To the best of your ability, specify which kinds of disciplinary specialists (e.g., toxicologists, hydrologists, economists) would be needed to conduct these investigations.

2. Imagine that you work for a national environmental organization and you have been sent to collaborate with community activists trying to get something done about local groundwater contaminated by a manufacturing plant. Both the corporation which owns the plant and the state Department of Public Health maintain that the toxins in the water are at levels too low to be a threat to public health. How would you help local residents go about launching an attack on the corporate and government scientific investigations used to back up claims of limited risk?

Notes

1. Thoreau (1952), 310–311.
2. Case material from Yaffee (1994).
3. Kline (2000); Gottlieb (1993).
4. *Selected Environmental Law Statutes* (1995), 126.
5. Ibid., 127.
6. This act was first passed in 1966, but without the regulatory teeth of the 1973 version.
7. *Selected Environmental Law Statutes, 1995–1996 Educational Edition* (1995), 156.
8. Yaffee (1994), 12–13.
9. Ibid., 24.

10. Ibid., 53.

11. Ibid., xvii–xix.

12. Ibid., 171.

13. Fowlkes and Miller (1982), 44.

14. Endocrine disrupters would also lend support to this suspicion; see Colborn, Dumanoski, and Myers (1997).

15. Harte, Holdren, Schneider, and Shirley (1991).

16. Busch, Tanaka, and Gunter (2000).

17. Dobbs (2000).

18. Beck (1995).

19. Clarke (1999).

20. Maples and Snell (1988), 19.

21. Weisaeth (1991), 53.

22. Case material from Wynne (1992, 1996).

23. Wynne (1992, 1996).

24. Weisaeth (1991), 54.

25. Wynne (1996), 62.

26. Wynne (1996), 64.

27. Wynne (1996); McSorley (1990).

28. Wynne (1992).

29. Wynne (1992).

30. Freudenburg (1988).

31. Stern and Fineburg (1996).

32. Glazer and Glazer (1998).

33. Stern and Fineburg (1996).

34. Allan (1992), 4; as summarized in Irwin (1995), 119.

35. Case material from Irwin (1995).

36. Irwin (1995), 17.

37. Ibid., 112.

38. Ibid., 113.

39. The second and third dimension of power, as discussed by Lukes (1974).

40. Kroll-Smith and Couch (1990), 146.

41. Couch and Kroll-Smith (1997).

42. Brown (1991), 135.

43. Vyner (2000), 32.

44. Irwin (1995), 20.

45. Ibid., 21.

46. Case material from Alario (2000) and Helford (2000).

47. Alario (2000), 491.

48. Helford (2000), 125.

49. Alario (2000).

50. Helford (2000), 125.

51. Ibid.

52. Alario (2000).

53. Helford (2000), 126.
54. Quoted in Helford (2000), 136.
55. Helford (2000), 137.
56. Mileti, Drabeck, and Haff (1975).
57. Quarantelli and Dynes (1976).
58. Couch and Kroll-Smith (1985).
59. Levine (1982).
60. Walsh (1981).
61. Kasperson and Pijawka (1985).
62. Fowlkes and Miller (1982), 6.

5

Perceptions of Fairness

Is it fair to locate a hazardous waste site in an historically black community already surrounded by these sites? Is it fair to build a chemical plant down the road from a high school? Is it fair to bust unions who represent workers who are exposed to all kinds of nasty, toxic stuff while at the job site? Is it fair? No. Does it happen? Yes.

Resident of St. Gabriel, Louisiana[1]

You know what's not fair? Lots of people in this town who say, "Keep the jobs out. We don't want your jobs!" That's what they're saying when they oppose this landfill expansion. Sixty-five new jobs will be created by this expansion and a good deal of additional tax revenue. We need it. I need it. My family needs it.

Resident of Agricultural Street, New Orleans[2]

Behind, perhaps partially hidden, but always adding emotional freight to local environmental conflicts are people's feelings and ideas regarding how they are being treated by both their neighbors and more distant stakeholders such as industries and government agencies. These feelings and ideas can be grouped together under a broader, but more serviceable, category as *perceptions of fairness*. Perceptions of fairness will inevitably arise as people confront an environmental disaster, debate a proposed environmental change, or suspect they are being exposed to an environmental hazard. There are a variety of ways in which fairness issues enter into local environmental conflicts.

People's cognizance of unfairness is likely to first center around distributions of costs and benefits, of rewards and punishments. If you have a coworker who makes the same hourly wage as you, even though he is often out back smoking or on his cell phone talking to his girlfriend while you work, you are likely to regard this situation as "unfair." The activities which undergird local environmental conflicts frequently differentially distribute costs and benefits to different groups of people, laying the groundwork for outrage. Outsiders who like to hike and commune with nature benefit from the preservation of local forests, while community residents bear the costs in reduced employment opportunities. Corporate executives and stockholders reap the benefits of profitable plant operations, while local residents breathe in the noxious fumes. Politicians benefit from pork barrel projects which bring in massive federal subsidies to build dams, while local communities must relocate to avoid being inundated.

While conflict is most likely to surface around these obvious kinds of costs and benefits, these tend to quickly become embroiled in more complex disputes over value judgments and moral stances. Indeed, the simple act of designating something as a "cost' or "benefit," or as "fair" or "unfair," "just" or "unjust," is a value judgment which can only be made through the evocation of a moral position. Neither values nor moral frames are given in the nature of the universe but rather are human constructs open to endless disputes. Conflict participants may make drastically different evaluations about the fairness of a particular outcome simply because they are operating from radically different, and ultimately irreconcilable, moral points of view.

Finally, the perception that one is being treated unfairly often gives rise to visceral, intense, volatile emotional responses. These emotions may gain expression in such acts as name calling, vandalism, and death threats. If the target of these outbursts are other conflict participants, these individuals may respond in kind, thus escalating the conflict. Escalation can also occur through the intentional inflaming of emotions as a mobilizing strategy.

The case vignettes presented in previous chapters provide ample testimony to the pervasiveness of acrimony stemming from perceptions of unfair, unjust treatment in local environmental conflicts. For a more extensive discussion of the connections between material covered in this and previous chapters, see Box 5.1.

Box 5.1   Making Connections With Previous Chapters

Many of the basic descriptive questions outlined in Chapter 1 intimate fairness issues. In Box 1.4, for example, questions pertaining to the demographic and economic context of a community address the extent to which the local area has reaped (or failed to reap) benefits from economic development. These may also be suggestive of long-standing patterns of marginalization or exploitation. The question from that box which addresses key features of the local landscape provides a means to assess the extent to which local residents have accrued the benefits of environmental protection or borne costs of ecological degradation. As ground zero, communities are the touchstone where people come into direct contact with the ugly, inconvenient, or dangerous landscapes which comprise "the end of nature as we know it."

Conflict participants advocate different agendas embodying divergent ideals of acceptable and desirable distributions of costs and benefits stemming from conservancy efforts, siting initiatives, or exposure problems (see Box 1.2). Fairness issues may be quite prominent among the claims and frames raised in a controversy. Participants are likely to react to actions of others they perceive as unjust with their own mobilized efforts for redress, thus fueling conflict dynamics (see Box 1.3).

Loss of irreplaceable tradition-bound resources and places is likely to be viewed as a gross unfairness by the group experiencing the loss. The sense of injustice and the accompanying emotions of outrage may be further fueled if the group has been involved in a long-standing battle to preserve its traditional way of life and if the threatened places and resources are among the last remnants of the local environment still available for traditional use (see Box 2.3). On the other hand, conservancy issues which remove places and resources from traditional uses may also be perceived as an injustice, as seen in the Inuit's desire to continue whaling even in the face of international treaties banning the practice.

Long-standing exploitative relationships with outsiders shape the kinds of assets and liabilities present in a community's cultural toolbox (see Box 2.4). Accusations of unfairness may become a central focus of invented histories (see Box 2.5). Tradition, invention, and fairness issues may intersect in complex ways, such as when one group claims traditional access to a resource (such as fishing stock) but uses modern equipment to extract the resource. Other users of the resource, denied the same level of access, may regard such "inventive" uses of tradition unfair.

Premeditated betrayal also constitutes a gross unfairness and can be expected to engender strong emotions of anger and outrage when encountered (see Box 3.3). Few things can produce a strong visceral reaction like discovering that government agencies and officials have not only put one's community in harm's way but lied about it as well. Such strong emotional reactions are also likely to occur in residents' encounters with structural betrayal, also perceived as unjust treatment, even though here powerful social actors are not intentionally acting in a negligent or malfeasant manner (see Box 3.4).

Scientific studies may be used to legitimate decision outcomes some participants believe are unfair. The veracity of such studies may be called into question by local residents, who may use popular epidemiology to conduct their own investigations. Dismissal of local knowledge by outside experts also deeply implicates fairness issues and can be a source of rather volatile emotional responses (see Box 4.4).

Fairness and Equity Issues

Land Use Disputes on Wye Island

Over the course of the 20th century, automobiles and expanded road systems facilitated suburban development around metropolitan centers. People left the city for a number of reasons. For some, it was the allure of owning land and having more contact with nature. Others worried about crime in the city and the poor quality of urban schools. The motivations of an indeterminate number was to join that great migration stream known as "white flight." Whatever the reasons underlying it, this steady exodus had implications for the agricultural lands, small towns, and sparsely settled rural areas that fringed the crowded, bustling cities.

One such area vulnerable to suburban expansion was the eastern shore of the Chesapeake Bay.[3] In 1973–1974, Wye Island, located just offshore the eastern Chesapeake, became the subject of a heated land-use dispute. This was a complicated conflict, involving several alternatives for the island and numerous participants with diverse concerns and interests. The lines of divisiveness crossed race and class, outsiders and insiders, old-timers and newcomers, allowing present conflicts to become entangled with long-standing grievances.

Six miles long and approximately 2,800 acres in size, Wye Island had reached its population peak of roughly 100 people in the late 19th–early 20th centuries. By the early 1970s, Wye Island, containing only three farms, was almost uninhabited. Two brothers who were major landowners on the island convinced the land developer Jim Rouse to take out an option, with plans for eventual purchase and residential development.

Jim Rouse was a businessman with the expected concern for profit, but he was also a bit of a visionary who believed good development was possible. One admirer put it this way: "Rouse has many lofty goals, but his highest is that people of different races and backgrounds can live together without conflict, and that poorer people should have decent housing."[4] At a development undertaken by Rouse's company in Columbia, Maryland, prior to the Wye Island venture, about one fifth of the residents were African American, a remarkable achievement at the time considering the country was barely out of the height of the civil rights era.

Rouse also believed good development meant planned, environmentally responsible development. Rouse had grown up on the eastern shore of the Chesapeake and regarded suburban encroachment from nearby Baltimore, Annapolis, and Washington, D.C., as inevitable. He also thought if proactive measures were not taken to control development, the shore would end up with the worst kind of suburban landscape: chaotic sprawl. While his company struggled through a number of plans to hammer out specific details, Rouse was clear about some of the general features he wanted on Wye Island. He wanted to concentrate most of the residents in one larger or several smaller villages, leaving much of the island for agricultural or wilderness uses. He wanted to establish a bird sanctuary. He wanted one centralized marina, rather than letting every home with waterfront property build a private deck and boat launch. He wanted to ensure sewage was adequately treated and that development on the island did not add any pollution to the Wye and Wye East Rivers which flanked the island.

On the downside, development on Wye Island would not meet some of Rouse's loftier social goals. Given the price of land, only the financially well-off could afford to buy there. While Rouse was not crazy about building a resort community for the wealthy, he felt the benefits outweighed the costs. He also expected to receive support from the local area, not only because he offered the prospect of well-planned development but also because he would bring jobs to an economically depressed area. Residential development of Wye Island was expected to bring around 350 permanent jobs to the area; 250 temporary jobs would be created during the 10-year construction phase. Rouse's company also calculated the development would bring about $700,000 in tax revenue to the coffers of the county where the island was located. At the time, the annual tax revenue for Queen Anne's County was around $12,000.

The county population was a mix of wealthy retirees, professional people willing to undertake long commutes to work, watermen and women (commercial fishers and crabbers), farmers, and individuals employed in marginal working-class jobs like road repair and house painting. The wealthier inhabitants had generally moved into the county from elsewhere, while working-class inhabitants were typically local folk. At the time Rouse announced his proposed development, "[n]ineteen percent of all year-round houses in Queen Anne's County [had] only an outhouse for a toilet,"[5] providing some indication of the general impoverishment of the area. "There are few well paying jobs in the county—many are barely at subsistence levels."[6] Young people left the area in droves.

At the time of Rouse's proposal, Wye Island was zoned for 5-acre lots. Despite Rouse's expectation that the local people would support his plan, the county commissioners displayed no interest in changing the zoning ordinance to accommodate Rouse's development. Long-time county residents were dismayed at the changes that had occurred in the local area since the construction of the Chesapeake Bay Bridge in 1952. The bridge had allowed for the intrusion of wealthy outsiders who had bought up waterfront property, making it prohibitively expensive for most county natives. The bridge also provided access for recreational boaters and "chickenneckers" (individuals who used chicken necks as bait for the Chesapeake blue crab), who congested waterways, produced litter, and presented competition for the local watermen and women. A politically conservative lot, local residents did not welcome any influx of "strange new people" to the area.

The newcomers to the shore, the wealthy retirees and commuters, had settled in the area because they liked its rural ambiance. "In purchasing their vast estates, the wealthy were buying privacy and, in a sense, walling off themselves. . . . Land is the ultimate means of exclusion."[7] Increased population would threaten the very amenities which had drawn these people to the shore in the first place. So, despite the fact there was long-standing animosity between old-timers and newcomers, for the most part all agreed that the best plan was to leave Wye Island just as it was.

Yet Rouse's plan was not the only option on the table. Another possibility was to have the State of Maryland purchase the island and turn it into a state park. This option was also vigorously opposed by locals, who thought an island open to public access would be overrun by chickenneckers from Baltimore. Local stereotypes painted chickenneckers as black folks from the city. In reality, many chickenneckers were white and from the local area.

During the antebellum period, Queen Anne's and nearby Talbot Counties were home to plantations run with slave labor. African Americans continued to live in the area, making up about a quarter of the population of both Queen Anne's and Talbot Counties, but they were marginalized and ignored by local leaders. In the early 1970s, on the eastern shore of the Chesapeake, racism ran deep. "There are still natives around who proudly remind a visitor that in 1860 Abraham Lincoln received not a single vote in Queen Anne's County."[8] Locals did not want the island turned into a public space which would attract a lot of "undesirables" to the area. Since there were almost no public access spots in Queen Anne's and Talbot Counties, outsiders who wanted to launch power boats or crab from the shore did congregate in those few areas which were open to them.

Another possibility for the island, though one which surfaced only briefly, was to have the Nature Conservancy purchase the island. The Nature Conservancy is a private environmental organization which buys wilderness areas for preservation purposes, sometimes maintaining the land itself, sometimes turning it over to the government. At the time of the Rouse controversy, the Nature Conservancy had been looking to purchase land in the eastern Chesapeake that was home to endangered species and/or characterized by rich biodiversity. Wye Island did not meet either of these criteria, but because it was almost uninhabited and because local people were interested in preserving it, the Nature Conservancy thought it worthy of their attention. The Nature Conservancy needed private donations to make the purchase, however, and in the end none of the wealthy people in the area so interested in maintaining the island in its present state were willing to contribute the necessary funds.

After over a year of effort and the expenditure of close to $1 million in preliminary studies, Jim Rouse also abandoned his plans for Wye Island. The combination of a poor national economy and the lack of any support government simply made the residential development too risky of a venture. In the end, the State of Maryland did purchase the island, but not with the intention of turning it into the park so dreaded by locals. What the state did intend to do was lease the land out for agricultural use, thus providing a continuation of existing uses of the island.

❖

At its most straightforward, fairness pertains to the equity of the distribution of costs and benefits, rewards and punishments, socially desirable and undesirable things.

In the environmental arena, it is useful to think about the distribution of costs and benefits which stem from economic development, ecological degradation, and environmental protection.[9] On the plus side of economic development are jobs: jobs create consumers; consumers create and grow local businesses. Economic growth results in increased housing, the availability of medical care, good schools, and other spoils of success. On the minus side, ecological debasement is often a cost of economic development. Soil erosion, loss of habitat, air and water pollution, and chemical contamination of soils are just some examples of the ways extraction and manufacturing activity may affect local environments.

Environmental protection also has costs and benefits. Examples of the latter include safer, healthier, more aesthetically pleasing spaces for homes, work, and recreation. Environmental protection also raises the costs of extraction and manufacturing activities, may remove some resources from use altogether (such as endangered species habitats or wetlands), and may result in higher taxes and more government intrusion into what were previously private economic and lifestyle decisions.

What becomes important from the standpoint of local environmental conflicts is the perception of the distribution of these various costs and benefits. Any group which sees itself as bearing many costs and few if any benefits is likely to become outraged. This is one place where the distinction made between local and extra-local conflict participants introduced in Chapter 1 can be especially useful: when a disproportionate share of the costs is seen to fall on local residents, while benefits go almost exclusively to outsiders, then unified local action is more likely. When costs and benefits are inequitably distributed within the community, factionalism may result.

Anger and outrage may be heightened if local residents believe they have been targeted to bear costs for political expediency. Recall the conflict over turtle exclusion devices (TEDs) on the Louisiana and Texas coast presented in Chapter 3.[10] While the precipitous decline in sea turtle populations is well documented, it is possible to identify several likely causes for this phenomena. Certainly these include turtles drowning in shrimp trawls, but also on the list are pollution and coastal land development. Indeed, Texas and Louisiana shrimpers sought to remove their own activities from the list by denying that turtles drowned in shrimp trawls. While that claim is probably specious, there are good reasons to suspect that incidental drowning of sea turtles in shrimp trawls is a minor part of the problem next to the other two culprits of pollution and coastal land development.

Yet, trying to protect endangered sea turtles by taking on these two culprits would be a daunting task. For starters, we are talking about millions of separate acts spread across a vast geographic territory. Furthermore, efforts to regulate these activities would require going after some of the wealthiest and most politically powerful entities around, including large coastal metropolitan cities which are hardly going to be interested in limiting economic development. Shrimpers present a far easier political target. As members of a small-sized, working-class occupation, shrimpers have little political clout and are unlikely to attract many powerful allies. As such, they can be forced to shoulder the costs of protecting sea turtles while other culpable parties continue reaping benefits from their ecologically degrading activities with impunity.

The environmental justice movement formed in the early 1980s around just these kinds of issues.[11] (See Box 5.2.) The costs of ecological degradation are inequitably distributed in this country across the lines of both class and race. Poor and working-class communities in general, as well as poor, working-class, and middle-class communities of peoples of color, are more likely to host polluting and/or hazardous facilities than are white middle-class communities or any community higher on the socioeconomic scale. The extent to which this discriminatory pattern is intentional is open to dispute, though there is compelling empirical evidence that in at least some cases these communities are chosen precisely because they are seen to be politically powerless.[12]

Box 5.2   The Environmental Justice Movement at a Glance

The idea of environmental justice and the social movement it inspired can be traced to a small, rural county in North Carolina. The year was 1982. The issue was a landfill in Warren County built for the disposal of highly contaminated and toxic soils.

The landfill was built in the midst of a number of poor, black communities. The fiery term *environmental racism* was coined in response to this episode. A year later, in 1983, prompted by a prominent civil rights leader and congressman, Walter Fauntroy, the U.S. General Accounting Office examined the distribution of hazardous wastes by demographic characteristics in eight southern states. The study, *Hazardous Landfills and Their Correlation With Racial and Economic State of Surrounding Communities,* concluded that three out of four commercial hazardous waste facilities were located in African American communities. Shortly after the publication of this landmark study, the federal government and Olin Chemical settled a $25 million lawsuit with black residents of Triana, Alabama. Contaminated with DDT, this small, historically black, community was called the "unhealthiest town in America."

The idea of environmental justice linked civil rights to environmental equity, creating a powerful appeal that captured public attention. It also linked the environmental movement with the civil rights movement to forge a powerful united front against both the manufacture of toxins and their inequitable distribution. This was indeed a new chapter in the history of environmentalism in the United States.

In 1991 scholars and activists from around the country held the First National People of Color Environmental Leadership Summit. In 1992 the Environmental Protection Agency (EPA) created the Office of Environmental Equity. In 1994 the federal government issued Executive Order 12898, which directed the EPA to dedicate resources to examining and ameliorating the environmental health problems among poor and minority communities. Not surprisingly, the enforcement of this order is not uniform and varies widely with different political administrations.

The environmental justice movement continues to address the inequality in the distribution of environmental hazards among disadvantaged groups. African American children, for example, are five times more likely to suffer from lead poisoning than white children, while half of all Native Americans live in communities with uncontrolled hazardous waste sites. The struggle, in short, continues.

NOTE: For a compelling case history of environmental justice, see Lerner (2005).

Concerns with environmental justice provide an avenue for powerful linkages of present troubles with past histories of inequitable burdens. The costs and benefits of economic development have long been inequitably distributed across class and race lines; each of these has been the target of formative and influential social movement activity. The labor movement was at its peak during the latter 19th and early 20th centuries, while the civil rights movement was at the forefront of public attention during the mid-20th century. These movements were fought not only on the national (and, in the case of the labor movement, international) stage but also, more important, at the local level. The forms these local battles took were as varied as coal miners' struggles to secure higher wages and safer working conditions from the coal companies[13] to African Americans' struggles against discrimination, oppression, and violence in such places as Birmingham, Alabama.[14]

What organizing around issues of environmental justice entails, then, is adding inequitable pollution and hazard burdens to an already existing list of injustices.[15] To the extent these claims tap into long-standing resentments, they present a powerful organizing tool. The way they play out in particular local contexts can be tricky, however. Trade-offs often must be made between economic development and environmental protection. When community residents fall on the high costs/few benefits side of both of these, then the stage is set for considerable disagreements about whether economic development or environmental protection is more desirable.

Consider, for example, the case of Robbins, Illinois.[16] A small (population approximately 7,000) African American community in the Chicago area, Robbins developed plans to attract a waste-to-energy incinerator in the 1970s. Little became of these plans until the latter half of the 1980s, when social and political changes made siting an incinerator in Robbins an attractive option to the waste treatment industry. Foremost among these changes was mounting local opposition to solid waste landfills and the 1987 passage by the Illinois State Legislature of the Retail Rate Law, which provided "significant tax subsidies to incinerator companies that choose to locate in the state."[17]

Robbins is one of the poorest communities in the country. The village had tried for years to attract business and industry, to no avail. "This is a ghost town as far as most businesses are concerned, a barren landscape with few prospects for economic development."[18] The local government had long been in financial straits, facing mounting debts and periodically having trouble meeting its payroll. "Since the 1980s, the city has held charity drives to raise funds for its own management!"[19] With the perception of no other viable prospects on the table, the siting of a trash incinerator seemed like a welcome development to many.

Not all Robbins' residents agreed with this assessment, and some of the dissenters joined forces with such outside opponents as Greenpeace, the Sierra Club, Citizens for a Better Environment, and the South Cook County Environmental Action Coalition. Many residents, however, supported the incinerator. "At a hearing . . . in 1992, scores of incinerator supporters (outnumbering opponents) showed up, wearing painters' caps that read 'Yes, in my backyard,' 'Don't trash jobs,' and 'Right 4 Robbins.'"[20] While incinerator opponents cast the siting effort as a case of environmental racism, efforts to link with past injustices cut both ways. "The mayor . . . used the observation that whites were universally against the incinerator as 'evidence' that white folks did not want to see an all-black town pull itself up and out of poverty."[21]

One strategy that can be used to highlight unfairness is to draw comparisons between assistance and other resources received by local people versus those received by other communities (or other relevant comparison groups) facing similar problems. Consider the case of Press Park, a New Orleans housing development built on top of a "reclaimed" landfill.[22] After severe contamination problems were found at the site, many residents in the African American neighborhood wanted to be relocated. The Environmental Protection Agency (EPA) rejected this option, however, preferring instead to try to clean up the site by scraping off contaminated soil from people's lawns. Outraged, local residents pointed to a community facing a similar exposure calamity in Florida; the residents of this white community had been bought out by the government. Indeed, Press Park residents took these comparisons even further, pointing out that 16 of the 17 EPA relocations had been in white communities, while only one had occurred in an African American community.

These types of comparisons were also made in the contamination of Prince William Sound. Addressing his perceptions of the lawsuits following the *Exxon Valdez* oil spill, a local resident remarks:

> It doesn't seem fair. . . . There's just so much tort law that just seems so ridiculously unfair. How can somebody that's been smoking cigarettes get a billion dollar reward for having lung cancer and yet a court can't see the economic impact that the oil spill has had on us?[23]

Another factor which can add intensity to distributional conflicts is if participants perceive outcomes to be zero-sum in nature. In a nutshell, a zero-sum situation is one that by necessity produces winners and losers.[24] In zero-sum conflicts the gains achieved by one set of conflict participants come at the expense (loss) of other participants. Suppose two hungry people stranded on a desert island come across two coconuts. If resources are to be distributed equitably, each of the individuals would get a coconut. That resolution, however, might not appear attractive under conditions of extreme scarcity. Yet the only way one of these individuals is going to get more coconut is if the other person gets less.

Local environmental conflicts abound with examples of scarce resources. Endangered species, relatively untouched wilderness areas, ecologically unique areas, places of spectacular natural beauty, culturally important places, as well the health of oneself, one's family, and one's community—these are resources which are irreplaceable or that exhibit what we referred to in Chapter 2 as incommensurable value.[25] Furthermore, once degradation of these resources occurs, recovery might be impossible, and once destroyed, loss is often irreversible. These types of situations are easy to read as zero-sum and as such lend themselves to absolutist stances that book no compromise. As such, zero-sum situations can be created both by resource scarcity as well as by the intransigence of conflict participants who adopt an "all or nothing" attitude.

A summary of the types of questions students need to ask about equity issues in local environmental conflicts is presented in Box 5.3. Conflicts over the distribution of costs and benefits hardly exhaust the types of fairness issues which surface in local environmental conflicts, however. Indeed, as we will see in the following section, the very meaning of "fairness" itself may come under dispute.

Fairness, Moral Frames, and Value Judgments

The Moral Construction of Egrets

Conway, Arkansas, is a small town of slightly less than 45,000 people located 30 miles from Little Rock.[26] It is solidly middle class and white. Conway is home to a variety of birdlife, including the common cattle egret. The cattle egret probably originated in Africa, but it is now found in

---

Box 5.3   Adding to the Portfolio: Fairness and Equity Issues

1. What are the costs and benefits associated with the proposed action or existing problem, and what is the distribution of each among local residents?

2. Do some conflict participants believe they have been targeted to bear costs for reasons of political expediency?

3. Do some conflict participants link their present woes to a broader history of inequitable burdens?

4. What types of comparisons do conflict participants make to highlight unfair treatment?

5. Is the conflict seen to be zero-sum in nature?

several places throughout the world. It was first spotted in North America in 1953. Cattle egrets nest in large colonies. In 1983 the birds founded a nesting site close to Conway. In time, this colony grew to include approximately 20,000 nesting pairs.

Cattle egrets are attracted to the rural landscape around Conway for the same reasons that they have settled in pastureland environments worldwide. They appear to have evolved a "commensal" relationship with a variety of grazing animals who stir up bugs for the birds to eat.[27]

A small town seeking to grow, Conway supports housing developments. On July 24, 1998, as men were clearing land with wheel loaders and dozers, they rolled over the cattle egret nesting colony, killing or maiming approximately 5,000 birds. Surviving birds, who were still able to walk, wandered around stunned, seeking respite from the stifling heat.

Videotapes and newspaper photographs showed images of birds inundating local streets and yards, struggling to survive. Some of the birds huddled around air conditioner condensers, and mothers tried to shelter their chicks. Passing cars killed some of the egrets, and curious onlookers aggravated the problem.[28]

Routed from their nests, the surviving cattle egrets appeared to some residents as hapless victims of an overzealous developer and community bent on expansion. To other residents, however, the homeless egrets were at best pests and at worst health hazards. Each side in this burgeoning dispute constructed the cattle egret in its own way: as innocent sacrifice on the one hand, as a nuisance and health risk on the other.

Consider the plaintive words of a rescue volunteer who laments the plights of the birds: "They were very beautiful and very vulnerable. There was a snow of beautiful white feathers, but a feeling of blood. The numbers. Everywhere you look there is vulnerable life trying to survive, and dying."[29] Now examine the quite different account from a resident who shifts the focus from the tormented birds to the tormented residents of Conway:

> [We] went from a neighborhood of people who had swimming pools [to people] who could not swim in their pools because there were dead egrets every day. [We] were afraid of disease. . . . We were prisoners in our own homes. For three months straight . . . some people just locked their doors, went to work, came home, locked the doors, kept their kids inside, playing Nintendo.[30]

For the ornithologist, the cattle egret is, and always will be, a bublucus ibis, a stocky heron with a thick neck. For the residents of Conway, however, the bublucus ibis was something more complicated than a stubby member of the heron family sporting a wide neck. For one group, cattle egrets "were beautiful . . . innocent creatures unable to defend themselves . . . God's creatures."[31] For others, the egret was "just an old cowbird . . . useless . . . [and likely to] carry the disease histoplasmosis."[32]

In the end, the almost diametrically opposed social definitions of the cattle egret expressed a volatile community friction between residents who favored development and those who opposed it. Like a Rorschach inkblot, this simple bird became an object of apperception, encouraging residents to connect it to their feelings about preservation and conservation, on the one hand, and growth and development, on the other. However we choose to characterize this dispute over the cattle egret, a question of fairness is at the heart of the matter.

In this instance, the question is one of who or what is being treated unfairly. Is it the cattle egret who is being treated unfairly by a development-crazed population? Or is it those residents of Conway who suffer emotional turmoil at the sight of the birds' plight? Or is it that community cohort who believe they should be able to enjoy their community and its amenities free of a "hazardous nuisance"? The fate of the birds, their defenders, and those who subscribe to the "growth is good" ideal is decided, in part, by how these questions are answered.

❖

For our purposes, the important lesson in the contested questions over the cattle egret in Conway, Arkansas, is that none of them is amendable to resolution by science. Data, facts, numbers, more and better information, none of these will settle this dispute. Only a *value judgment,* a collective accord that one party is being treated unfairly, will settle it. It's not hard to see why disagreements over perceptions of fairness are most difficult to resolve. In many cases, to resolve the fairness question in environmental controversies is to ask and answer the most difficult of questions. Among them, "What kind of community do we want to be?" and "What is our relationship to nature?" Attention to values complicates considerations of costs and benefits, since determinations of what is socially desirable are inevitably linked to broader value systems.

Perceptions of fairness frame environmental controversies as moral contests. More Platonic than Aristotelian, fairness exists as an ideal. Ultimately it is in the arena of justice, not science, that workable resolutions to environmental controversies must be forged. Emile Durkheim drew a distinction between "judgements of reality" and "value judgements" that is worth considering here.[33] While specific findings of science may be challenged, as we demonstrated in the previous chapter, science itself is still approached as a judgment of reality; its goal is to make factual assertions about the world. "Nicotine is a carcinogen" is such an assertion. "On average, women live longer than men" is also an assertion of fact. "More tornadoes touch down in Kansas than in any other state in North America" is a judgment of reality based on longitudinal counting and comparison. It makes practical sense to approach these three statements as facts.

Value judgments, on the other hand, are expressions of moral purpose, principled intentions that author a version of the world based on ideas of good and right. Referring to physical disability, for example, Francis and Silvers argue that no one should suffer "an attenuation of the right to be in the world."[34] The EPA takes the position that "[e]nvironmental justice is the fair treatment . . . of all people regardless of race, color, national origin or income with respect to . . . the enforcement of environmental laws."[35] While facts are assertions about *what is,* value judgments are assertions about *what should be.*

We can always hold out for the possibility that disputes about the nature of reality can be resolved through scientific investigation; objective reality forms the ultimate authority against which beliefs can be measured. Think of a judgment of reality as a proposition that could be stated in the manner "It is, or it is not." "The cattle egret does not migrate" is a reality-based judgment of the "does or does not" variety. Values, in contrast, are human constructs; when values come into dispute, there is no ultimate external authority to whom we can turn to determine which values are the correct, right, truthful ones.[36] Science may provide us with the knowledge of how to build a nuclear bomb, but it cannot tell us whether or not it is morally responsible or reprehensible to use such a device.

As value judgments, perceptions of fairness are essentially contested positions, arguments, and so on that could be perpetually debated. At the root of the statement "In your unholy push to develop this county you are destroying cattle egrets" is a value judgment about both fauna and a quality of life. A value judgment is not based on the calculating "it is, or it is not" assessment but on the far more combustible language of "thou shalt, or thou shalt not," accompanied, perhaps, by a "How dare you!" Value judgments are almost always moments of high drama.

The Idea of the Moral Frame

Think of the perception of fairness as a moral frame. A well-worn sociological idea, a frame is a lingual strategy for casting a controversy or problem in a broader, more commonly recognized language game.[37] A moral frame is a scheme of interpretation that both enables action and constrains it and does so through its peculiar use of normative and ethical language. A moral or ethical frame seeks to change behaviors and beliefs, reward the righteous, condemn the wayward, and so on through the panoply of right-minded stances humans might take toward their worlds. From animal rights, to civil rights, to environmental justice, the artfulness of moral appeals is expressed with varying intensity. Different frames shape radically different perceptions of the same phenomenon, as seen in these two quotations:

No other creature seems more a shape of the moonlight than does the deer.[38]

Deer are the same as any pest. They're not beneficial as far as I can see; they just come and eat your crops.[39]

Moral frames make a particularly persuasive claim on our attention, in part, because they typically do more than define a problem: they are also likely to point to its cause and imply—if not propose—a solution. Consider the assertion "Radon exposure in homes poses an unfair health risk." In this case the source of the risk is identified as a rock bed. And the remedy? Forcefully request the city council to recognize the risk and petition the state for money to retrofit homes with radon detection and remediation technologies. At a more general level, the moral frame "environmental justice" both defines an issue (discrimination in exposure to environmental risks) and points to the cause (the unjust distribution of risks). It also, of course, strongly intimates a remedy: reduce the risks and redistribute them in a more equitable manner.

By paying attention to the way in which a problem is defined, and the means and ends which are offered as a resolution, we address some very important questions: What is a just way of defining this issue? Is the process for resolving it fair-minded? Is the resolution itself equitable and fair? At initial blush, it might seem answers to such questions are relatively straightforward, but this is hardly the case. Before we can make a determination about whether a particular distribution of costs and benefits is fair, we must first have general agreement about the fundamental nature of fairness. But here's the rub: fairness, equity, and justice are all essentially contested ideas.[40]

To say something is contested is to mean more than that it provokes spirited debate. An idea or concept that is essentially contested cannot be resolved using an agreed-upon principle.[41] In the absence of such common ground, we must deal with a world where different moral frames shape different value judgments about what is equitable, just, and fair.

"It isn't fair!" railed Sarah at the Goblin King, who replied, "Who keeps saying that? I only wonder what is your basis for comparison?"[42] Comparison, indeed. If comparison was based simply on quantity, then the determination of fairness would be rather straightforward. Consider a father who has four quarters and two children. He gives each child two quarters. Is that fair? Yes, if only quantity mattered; but it rarely does. What if one child is three years older than the other child? The older child notes that he washed the dishes that morning and therefore deserves an extra quarter. Fairness is rarely as simple as distributing a common good in equal measures.

The choices and resolutions advocated in any particular conflict, of course, do not exist in isolation but have implications for other venues of concern. Actual and proposed environmental actions generate costs and benefits, but these coexist with costs and benefits generated from other sources and activities. At its most fundamental, fairness addresses a broad system of rules for distributing rewards and punishments. Conflict participants will embrace values and moral frames which fit with their own visions of "the good society."

Let's consider the moral frames of capitalism, individualism, and humanitarianism.[43] Capitalism as a moral frame emphasizes the importance of "private property, a free market for goods and labor based on competition, and the right to profit."[44] Individualism exalts the value of individuals over social collectivities such as families and tribes and stresses both individual freedoms or rights as well as individual responsibilities (especially the responsibility to work hard and to financially take care of oneself and one's family). A humanitarian frame focuses on human well-being and the elimination of pain and suffering. Individualism and capitalism are complementary moral frames, while humanitarianism is in marked tension with the other two.

Note how these frames shape different perceptions of fairness. Individuals who embrace the first two frames are likely to consider *any* policy or activity which limits their right to enjoy, and profit from, their private property as "unfair." Individuals who adhere to a humanitarian frame are likely to define *any* policy or activity which either causes, or does nothing to alleviate, pain and suffering as "unfair." Cattle egrets are the Rorschach inkblot test within which one sees one's own vision of the good society, and the very definition of fairness itself remains contested because people operate from incompatible moral frames.

Consider another example: the case of conflict over the construction of the Seabrook nuclear plant on the Atlantic shore of New Hampshire, a battle which raged for most of the 1970s and 1980s. As Bedford describes it:

> New Hampshire's small towns treasured independence. They raised their own taxes, paid for their own schools, fire trucks, and snowplows, and minded their own business. . . . Citizens defended their own independence as well as that of the town, and they respected self-reliance in others. You stand on your own two feet; you pay your own way. Live Free or Die, the state's motto, was descriptive as well as hortatory.[45]

One major source of contention was over emergency evacuation plans. These plans were made by outside experts, with little or no consultation with local people or consideration of local resources and circumstances. Evacuation complications posed by the influx of tourists to nearby beaches in the summer months was not taken into account, for example. Buildings were designated as public shelters without the permission or cooperation of their owners. School teachers were supposed to assist the orderly evacuation of students; the teachers argued that this assignment of extra duties constituted a violation of their contract. Bus drivers were expected to pick up the handicapped and elderly; local police said they did not have the resources to enact the emergency plans. Time after time, local people insisted at hearings on the emergency evacuation plans that they would not, and often could not, fulfill the functions the plan had proscribed for them. Nonetheless, the licensing board discounted their testimony in favor of the outside experts.

> This was not the way Live Free or Die, town-meeting democracy was supposed to be conducted in New England, where home rule was more than a slogan. . . . For some opponents, the nation's system of governance was at issue, not a mere nuclear power plant.[46]

A final point: Fairness as a moral frame is never far removed from the ugly idea that a person, group, or community is a victim. Indeed, once fairness surfaces as a contested issue, it is probable that all parties to the dispute are likely to perceive themselves as victims of one another's choices and actions. The Latin root for victim is *victima* or sacrificial beast. It is disquieting, to put it mildly, to believe that you or your town are being sacrificed by others who claim to know what is best for you, or worse, simply want you to accept your fate for a greater common good. The ideas of victim, sacrifice, and failed redemptions are often salient features of environmental controversies and ensure that these disputes will be freighted with mercurial convictions, emotions, and sentiment.

Box 5.4 lists the kinds of questions students need to ask about the role of fairness, value judgments, and moral frames in local environmental conflicts. We turn now to an issue which has threaded its way through both of the conflict cases already presented in this chapter, as well as many cases

---

Box 5.4   Adding to the Portfolio: Fairness, Moral Frames, and Value Judgments

---

1. What aspects of claims can only be resolved via appeal to value judgments rather than appeal to objective facts?

2. What types of moral frames are evoked to undergird claims of injustice?

3. Is the very definition of fairness itself contested?

4. In what ways are the particular values and moral frames embraced in a specific conflict linked with broader visions of "the good society"?

5. To what extent do conflict participants come to see themselves as victims of others' actions?

---

presented in other chapters: that of the volatile connection between fairness and emotions.

Fairness and Emotions

"Spillionaires" in Prince William Sound

At 12:26 a.m. on March 24, 1989, Captain Joe Hazelwood radioed these now famous words to a Valdez, Alaska, water traffic controller: "We've fetched up, ah, hard aground . . . off Bligh Reef and, ah, evidently leaking some oil and we're gonna be here for a while . . . so you're notified."[47] In what must be one of the grandest understatements in the history of environmental calamities, Captain Hazelwood signaled the beginning of a prolonged, painful, and demoralizing period for thousands of local Alaskan residents. Like the near core meltdown at Three Mile Island and the discovery of toxic waste buried at the Love Canal, the *Exxon Valdez* oil spill (the EVOS) has quickly become an iconic event in the history of environmental disasters.

The *Exxon Valdez* was a new tanker, almost 10 football fields long, designed to carry 55 million gallons of crude oil. On this fateful trip, the *Valdez* was carrying 53,094,510 gallons. Assisted by two tugboats, the ship left the dock at approximately 9:00 p.m. on the evening of March 23rd. Three hours into the trip, this supertanker, almost 1,000 yards long, was maneuvering with little trouble through an icy patch of water, attempting to enter a shipping lane that would take it from the bay to the sea. A surprised lookout reported that the light on Bligh Reef was visible off the starboard bow (right side) of the ship. It should have been visible off the port or left side. Requiring hours to recalibrate the direction of a vessel this large, the *Exxon Valdez* was in serious straits. At 12:04 a.m. the supertanker ran aground on the reef. Eight of its 11 cargo tanks were punctured by sharp rocks. Approximately 6 million gallons of crude oil surged into Prince William Sound during the next 3 hours. All told, 11 million gallons of oil escaped from the hull of the *Exxon Valdez*. The oil formed a sheet of carbon-based poison that covered a complex and pristine ecosystem. Among the immediate victims were "more than 350,000 seabirds, 144 bald eagles, approximately 5,500 sea otters, 30 seals, and 22 whales."[48]

Arguably one of the most complex environmental disasters on record, the EVOS had both immediate and long-term, indeed seemingly endless, repercussions for residents and their communities. From the devastation of the spill itself, to the protracted and expensive cleanup attempts, to the interminable legal struggles with Exxon itself, the question of fairness has framed many and varied conflicts.

During the early stages of the disaster, perceptions of fairness were likely to be directed outward from communities around Prince William Sound to Exxon and state and federal government agencies. Perceptions of a horrible injustice were shared among residents who, like this commercial fisherman, spoke for many when he confessed, "I was pretty devastated. . . . I felt outrage that we hadn't been dealt with more fairly and recognized immediately what the impact was going to be on our fishing."[49] But very quickly a quite different problem emerged that was immediately recognized as an equity and fairness issue, and it rent apart these once close-knit communities.

Shortly after the spill, Exxon was forced to acknowledge it had little in the way of a formal spill response policy. To quote one local resident, "It was apparent that a lot of the cleanup stuff that was going on wasn't any use at all and it was poorly organized."[50] When it was clear to Exxon that it could not manage the cleanup without the help of local residents, the company literally redefined local fishermen as "independent contractors" and hired some of them to begin mopping up the oil. The contractors, in turn, were to hire crews to work the boats. The *Anchorage Daily News* reported:

> Exxon began signing contracts with fishermen. Amazement spread at how much the oil company was paying. Exxon . . . paid in the range of $3,000 a day for an average fishing boat. Some fishermen have worked two months straight since then.[51]

A profound difference quickly emerged among residents of these small villages between people who worked on the spill and those who either chose not to or were not given an opportunity. A caustic intramural conflict developed over what was perceived as an equitable distribution of cleanup money. A local woman gets right to the heart of the cleanup controversy:

Money makes people real creepy. There was just a lot of bad blood that was created. There were people who felt self-righteous because they never got involved. Those people were looking down on the people [who did].[52]

Some residents framed the activities of their neighbors who worked on cleanup using an excoriating voice: "Cleanup workers and contractors were called 'Exxon whores' who accepted 'blood money' and became 'spillionaires.'"[53] Three divisions appeared among residents over what was perceived as a fair, equitable, and honest response to the appeals from Exxon to get local fishermen involved in mopping up the oil. There were those who sought and received cleanup contracts from Exxon. There were those who sought contracts but did not receive them. And finally, there were those who refused to work for Exxon.[54] Significantly, each group sounded its stance toward the mop-up work in the language of fairness.

For the first group (those who sought and received contracts), what happened could be framed in the righteous distinction between the haves and the have-nots.

[O]ne of the things that has been hard on the town is the "haves" and "have-nots" of the spill. Clearly, I was a "have." . . . [I]t all boils down to how you responded to the oil spill. . . . [I]f you seized the opportunity then you were a "have" and if you were emotionally distraught or dysfunctional . . . then you may have become a "have-not."[55]

And, apparently, some of the have-nots did not accept their fate quietly. As one resident observed, "A lot of the people that weren't spillionaires were so self-righteous."[56]

For the second group, those that wanted to work on the cleanup but were unable to, the idea of fairness was compromised by what appeared to them as suspicious, if not unethical, behavior on the part of their neighbors. A man who lived in the area seasonally returned to participate in the cleanup. When he arrived he "realized I had already been 'had' a little. [My friends] wanted to sew that little deal up for themselves and it's taken me many years to get over that because . . . that wasn't what I was about."[57] The perception of a covetous, unjust pattern of conduct among those who received contracts is addressed in this rustic commentary on the problem of fairness:

People abused some of this stuff Exxon was offering. I know they meant right on some of it, but people abused the system. . . . Some people . . . [were] greedy. I have hard feelings on them.[58]

Finally, there were those people who perceived the activities of their neighbors who worked on the spill as "selling out" to Exxon, violating the idea of a close-knit community facing the faceless and immoral corporate giant. One resident recalled the anger of those who refused to cooperate with Exxon: "I heard those angry words. They were ugly. . . . Some people would say people were traitors, that they sold out and took one of those contracts."[59] What is fair here? To work for the company responsible for this ecological disaster and make some good money? Or to refuse to work for Exxon and try to fish? Once the dispute is framed in the grammar of fairness, its moral and emotional tenor is rendered in the stark terms of "either/or."

> There were people who were making literally $4,000 or $5,000 a day on the oil spill and then there was [sic] people who were fishing. [Some people] believed that fishing was their livelihood and that's what they should be doing for a living. . . . I guess it depends on how you value a dollar and what kind of person you are deep down inside and whether money makes you tick or . . . community makes you tick.[60]

❖

The dispute over the "spillionaires" in the Prince William Sound provides a telling example of the deep feelings and volatile emotions to which perceptions of unfairness can give rise. The division of the community into haves and have-nots is far more visceral than empirical, a heartfelt expression of difference between those residents who "made the best of a bad situation" and those who, perhaps for psychological reasons, were unable to act on their own behalf. For those residents who wanted to get a contract to work on the cleanup but were unable to, their more successful neighbors were "greedy" and "abused the system." Add the third group to the scenario, and the moral confusion over what, in fact, is a fair, equitable, indeed ethical response to this ecological nightmare becomes even more labyrinthine in character. For this group, those who sought the cleanup contracts and worked for Exxon betrayed their idea of the small town fighting the corporate giant. Framed in the highly charged language of "traitor" and "betrayer," there was little room for a civil discussion of differences and, perhaps, compromise.

Toward a Sociology of Emotions and Environmental Controversies

It should go without saying that emotions—as strong visceral feelings—are always a part of conflict. Perhaps more latent than manifest at times, emotions are nevertheless what makes conflict animated, moving, possibly dangerous. Indeed, the Latin etymology of *emotion* is to move something. The centrality of emotions to local environmental conflicts is evident in many of the case studies introduced in this book: from the anger which led some of the citizens of Owens Valley, California, to engage in violent acts of sabotage (see Chapter 2), to the fear and anger which spurred a group of ordinary middle-class citizens at Love Canal, New York, to hold two EPA officials hostage (see Chapter 3), to the hostility and resentment that led former friends and neighbors in Centralia, Pennsylvania, to stop speaking to each other, and even engage in vandalism and death threats (see Chapter 1), to the fierce love of the Yavapai for their land and culture (see Chapter 2).

Certainly intense feelings are generated by more than just perceptions of unfairness, including fear, anxiety, and loss. Apart from any of the specifics involved, conflict itself is a generator of emotions, as many people find conflict stressful, while others find it exhilarating. We suspect, however, that perceptions of injustice undergird much of the strong emotions experienced by participants in local environmental disputes. Consider this exchange between a logger, his wife, and their son. The dispute is over logging old-growth forest in Oregon. The loggers are aware that they have a compromised public image, one based on chopping down ancient trees and bullying local environmentalists who want the cutting to stop. The topic is, specifically, fairness and emotion.

Gary: I think there's a lot of emotion but it doesn't do any good. It doesn't settle the problem.

Chris: No, but . . . the other side gets emotional—

Gary: Real one-sided.

Chris: [They] think that if they don't do something . . . disaster's coming. . . . [I]t's very personal thing to them, . . . And it's very personal to us, . . . When the paycheque [*sic*] stops flowing you get pretty upset. You know, people get pretty violent even—

Arlene: Yeah. That's the emotional part for me . . . like the time I thought that I was going to . . . you guys were arguing with that little weasel in front of the Wilderness Society [booth] . . . and then I become emotional when he called me a name. So, you can lose it real easy.[61]

Emotions such as fear, anxiety, and loss are amplified when the conditions seen to give rise to them are believed to be unfair. While it is certainly difficult to handle the unexpected death of a close family member from natural causes, those feelings are much more intense if that death was the result of negligent actions of others (such as a drunk driver). Indeed, anger stemming from encounters with unresponsive agencies or official dismissal of local knowledge, discussed earlier in the book, are also, at heart, issues of justice and fairness.

We use the qualifying language of "we suspect perceptions of injustice undergird much of the strong emotions associated with local environmental conflicts" because, to be frank, the sociologists and anthropologists who study local community conflicts do not typically include emotions as an analytical part of their accounts. Emotions, sentiments, feelings, and so on might be described,[62] but they are not conceptualized or interpreted as meaningful in the analysis. This is not surprising. The sociology of emotion is of recent vintage, emerging in the early 1980s.[63] In short, there is no well-established road to inquiry here, but a path is worth breaking.

Aristotle reasoned that emotion was a constituent part of our mental and physical life. It pervades everything we do, coloring, shading, or perhaps forcefully defining our day-to-day lives. We are suspicious of people who are unemotional. In truth, we view them as "cold"—in some fashion, dead. On the other hand, as the father of the golden mean knew only too well, too much emotion, the kind that becomes frenzy or zeal, is also a problem. We might refer to those prone to emotional outbursts as hot heads, people who, for whatever reason, cannot control themselves. Hot or cold? What's our emotional temperature? Aristotle's idea was that we seek to be tepid, lukewarm, a little of each. There is nothing wrong with this idea, in principle. The problem is that life—with its inevitable trials and tribulations—does not readily encourage the development of tepid people or, as we are likely to say, "people who keep their cool." We return to this idea in a moment.

Many of us believe that emotions are primitive or instinctual, while reflection and thoughtfulness are rational or reasonable behaviors. On the contrary, emotions are shaped, organized, and regulated by culture.[64] The Llongot people who live in the Philippines, for example, fear anger and avoid it at all costs.[65] The medieval knight, on the other hand, like the modern gangbanger, embraced battle if honor was at stake. Erikson found the people of Appalachia slow to anger (see the discussion of the Buffalo Creek flood in Chapter 2). But once riled, these kind people could become demonstrably aggravated and difficult to mollify.[66] Emotions, in short, are both visceral and somatic, on the one hand, and governed by culture, on the other.

Not only the emotions being expressed, but also the target of those emotions are important to an understanding of how feelings play out in local environmental conflicts. Reflecting on our fieldwork, one particular manifestation of the role of emotions in community environmental conflicts seems especially salient. Posed as a question, it would sound like this: "Who or what am I upset or furious with?" "Who or what" introduces poignant differences between directing combustible emotions toward a person or group or toward a situation or state of affairs. Consider a field note account of a strategy session called by the Concerned Citizens Against the Centralia Mine Fire (CC). At issue was how the group would confront the town council at the next community meeting.

Tommy: I say we go in both barrels blasting. The mayor and his little band of "merry men" are criminally negligent in their duties to make the state and feds do what is necessary to stop this disaster. Enough!

Sam: Okay, we're pissed off and should be. But if we go in there and start pointing fingers and yelling, we don't have the upper hand. Many people in town already think we're a little nutty.

Catherine: We are nuts. Nuts is the only way to be. . . . This is a crazy [way] to live.

Sam: Of course we're nuts. But let's consider making everyone else think we're knowledgeable and reasonable people who want the best for the community. . . . Let's not let them say we're nuts.

Tommy: Well, I for one am not going to that meeting and sugarcoat it for that piece-of-shit mayor and his buddies.[67]

More discussion of this nature occurred. It was decided that everyone needed to express themselves at meetings in their own way. But argued forcefully by several people in the group was the idea that getting emotional or "fired up," as they called it, was okay as long as one avoided *personal* attacks. Fashioning a public emotional encounter that targeted the other's personal defects or shortcomings, it was thought, would simply reduce the mine fire from a complex environmental hazard to personalities.

In general, however, Americans are more prone to direct volatile sentiments toward people, individuals, and personalities rather than toward social structure, history, or polity. A culture that places a high value on individual agency, choice, and free will is also likely to be one that faults, blames, and censures persons rather than something more abstract like a historical pattern or piece of legislation. Indeed, despite the caution advocated by some activists, the Centralia conflict often devolved to personal attacks, as we demonstrate below.

This is an important caveat, because emotions targeted at another are likely to increase geometrically as the targeted person is tempted to return an equally emotive salvo at his or her assailant. In the language of conflict resolution, this is referred to as escalation.[68] Escalation is evident in the following passage, again taken from field notes collected by Kroll-Smith. The scene is a town meeting with officials from the state Department of Environmental Quality and the federal Office of Surface Mining. At the meeting, several members of the CC fought with several members of the town council. The CC are lobbying for a government buyout of the town; the council opposes a buyout.

Charlie,
addressing an
official from the
Office of Surface
Mining (OSM): I'm tired. I work all day. And now I'm steamed! I come home and go to these meetings to get news about my house, my property. And what you got for us? Charts with funny numbers I can't read. S***t!

OSM Official: We are studying this problem. I can tell you that. And we're doing it as fast as we can. We're working with your borough council to find the best solution.

Charlie: Our borough council. Look at 'em. [Charlie points in their direction] They're looking to make a mint off this disaster. They smirk. They make deals. They disgust me!!

John, president
of the borough
council, stands
up and moves
toward Charlie: You're whining again, Charlie. Charlie the whiner. You want to take this outside?

Charlie: Go f*** yourself.

Emotions beget emotions when they are targeted at another. Moreover, they quickly move the focus from the real problem, in this case an underground mine fire, to personalities.

While strong feelings may be counterproductive to efforts at conflict resolution, they can prove a useful organizing tool. Indeed, activists may intentionally inflame emotions as part of their mobilization strategy, both to win broader public support and to gain the attention of the media.[69] During the late 1960s and the 1970s, for example, environmentalists and animal rights activists waged a campaign to halt the "slaughter" of baby seals in Canada, which were clubbed to death for their fur (note here the emotional overtones of the word *slaughter* as opposed to the more neutral term *hunt*). With their wide foreheads and wide round eyes, baby seals are reminiscent of human infants. Indeed, environmentalists and animal rights activists have intentionally conducted campaigns to save animals toward which humans have strong, positive emotional reactions, including ones which resemble human infants, domesticated animals used in laboratory experiments, and megafauna such as big cats, elephants, and whales. Species which produce either no emotional reaction, like worms and lichen, or negative emotional reactions, such as spiders, have seldom been on the receiving end of beneficial social action.[70]

Kenneth Burke makes a fundamental distinction between what he calls human motion and human action which is useful to an understanding of the intentional inflaming of emotions as a mobilization strategy.[71] The first, human motion, is visceral, while the second, human action, is a symbolic act. The goal of activists is to use emotion-laden, iconic symbols—baby seals, threatened children, cooling towers, leaking drums—to spur kinetic, somatic motion of affect, feelings, and sentiments.[72] When these campaigns are successful, motion and action combine in perceptions of fairness to amplify (literally and figuratively) local environmental hostilities.

Box 5.5 is a list of questions that will allow students to inquire about the role of emotions and fairness in local environmental conflicts. In the following chapter we explore in greater depth the effect of mobilizing strategies on local communities.

Box 5.5   Adding to the Portfolio: Fairness and Emotions

1. To what extent do conflicts over fairness and equity give rise to deep feelings and volatile emotions?

2. What is the emotional repertoire present in the local culture?

3. Are volatile emotions directed toward social structures, history, and polity, or toward people, individuals, and personalities?

4. Does emotion targeted by one set of conflict participants toward other participants increase geometrically as the targeted groups or individuals respond in kind?

5. To what extent are emotions intentionally inflamed as part of a mobilizing strategy?

A Concluding Word

In this chapter we addressed the role of perceptions of fairness in local environmental conflicts. Whether one is talking about the distribution of costs and benefits of proposed or existing actions, the moral frameworks which shape how we define fairness in the first place, or the volatile emotions which erupt when people believe they are victims of unfair actions, concerns about equity, justice, and fairness are mainstays of local environmental conflicts. After all, if all involved parties thought the benefits they received from particular actions exceeded the costs they were asked to bear, there would not be any conflict to begin with. Perceptions of unfair and unjust treatment make conflict resolution difficult, divide communities, and produce resentments which can linger for years.

The sociology of emotions is a promising field and particularly suited for the study of environmental controversies. There is something particularly incendiary about people and their relationships to environments. Rarely are questions and differences about the use, purpose, or quality of environments debated and resolved in a sedate and placid manner. For whatever reasons, matters of environment are also likely to be matters of the heart.

In the following chapter we address the question of what happens when local residents use their feelings of outrage to forge oppositional activity to conservancy efforts, siting initiatives, or exposure problems. As the present chapter has illustrated, the very definition of fairness may be divisive among local residents, and hence there is no guarantee that local support will crystallize behind activists. Indeed, oppositional activity may engender anger from one's neighbors, and can have quite devastating effects on the fabric of local social life.

STUDENT EXERCISES

1. Recount three past experiences where you felt you were being treated unfairly. What were the rewards and/or punishments at stake? What moral frame did you use to judge the situation as "unfair"? Elaborate an alternative moral frame which would promote a different conclusion about the fairness of these situations.

2. Speculate on characteristics of conservancy, siting, and exposure disputes which would likely produce zero-sum and non-zero-sum situations.

3. What costs and benefits from economic development, ecological degradation, and/or environmental protection do we see in the cases of Scotia, California

(Chapter 1), and Chicago Wilderness (Chapter 4)? What was the distribution of these costs and benefits, and how did this influence the nature of conflict in each case?

4. Using the conceptual lens presented in this chapter, reexamine either the Convent, Louisiana, case (Chapter 1) or the Grand Island, Nebraska, case (Chapter 3). What new insights have you gleaned about the case by explicitly addressing fairness issues? What additional information about fairness not included in our case vignettes would you like to know?

5. In Chapter 2 we argued that knowing something about the history of a local area may provide valuable insight into the dynamics and outcomes of conflict. Choose four questions from the list of 15 presented in Tables 5.3, 5.4, and 5.5 and explain how history might be useful in helping you answer those questions.

Notes

1. Interview with resident of St. Gabriel, Louisiana, July 1997. Interview conducted by Steve Kroll-Smith.

2. Interview with resident of Agricultural Street, New Orleans, Louisiana, April 1998. Interview conducted by Steve Kroll-Smith.

3. Case material from Gibbons (1977).

4. Gibbons (1979), 20.

5. Gibbons (1979), 21.

6. Gibbons (1979), 22.

7. Gibbons (1979), 90.

8. Gibbons (1979), 148.

9. Bell (2004).

10. Margavio and Forsyth (1996).

11. Cable and Cable (1995).

12. Allen (2003).

13. Gaventa (1980).

14. McWhorter (2001).

15. Allen (2003); Checker (2005).

16. Pellow (2002).

17. Ibid., 90.

18. Ibid., 91.

19. Ibid., 91.

20. Ibid., 93.

21. Ibid., 95.

22. Roberts and Toffolon-Weiss (2001).

23. Quoted in Ritchie (2004), 408.

24. Kriesberg (2003).

25. Espeland (1998).

26. Case material from Capek (2005).

27. Capek (2005), 196.

28. Ibid., 199.

29. Ibid., 200.

30. Ibid.

31. Ibid., 201.

32. Ibid.

33. Durkheim (1974), 80.

34. Francis and Silvers (2000), xiii.

35. Environmental Justice (2006).

36. We do realize religious fundamentalists will disagree with this statement. However, at present there are fundamentalists of different religious traditions asserting the absolute truth of their sacred texts, and hence from a sociological perspective these disputes remain intractable.

37. Loseke (1999), 73.

38. A 1918 statement by Archibald Rutledge; quoted in Nelson (1997), 10.

39. Organic farmer quoted in Nelson (1997), 189.

40. Bell (2004).

41. Gallie (1956).

42. From the movie *Labyrinth* (1999).

43. Loseke (1999).

44. Ibid., 52.

45. Bedford (1990), 6.

46. Ibid., 186.

47. Alaska Oil Spill Commission (1990). Case material from several sources, but most notably from Ritchie (2004). See also Picou, Gill, and Cohen (1997) for an extensive overview of the disaster and its impacts.

48. Picou, Gill, and Cohen (1997), 3.

49. Quoted in Ritchie (2004), 267.

50. Ibid., 293.

51. *Anchorage Daily News* (1989), 2.

52. Quoted in Ritchie (2004), 370.

53. Robbins (1993), 242.

54. Ibid., 244.

55. Quoted in Ritchie (2004), 373.

56. Ibid., 354.

57. Ibid., 294.

58. Ibid., 374.

59. Ibid., 367.

60. Ibid., 367–368.

61. Satterfield (2002), 138–139.

62. See, for example, Freudenberg and Gramling (1994) and Kroll-Smith and Couch (1990).

63. Thoits (1989).

64. Russell (1991).
65. Rosaldo (1984).
66. Erikson (1976).
67. From field notes taken by Steve Kroll-Smith.
68. Kriesberg (2003).
69. Goodwin, Jasper, and Polletta (2001).
70. Jasper and Nelkin (1992); Singer (1998).
71. Burke (1989).
72. Cf. Szasz (1994).

6

Oppositional Activity
and Social Capital

*From the very beginning [of New York state's announcement of
the possible siting of a nuclear waste dump in the area] I felt I was
part of a hive of bees, threatened with destruction. People called
everyone they knew. I talked to Stuart and Sally, to a farmer
down the road, to Steve Myers, to you and Megan. There was a
general buzz that seemed to connect us all. I sometimes think we
are part of a larger organism, even though we usually pretend
that we're separate individuals. When there's a crisis, we pull
together, subconsciously recognizing we're part of something
much bigger.*

Jessie Shefrin[1]

Local environmental activism occurs in communities. This is more than
a prosaic observation; it is the guiding focus of this book. Environmental activists are not only strikingly committed people; they are also
teachers, mechanics, Girl Scout leaders, neighbors, in short, fellow citizens.
Individually and collectively, these are the men and women who decided to
step outside their ordinary routines to follow the uncommon path of civic
engagement. Activists are more likely than others to experience local environmental troubles as, in James's words, forced options (see Chapter 1).[2]

Their proclivity for grassroots organizing and dramatic actions are likely to alter the social and cultural life of a neighborhood, village, or town. It is this exchange between citizen activists and their social milieus that interests us in the present chapter.

When journalists or sociologists write about local environmental conflicts, what they typically focus on is the story of the struggle. A typical story goes something like this: a group of local residents decide they do not want a nuclear power plant located near their community. They form a grassroots organization, pool their resources, and begin agitating to halt construction. They do not proceed unchallenged, however. Indeed, just as the activists are struggling to stop the process, those who back the plant will be equally intent on stopping *them*. Victory and defeat are measured by decisions and developments that favor one position and threaten the other. So, as the story proceeds, organized opposition unfolds over time through a series of action-reaction encounters.

Social Capital and Its Two Variations

Our goal in this chapter is to alter the narrative line in this conventional story with a more contextual approach that examines oppositional activity in its relationships to community as a source of *social capital*. Think of social capital as a web of relationships, experiences, and sentiments that make community a resource in our lives. More concretely, it facilitates coordination and communication. It opens channels of information that enhance human agency. By promoting civic engagement it helps to ensure that the whole (the neighborhood, community, county, and so on) will be greater than the sum of the families and individuals who inhabit it. Social capital, in short, is a resource that adds appreciably to human well-being.

It was probably Lyda Judson Hanifan who first introduced the idea of social capital in her study of rural schools.[3] The idea was picked up by Robert Putnam in 1993 and launched as a useful tool in evaluating the viability of civil society.[4] *Physical* capital refers to material, biology, anatomy, and other objective resources. Human strength is a type of physical capital. *Human* capital refers to the qualities of individuals, their capacity to trust, for example. *Social* capital is measured in the strength of social ties, collective goodwill, mutual caring, and similar bonding resources. Like other forms of capital, social capital is a resource that can be both accrued and forfeited. Consistent with our attempt to provide lenses through which readers can visualize key dynamics and processes, social capital will serve as the lens for this discussion.

Students of social capital draw a distinction between two different dynamics in the formation of social capital: bonding and bridging.[5] *Bonding capital* is more local, and inward looking. It operates on a horizontal plane, drawing together neighbors, fellow residents, and people who live or work in the same geographic milieu. As its name implies, *bridging capital* links local residents and groups to external social and cultural assets. Its plane is more vertical, creating meaningful social ties between a local community and distant communities, organizations, and agencies.

In this chapter we explore how oppositional activity alters the quality and quantity of both bonding and bridging capital. In the first section we present an exposure dispute which provides a striking example of oppositional activity that creates both bonding and bridging capital. We trace the chronological sequence at work in this particular case, showing how it was the initial employment of bridging capital (in the form of an outside organizer) which facilitated the formation of bonding capital, as well as additional forms of bridging capital. From the perspective of movement sympathizers, coalitions which unite local residents and outside supporters constitute the best case scenarios for producing successful outcomes.[6]

Next, we consider a case where bonding capital is formed in the absence of bridging capital. Here local people, under their own direction and initiative, forge a broad-based community coalition, even reaching out to former enemies. In the process, they undertake symbolic displays of local unity and engage in actions which build trust. We consider two different circumstances which could result in the absence of supportive bridging capital: first, outsiders' rejection of local environmental campaigns, and second, locals' rejection of outsiders' assistance.

In the final section we consider a case where oppositional activity resulted in the simultaneous creation and destruction of bonding capital. As we pointed out above, individuals are moved to civic engagement by problematic local conditions they feel they cannot ignore. As these individuals spend time talking with like-minded individuals, they establish meaningful social connections and reinforce their mutual understanding of the situation. As they plan and execute oppositional activity, they build up a fund of trust and goodwill. Yet these actions may upset and alienate other residents, who may reject their definition of the problem entirely or who may agree there is a problem but disagree with the tactics the activists employ to redress it. Oppositional activity, in short, may forge active and meaningful connections among only a subset of local residents, creating, at times, dramatic schisms between them and their neighbors.

These three cases hardly constitute an exhaustive listing of the ways in which oppositional activity may affect a community's fund of social capital. Indeed, the most likely scenario is that over the course of an environmental conflict, a community will accrue both bonding and bridging capital; it is also likely to lose some of each type as well. What distinguishes different cases is the degree of gain and loss of different types of capital, the chronological sequence in which these gains and losses happen, and the social processes which erode or build mutual understanding, trust, goodwill, and meaningful social connections. Obviously, this opens the door to many possible combinations; our goal in this chapter is to provide readers with a general sense of a few of these.

Indeed, we use these cases as a vehicle to drive home the broader, underlying lesson: social capital is a powerful tool in a community's struggle with environmental troubles, but it is a two-edged sword. In its propensity to cut both ways, it invites a careful and considered analysis in each case. Keep this lesson in mind as you read through this material. You might also want to note how the concepts of oppositional activity and social capital start to pull together the disparate material covered in previous chapters. This is most evident in Box 6.1 and in the student exercises introduced at the end of the chapter. We return to this point in the conclusion, for it sets the foundation for the chapter to follow.

Box 6.1   Making Connections With Previous Chapters

Throughout this book, we have been talking about oppositional activity. After all, without opposition there would be no conflict. Accordingly, many of the questions presented in the portfolio boxes in the first five chapters are pertinent to the material covered in the present chapter. For this reason, this Making Connections box is a bit longer than its predecessors.

The first portfolio box, for example, lists a series of questions designed to yield descriptive information about conflict participants and their claims (see Box 1.2). The concept of social capital provides insight into how we can push the answers to these basic "who is involved" and "who said what" questions in a more analytic direction. For example, issues can be framed in ways which draw on and reinforce (or perhaps even create) bonding capital, such as calls for the entire community to pull together to face a common threat. Of course, issues can also be framed in a divisive fashion. Knowing there is a mix of local groups with divergent agendas suggests potential for bonding capital to be simultaneously created and destroyed over the course of the controversy.

The concept of bridging and bonding capital once again draws attention to the distinctions between local versus extra-local (outside) participants. Conflict participants which span the local/extra-local divide are likely to prove an especially valuable source of bridging capital. Box 1.3 directs students to address other key descriptive components of local environmental conflicts, including the major strategies nongovernmental conflict participants use to influence the course and outcome of the controversy. This chapter allows us to take this basic descriptive information and wrap it into a more analytic account, by focusing on the intentional and unintentional ways these strategies create and strengthen, and undermine and erode, social capital.

While our focus in this chapter is on the creation and destruction of social capital over the course of a controversy, communities enter a conflict with a stock of social capital in place. Indeed, social capital is an important element of a community's cultural toolbox, and as such can also play a harbinger role in any conflict. It is important, therefore, to examine the effect of past crises, calamities, challenges, and conflicts on both bonding and bridging capital (see Box 2.4). The enactment of traditional cultural practices, as well as the oppositional activities directed toward preserving the places and resources upon which these practices depend, can be a potent means of strengthening and reinforcing bonding capital (see Box 2.3). Invented histories can also facilitate the formation of bonding capital, though they may do this by romanticizing the past, that is, ascribing (perhaps significantly) higher levels of harmony, meaningful social connections, and shared goodwill in previous times than actually existed (see Box 2.5).

In Chapter 3 we discussed how many local environmental conflicts result in a breakdown in citizen trust of powerful social actors. Local perceptions that government agencies and other major conflict participants are acting in a deceitful, evasive, or self-serving manner, therefore, always represent a loss of bridging capital, regardless of whether the powerful outsiders are intentionally engaged in malfeasance (see Boxes 3.3 and 3.4). The difficulty in ascertaining others' intentions can produce conditions of uncertainty which can also lead to horizontal knowledge disputes and their accompanying erosion of bonding capital (see Boxes 3.5 and 4.5).

Uncertainty can have erosive effects on both bridging and bonding capital. The former can occur if community residents and outside experts clash over the "true state" of environmental conditions (what we refer to in Chapter 4 as the vertical axis of knowledge disputes; see Box 4.4). The horizontal axis of knowledge disputes, where community residents dispute among themselves about the true state of local environmental conditions, illustrates how uncertainty can undermine bonding capital (see Box 4.5). While we suspect that erosion of social capital frequently occurs in the face of uncertainty, we do not want to suggest it is inevitable. The BASF/Geismar case, recounted in this chapter, shows how bridging capital was strengthened through the use of outside experts.

Social capital will be eroded when one group thinks another group of conflict participants is treating them in an unfair, unjust manner. This erosion process may be magnified if participants perceive the conflict to be zero-sum in nature (see Box 5.3). Unfair treatment wielded at the hand of outsiders may result in a pattern where bridging capital is undermined but bonding capital strengthened, as seen in several cases reported in this chapter. On the other hand, if the costs and benefits of a siting, conservancy, or exposure dispute are inequitably distributed in the community, and/or if local residents bring to the conflict different value systems and different conceptions of "fairness," then residents may fight among themselves, undermining and eroding bonding capital.

Creating Both Bridging and Bonding Capital

BASF Lockout in Geismar, Louisiana

In 1970 a giant transnational corporation based in Germany, known by the acronym BASF, bought out the Michigan-based Wyandotte Chemical Company. Included among BASF's new acquisitions was a 2,400-acre chemical factory complex in Geismar, Louisiana.[7] A modest-sized community, Geismar is located along the 90-mile stretch of the Mississippi River that runs between Baton Rouge and New Orleans. Chemical factories began sprouting up in this area during the post–World War II era, a time when the industry in general was undergoing a major expansionary phase. An abundance of nearby natural resources (especially petroleum from offshore drilling), ready access to interstate, rail, and river transportation, and a state government that went out of its way to accommodate business (including lax environmental regulation) provided an attractive mix for companies looking to site new facilities. By the 1970s, over 20% of all chemicals produced in the United States were manufactured in this 90-mile corridor.

Unlike most of its neighbors, the Wyandotte (subsequently BASF) Geismar plant was unionized from its start in the late 1950s. Company executives, based in the heavily unionized state of Michigan, were accustomed to dealing with a unionized workforce and presented few obstacles to the formation of Local 4-620 of the International Oil, Chemical, and Atomic Workers (OCAW) union. For about two decades (one before and one after the BASF takeover), labor-management relations at the Geismar plant were relatively peaceful, with jobs there providing better pay and more job security than other employment options in the area.

This changed, however, in the early 1980s. The 1980 election of Ronald Reagan resulted in a federal probusiness administration. President Reagan's firing of striking air traffic controllers in 1983 signaled a new, get-tough-on-unions mentality. Many companies throughout the United States took the opportunity to greatly decrease the power of unions or to break them entirely. BASF saw the political climate as opportune for abolishing OCAW at the Geismar plant. In contract negotiations beginning in the early 1980s, the company demanded a number of significant concessions from the union, which the union fought. Failing to ratify a new contract after months of negotiations, union members were suddenly and unexpectedly locked out of the plant. What followed was the longest lockout in U.S. history. It was over 3 years before union members began to return to their jobs and 5 years before all members were reinstated.[8]

During the first year of the lockout, members of Local 4-620 engaged in conventional labor-management negotiations, to no avail. During the second year, the international union sent a full-time organizer, Richard Miller, to assist the local's efforts. Miller would spend a total of 5 years living in the area and working with the locked-out workers.

Under Miller's direction, an important shift in union strategy was undertaken. Rather than continue to keep the conflict an in-house affair between labor and management—the conventional negotiation model—a decision was made to take the dispute outside the company gates in hopes of winning broader public support for the union. This tactic, known, somewhat facetiously, as a "corporate campaign," was a recent and as yet little used addition to the repertoire of tools unions deployed to increase their negotiating clout with management.[9] Because it involved generating negative publicity about the company, including the possibility of airing dirty laundry in public, it was not a tactic to be pursued lightly. Workers are dependent on their employers and therefore vulnerable to repercussions if damage to a company's reputation costs the company economically. Declines in sales and stock values and increases in regulatory oversight hurt employees as much or more than employers.

With little to lose, the union began to cultivate alliances in Geismar and the surrounding areas. The strategy was to bring pressure on BASF through making the conflict a public, civic issue. The logical place to start looking for allies was among groups who had preexisting grievances against the plant.

One of the most promising locations for finding confederates was the town of Geismar. Residents of Geismar had endured two-and-a-half decades of double-fisted assault from the factory: on the one hand, they were saddled with costs in the form of a polluted, degraded environment; on the other hand, these costs were not offset by commensurable benefits, since the plant employed very few local workers. Most of the workforce was drawn from the Baton Rouge area, about 40 miles away, making ties between town and factory tenuous at best. This social division was exacerbated by the fact that most of the workers at the plant were white, while most of the residents of Geismar were African American.

Indeed, BASF workers had previously given little thought to the fact that the town of Geismar had to live with pollution from the plant. The corporate campaign, however, was designed to bring just these kinds of problems to public attention. Spurred by the union's efforts at coalition building, Geismar residents formed their own grassroots organization, Ascension Parish Residents Against Toxic Pollution, and began to more aggressively fight environmental problems caused by the BASF operations. With assistance from union members and other environmental organizations that became active in the local area (see below), Geismar residents went on to successfully defeat several BASF initiatives, including one for expansion at the plant, one for waste incineration, and one for deep-well injection of hazardous wastes.[10]

Richard Miller recognized the plant was vulnerable on environmental issues and encouraged further efforts to connect with regional and national environmental organizations. Given the history of antagonism between environmentalists and labor,[11] this development was rather remarkable, though hardly without a few rough spots. At the beginning of the corporate campaign, members of Local 4-620 had neither contacts with environmentalists nor high opinions of them. Union overtures to the Delta Chapter of the Sierra Club, based out of New Orleans, were greeted with opposition by some club members. The chapter president, Darryl Malek-Wiley, was a former union member who was interested in cultivating stronger ties between labor and environmentalists. Together, Malek-Wiley and Miller spearheaded several studies in the area which were crucial in documenting pollution problems around the plant. The international union also hired toxicologists and hydrologists to assist in these studies.

Several outside environmental organizations provided assistance in securing media coverage of the union's struggles while also focusing on local environmental problems. These groups spanned the range from state-level (Louisiana Environmental Action Network, or LEAN) to national (the German Green Party) to international (Greenpeace). The LEAN was formed in 1986 as an umbrella organization designed to provide assistance to grassroots environmental groups in Louisiana. In 1988, the LEAN joined with the Gulf Coast Tenant Leadership Development Project, the Sierra Club, and Local 4-620 to sponsor the Great Louisiana Toxics March. This march involved a core of several hundred individuals (at times joined by additional people) walking the 90-mile stretch from Baton Rouge to the outskirts of New Orleans. The march was timed to coincide with the arrival of Greenpeace's ship *Beluga*. The *Beluga* had been traveling down the length of the Mississippi River, documenting environmental problems from the source of the river to its mouth.[12]

Modeled on civil rights marches, the Great Louisiana Toxics March was intended to draw public attention to pollution problems along the riverine corridor. Union members provided support and encouragement to the marchers as they moved through the Geismar area. Greenpeace activists tried to get a sample of effluent discharged from the BASF plant, but they were unsuccessful. The march, however, which lasted for over a week, did garner considerable media attention.

A Local 4-620 representative also reached out to the German Green Party, "as part of a broader effort to create pressure against BASF within Europe" (recall that BASF is based out of Germany).[13] In April 1986, several members of the Green Party, including two in parliament, came to Louisiana. They tried to gain access to the Geismar plant, but BASF officials denied their request for a tour. The Green Party representatives did make several public statements condemning the aggressive antiunion tactics of the BASF lockout. In addition, Local 4-620 worked with the International Federation of Chemical, Energy, and General Workers' Union, which provided them with valuable information about BASF.

After 3 tumultuous years, the majority of locked-out workers were allowed to return to their jobs. Maintenance workers continued to be locked out, however, probably as punishment for their role as union leaders. (Maintenance workers are also often union leaders because they are able to move more freely about the facility than line workers.)

In December 1989, BASF finally agreed to recall all of the workers who had been locked out of the plant, a move that paved the way for the signing of a new contract.[14] The agreement came after the union joined with local, regional, national, and international environmental groups to launch an effective campaign to expose the many dangerous work practices at the facility. It also forced BASF to clean up its more egregiously polluted sites located at and around the plant.

Expressed in this case is the idea that norms of reciprocity and, perhaps, shared goals exist in potentia between all manners of groups and individuals, even those currently marked by a lack of meaningful social contact and perhaps even enmity. It is the sociologist's job to understand the circumstances under which that potential becomes realized, for certainly there is no guarantee it will happen. We might easily imagine a situation where the BASF workers reached out to people living around the plant, only to find their overtures rebuffed, leaving them with fewer resources in their struggle with management. So too, regional, national, and international organizations may have ignored them or responded in a hostile manner. In this particular case, however, the OCAW was successful in expanding its radius of trust to include both local and extra-local people, groups, and organizations. By succeeding in creating both bonding and bridging capital, the OCAW created a cache of social wealth sufficient to achieve at least modest results for both itself and communities surrounding the plant.

To determine whether a local environmental conflict results in the creation of bonding and bridging capital, we must start with a baseline of social capital present at the start of the controversy. We can do this by mapping the configuration of local and extra-local social connections, paying particular attention to lacunae or "blank spots" on the map. Consider three of the blank spots on the BASF/Geismar map, places where communication and meaningful social connections *could* have existed, but did not: (1) between plant workers and community residents, (2) between plant workers and environmentalists, and (3) between community residents and environmentalists.

Once we have a sense of the baseline, we can determine how oppositional activity reconfigures social connections, facilitates mutual understanding, and builds trust.[15] When local activists decide to take on a conservancy effort, siting initiative, or exposure problem, they face a daunting challenge. We can expect they will confront opponents who possess considerable money and power. Furthermore, as shown in Chapters 3 and 4, participation in arenas of environmental decision making (such as permit hearings and court cases) requires levels of legal and technical expertise far beyond the ken of most laypeople. Given what they are up against, it is hardly surprising to find local people actively seeking help. What we want to emphasize here is the dualistic nature of this process, how the pursuit of assistance also builds and reinforces (and, as we show in a later section, also undermines and destroys) social capital.

Even with outside assistance, it is unlikely that local oppositional efforts can match the financial, legal, and technical resources of large corporations and government agencies. There is, however, one "resource war" grassroots activists actually have the potential to win (though there is no guarantee they will do so): the securing of public sympathy and support. Sheer numbers can matter, increasing the probability of attention from media and elected officials (who do not want to alienate constituents by failing to support a popular cause), as well as making it easier for activists to claim the moral high ground.

Reaching out to garner the support of fellow residents can create and strengthen bonding capital. Note that in the BASF/Geismar case, however, this "reaching out" process only occurred *after* the involvement of the outside organizer; for the first year of the lockout, the union members struggled in isolation. It seems unlikely that Local 4-620 union members would have undertaken a corporate campaign, with its accompanying strategy of seeking broad-based public support, in the absence of an external impetus. In this case, it was the strengthening and deepening of bridging capital which facilitated the formation of new forms of bonding capital.

Particularly noteworthy on this front was the formation of the grassroots organization Ascension Parish Residents Against Toxic Pollution and the collaboration between that group and locked-out workers. Union members were able to provide inside information about practices at the facility, including violations of environmental regulations, "accidental" releases, and questionable waste disposal practices. Local 4-620 also served as one of the sponsors of the Great Louisiana Toxics March, and some union members served refreshments to marchers as they walked through Geismar. These actions demonstrated mutual understanding between union members and Geismar residents, evoked norms of reciprocity, and engendered goodwill.

Remarkably, the collaborative effort pursued as part and parcel of the corporate campaign brought together groups that had been marked by deep social cleavages. These cleavages included divisions marked by race (union members and outside environmentalists versus Geismar residents) and social class (union members and Geismar residents versus outside environmentalists). Oppositional activity, spearheaded by an outside organizer, remapped the distribution of social capital in the local area. Where once there had been disengagement, mutual suspicion, and even animosity, we now find positive and supportive social relations.

We suspect many organizers and environmental sociologists would regard such a positive and productive joining of local and extra-local oppositional groups as a best case scenario. Allen, for example, who studied a number of environmental conflicts in Louisiana's cancer corridor (including BASF), reports:

> What I found was that the most successful activist strategies typically involved alliances: (1) between local citizens and expert-activists; (2) across lines of race and class; and (3) between local and national organizations.[16]

Box 6.2 presents a list of questions which will aid students in determining whether oppositional activity fostered the creation of bridging and bonding capital and if the formation of the first facilitated the development of the second. The BASF/Geismar case does not exhaust the possible patterns, however, as we see in the following case.

Box 6.2   Adding to the Portfolio: Creating Both Bridging and Bonding Capital

1. What is the configuration of local and extra-local social connections at the start of the controversy?

2. Do locals turn to outside organizations for assistance in their oppositional struggles, in the process forging new or strengthening existing social connections with extra-local associations?

3. Does an outside organization promote an organizing strategy of broad-based community support?

4. Does outside assistance facilitate the formation of one or more grassroots organizations?

5. Does outside assistance facilitate the establishment of new social connections between groups previously separated by deep social cleavages, and perhaps even marked by open animosity?

Creating Bonding Capital in the Absence of Bridging Capital

Allegany County's Fight Against Low-Level Nuclear Waste

In 1985, the U.S. Congress passed a law which required "that states take title to all the 'low level' nuclear waste generated within their borders by January 1, 1993."[17] In the aftermath of this federal directive, New York State identified 32 townships as possible locations for a disposal facility for low-level nuclear waste; 5 were in Allegany County. Upon learning of their inclusion on this list, many county residents became convinced that their county would in fact be chosen to host the facility. They also believed the decision would be made on political rather than scientific grounds.

The politics of New York State have always been heavily influenced by urban interests, especially those of New York City. State government, at the time, was in the hands of Democrats. Allegany County, in contrast, was a sparsely populated, economically depressed, conservative Republican rural county. Viewed from the centers of power, the county looked powerless and unimportant—an easy target to play the role of sacrificial lamb.

Some county residents decided early on, however, that they were not about to accept a low-level nuclear waste dump without a fight. In the first few months after the siting announcement, "hundreds of meetings were held all over the county. Representatives of the many citizens' groups met . . . to form a county-wide organization, becoming the 'Concerned Citizens of Allegany County'" (CCAC).[18] In time, the CCAC was joined by a second group, the Allegany County Nonviolent Action Group. These two groups worked closely together, with the CCAC pursuing more traditional and formal strategies like challenging the safety of the site on geological grounds (an earthquake fault had recently been found in the area), while the second group concentrated on organizing nonviolent acts of civil disobedience.

Over the next 2 years, these groups were able to forge a successful campaign, one that united county residents and kept the nuclear wastes out. Consider the following description of attendance at a public hearing held by the siting commission:

> For the first time in the history of Allegany County people from all walks of life showed up to protect their families and land—village dwellers and farmers, intellectuals and high school dropouts, business people and professionals, workers and those on welfare, Republicans and Democrats. Even the Amish, who normally avoid political meetings, had come.[19]

While the Amish are unusually adverse to political engagement, social protest was hardly a normal activity for the farmers and small-town residents of the county. For their efforts to win broad-based county support, activists had to frame their oppositional activity in ways which fit within the habits of mind, memory, and predispositions of the local culture. A politically conservative critique of the siting process was a reasonable starting point. For years the mantra of the Republican Party has been to get government off people's backs. From the perspective of rural conservatives, what better image to represent a distant, bloated state bureaucracy run amok than a government planting an unwanted nuclear waste dump in their backyards?

The collective memory of the county and its connections with the American Revolutionary War was another compelling image embedded in local culture. Indeed, in this case, past and present reinforced each other, forming a particularly compelling package. The Revolutionary War, after all, had been fought against a distant, tyrannical government; one of its rallying cries had been "No taxation without representation." The conservative citizens of the county saw themselves as carrying this fight forward. The heavy-handedness of the present governmental system had obviously strayed from the intentions of the Founding Fathers. Throughout the struggle, activists made use of Revolutionary War symbols like the tricorn hat. The battle they waged was both against a nuclear waste dump and for the "promise of democracy."

Commitment to nonviolence was also an important factor in rendering protest actions palatable to a conservative constituency. Activists worked hard throughout the conflict to keep their interactions with opponents civil. The emphasis was on passive resistance. At one protest 48 individuals engaging in civil disobedience (blocking public roads) were arrested without incident. Even the county sheriff, who had to make arrests when protesters engaged in civil disobedience, was reelected in the heat of the controversy.[20]

A significant challenge facing activists was the need to build a coalition that spanned several communities as well as diverse county interests. The possibility that government spies would try to infiltrate grassroots groups encouraged a general atmosphere of suspicion, a problem that required a solution. Similar concerns underscored activists' initial skepticism when local New York Assemblyman John Hasper took a public stance opposing the nuclear waste facility. Activists thought Hasper was a lying politician who would sell them out. For his part, Hasper was equally wary of the activists, whom he regarded as a bunch of hotheads who would discredit opposition to the dump and alienate county residents.

Over time, an effective working relationship did develop between Hasper and the activists, but this only occurred as the result of concrete and planned experiences which facilitated trust on both sides. On the part of the assemblyman, this meant engaging in actions which demonstrated that his opposition to the nuclear waste facility was sincere. On the part of the activists, this meant engaging in actions which demonstrated their commitment to passionate yet reasoned protest.[21]

The decision to pursue nonviolent tactics also provided a vehicle for building trust. A series of workshops trained several hundred county residents in the use of nonviolent techniques. Violence is far more likely to happen once people start to lose their tempers. Workshop participants learned to be more sensitive about their own flashpoints and to go stand next to calm friends when they felt on the verge of losing it. The workshops also trained people to watch their friends who appear to be overly distraught and volatile. When an individual was seen as getting too upset, another protester moved in to calm him or her. Activists were immersed, in other words, in training designed to keep themselves, and each other, in a pacific state of mind. As Allegany County activists practiced this restrained style of protest, they learned to trust one another while becoming a more credible movement in the eyes of the broader community.

Activists created an unintentional symbol of county unity when arrested individuals gave their names as "Allegany County." Initially this was done to slow down the entire arrest process, but once the power of this action was understood, it also assumed a potent symbolic meaning. County residents also found other means to express their unity. "Posters were plastered in every grocery store, restaurant, and bar in the county" informing residents of a public hearing the siting commission had scheduled in the county.[22] The county sheriff's department estimated attendance at that meeting to be about 5,000 people, roughly 10% of the county's population.

Other symbolic displays of local solidarity also occurred over the course of the controversy. After the state government announced that three of the five finalist sites were in Allegany County, "[p]eople in nearly every house in [the town of] Almond put bright orange 'No Dumping' signs in their windows."[23] An hour-long voluntary blackout was observed by the majority of the county's residents. During this time, people turned off their lights to express opposition to the dump. "The Village board in Alfred even had the streetlights turned off. It unified people in the county and was a positive statement about our willingness to conserve energy."[24]

❖

Nicely illustrated in this case is a dramatic increase in bonding capital created in good measure by oppositional activity. Only by increasing the stock of active connections among people in Allegany County, increasing social density, and encouraging cooperative behaviors did residents succeed in building a local coalition.

More important, from the vantage point of community, the bonding capital created in Allegany County worked to create more *inclusive* and *exclusive* community. On the one hand, it joined previously discrete and discontinuous communities into a common regional fellowship. On the other hand, it distinguished this newfound fellowship from other, external groups and agencies that sought to cajole and pressure the region to accept the nuclear waste facility.

Both the lockout at the BASF/Geismar plant and the state's efforts to site a low-level nuclear waste facility in Allegany County illustrate Walsh's idea of the suddenly imposed grievance.[25] Siting announcements, the discovery of chemical contaminants, or the listing of a species as threatened or endangered can all constitute an abrupt, unforeseen grievance. Local people, however, may also engage in oppositional activity, including coalition building, when faced with the intensification of existing grievances.

Consider the case of Quincy, California, a small community virtually surrounded by the Plumas National Forest.[26] Like many other towns in timber regions, this community was wracked for years by conflict between loggers and environmentalists. This conflict was especially intense and bitter during the 1980s, when environmentalists, frustrated with the prodevelopment stance of the Reagan administration, filed numerous lawsuits to stop the U.S. Forest Service timber sales in the Plumas National Forest and the nearby Lassen National Forest. Loggers, in turn, were frustrated not only by the environmentalists' actions but also by the Forest Service's increased efforts to promote recreational and environmental values seen to be at odds with traditional extractive values. This controversy was so acrimonious that some residents stayed away from public meetings held by the Forest Service for fear of violence.

By the early 1990s, however, local economic conditions were worsening. A 44% decline in timber production occurred between 1991 and 1992, with a reduction of equal or greater magnitude projected for the next couple of years. In 1992, three men who recognized that both the forest and the community were endangered embarked on an unusual coalition. These men included a Republican county supervisor and long-time supporter of the timber industry, a forester with the state's largest timber company (Sierra Pacific Industry), and an environmental lawyer and member of the Quincy-based

Friends of Plumas Wilderness. Recognizing that finding viable solutions to present problems would require overcoming past divisions, these men "assembled a group of their peers from within the Quincy community that included, among others, representatives from local timber and business interests, environmental activists, county supervisors, and local citizens."[27]

What we see in the case of Quincy, California, is a more divisive starting point than that seen in Allegany County. More than limited contact is going on here; loggers and environmentalists are more often than not openly hostile toward one another. Yet when the economic and ecological sustainability of the community was threatened, these competing factions pulled together to seek solutions to pressing local problems, in the process creating bonding capital. Similar coalition dynamics are seen in the Bakersfield, California, area in the early 1970s, when a coalition of area farmers and local environmentalists, who had long clashed over pesticide use in the Central Valley, came together to òppose a plan by the Los Angeles Department of Power and Water to construct a nuclear power plant (the San Joaquin Nuclear Project, or SJNP) in the vicinity.[28]

The formation of local coalitions and bonding capital can be facilitated by actions which demonstrate solidarity. Any visible sign of support—bumper stickers, flags, flyers, voluntary blackouts—repeated by many people over a wide area sends a strong message of local solidarity. As recounted above, the residents of Allegany County used a number of symbolic displays to express unity. In the SJNP case, local residents used the ballot as a venue to show their support of a common cause. In a countywide referendum, over 70% of voters said they did not want a nuclear power plant located in their county.[29]

In the process of reaching out to diverse community factions, activists facilitate meaningful social connections. In symbolic displays of solidarity, community residents signal their mutual understanding of local environmental problems. If these oppositional activities are viewed favorably by local residents, they will also engender goodwill. Meaningful social connections, mutual understanding, and goodwill are all important components of social capital. There is another important component of social capital, however, and it may well be the most difficult to establish and the most fragile once in place. Our topic is trust.

It is easier to talk to strangers or casual acquaintances than it is to trust them. Yet for the most part the coalition formed by Allegany citizens was comprised of individuals who had little or no personal contact with each other before their oppositional effort. As recounted above, concerns about trust surfaced on numerous occasions, including the fear that the government had sent spies to infiltrate the two local grassroots groups

(CCAC and the Allegany County Nonviolent Action Group), the concern that activists would pursue strategies which would alienate many county residents, and the worry that, in the heat of the moment, some protesters would break their commitment to nonviolent protest. Trust is an acquired virtue and it must be reaffirmed from time to time.

The Quincy case provides us with an even more daunting challenge in building this essential form of social capital: creating trust among long-time enemies. In recognition of the magnitude of this task, the local group which formed to address community problems decided to meet in the Quincy Library, partly because it was seen as neutral territory and partly because they thought it would foster civility.[30] (For this reason, the coalition became known as the Quincy Library Group, or QLG.) Early meetings were difficult, and it took awhile to build trust. In time, however, participants agreed on a plan they thought represented the best management option for the Plumas and Lassen National Forests, one largely based on a proposal developed by environmentalists in the previous decade. Calling for such measures as protection of old growth forests, use of selective logging rather than clear-cutting, and riparian buffer zones, this plan was seen by locals as the best option for preserving the forest resources upon which the local economy (and the local community) ultimately depended.

We have focused, thus far, on the ways in which oppositional activity initiated and undertaken by local activists may contribute to the creation and strengthening of bonding capital. Common to Allegany County, the San Joaquin Nuclear Project, and the QLG, however, is the absence of outside collaborators. The absence of such external connections precludes the possibility of the creation or strengthening of bridging capital. Furthermore, in all three of these cases, local opposition was aligned against outsiders, who were seen as the source of community woes. These adversarial relationships undermined and eroded bridging capital. All in all, these local areas appear to have experienced a net gain in bonding capital and a net loss in bridging capital over the course of their respective controversies. Indeed, the strength of the bonding capital originated, in part, with the common vilification of outside social and political actors.

There is nothing inevitable about this pattern. There are numerous conflict cases where the impetus to organize oppositional campaigns originated among local residents but where those activists then went on to reach out to, and receive assistance from, outsiders. The Shintech case presented in Chapter 1 and the Orme Dam case presented in Chapter 2 provide two examples. As recounted in the previous section, movement sympathizers such as Allen regard coalitions between local and extra-local oppositional groups to be the combination most likely to yield success.[31]

Yet as the cases of Allegany County, the San Joaquin Nuclear Project, and the QLG show, there is nothing inevitable about local/extra-local coalitions either. In the remainder of this section, we consider a couple of reasons why connections with and support from outsiders may fail to materialize. We hardly claim this is an exhaustive listing, but it will provide readers with some sense of the possibilities and dynamics at work here.

One set of circumstances in which local oppositional activity may proceed in the absence of bridging capital is when outside organizations reject local efforts. To a novice, it might seem to defy common sense that a regional, national, or international environmental organization would not be supportive of local environmental campaigns. Yet this can happen, and at least a few reasons are to be found in the conceptual ideas introduced in the discussion of structural betrayal (see Chapter 3). To wit, outside organizations have their own agendas, their own standard operating procedures, and a limited resource base. How extra-local organizations respond to local environmental campaigns will depend, then, on the extent to which those campaigns align with, or threaten, the external groups' goals and mandates.

Return, for a moment, to the case of the QLG.[32] When the QLG was first formed, the environmental lawyer who helped found the group had invited participation from environmental activists in Sacramento and San Francisco, but the 3- to 5-hour commute to Quincy made their involvement prohibitive. There were local environmentalists who joined the QLG, but not as representatives of state or national organizations. As the locally initiated collaborative effort progressed, it came under increasing criticism from national environmental organizations. Local environmentalists were cast as traitors who colluded with the Forest Service. National environmental organizations also fought against Forest Service adoption of the management plan put together by the QLG. This happened even though the QLG's plan was largely based on a forest management plan the environmentalists themselves had put forth in 1986.

One reason outside environmentalists did not seize the opportunity to finally bring to fruition their own earlier efforts to preserve the Plumas National Forest was a combination of economics and politics. During the 1980s, under first Reagan, then Bush senior, environmentalists had fought a rearguard action against administrations with proextraction, antienvironmentalist attitudes. By 1992 (the time the QLG was operating), a Democrat had been elected to the White House, and the timber industry wielded substantially less political power. Under these circumstances, it might be possible to wrestle even more concessions out of the timber industry than those laid out in the 1986 management plan.

Probably a more important reason, however, was the concern among regional and national environmental organizations with not only *what* decisions were made but also *how* they were made.[33] In the view of these groups, national forests were just that, national, not local, resources. Decisions about managing them, therefore, needed to be made at the national, not the local, level. Furthermore, national environmental organizations like the Sierra Club saw themselves as the logical defenders of the broader "public interests" in the forests. Allowing local communities to develop forest management plans set a dangerous precedent. Even if this particular plan was environmentally friendly, there were no guarantees that future plans, set by other community groups, would be as agreeable. If these decisions devolved to the local level, past experience with logger- and timber-industry hostility toward preservation efforts put the interests of the conservation-minded at considerable risk.

Rejection, of course, is a two-way street. Accordingly, another set of circumstances under which we see local oppositional activity proceeding in the absence of bridging capital is when local activists spurn assistance from outsiders. Again, to a novice, this might also seem to defy common sense. Why would a grassroots organization, most likely operating on a shoestring budget against powerful and well-financed adversaries, turn down assistance? It would be sensible, would it not, to seek aid from any and all possible sources?

There are circumstances, however, under which local activists may decide that outside "assistance" may do more harm than good. For an example, let's return to the case of the San Joaquin Nuclear Project (SJNP).[34] Like Allegany County, the Bakersfield, California, area in the 1970s was rural and politically conservative. A site of settlement for many "Okies" who migrated during the Dust Bowl, residents of the Central Valley were stereotyped by Los Angeles' residents as "hicks from the boondocks."

This demographic profile is a far cry from the typical antinuclear activists of the time, who "came from elements of the left wing of the Democratic Party such as environmental, remnant New Left, and peace groups."[35] In the Bakersfield area, in contrast, opposition to SJNP was spearheaded by "conservative farmers and whites at the lower end of the economic ladder who traditionally opposed environmental issues and would later vote for Ronald Reagan."[36]

What the local activists feared was that outside antinuclear activists would violate the conservative mores of the Bakersfield area, thus costing them needed community support. For this reason, activists rejected offers of assistance from two outside voluntary associations involved in antinuclear activity, Friends of the Earth and Ralph Nader's California group. As we indicated previously, there were some environmentalists who worked on the oppositional effort, but they did so as private citizens rather than as representatives of groups. In addition, they took a background role, letting local farmers lead the campaign. If needed, they cut their hair and changed their attire in order to better fit in with the appearance of the local population.[37]

Pursuing oppositional activity which fit well with local cultural norms was important to the success of the Allegany coalition. In the SJNP conflict, local activists also worked hard to make their opposition a comfortable fit with the conservative culture of the area. Their opposition to the plant was not framed in terms of environmental, antinuclear, or antiestablishment concerns. Instead, their rallying cry was that of "Protecting the Family Farm." The name given to the grassroots group which formed to fight the plant, the Agricultural Protection Council, was meant to emphasize the agrarian underpinnings of the movement.[38]

Indeed, far from promoting an antinuclear rhetoric, local activists made it clear their opposition to the SJNP did not represent a rejection of nuclear power per se. Instead, they spoke favorably of nuclear power, a position that fit well with conservative views on technological progress and economic growth and prosperity. Local activists made it clear that their opposition to the SJNP was not a wholesale rejection of nuclear energy; it was just that building a nuclear power plant in the Central Valley, with its limited water supplies and prime agricultural land, was a bad idea. As an alternative, they suggested siting these facilities in coastal regions, where there was an abundance of water.[39] In this sense, the Bakersfield opposition was a classic NIMBY (not-in-my-backyard) response: we do not care if you put this somewhere else, just do not put it here.

For a list of questions which will help students determine if they are examining a local environmental conflict where bonding capital is created and strengthened in the absence of bridging capital, see Box 6.3. We turn now to a consideration of a third way in which oppositional activity can affect social capital, this time examining conditions under which bonding capital is both created and destroyed.

Simultaneously Creating and Eroding Bonding Capital

"Don't Drink the Water"

In the late 1970s, some residents of Legler, New Jersey, learned there were toxic chemicals in their well water.[40] Part of Jackson Township, located near the Atlantic shore, Legler was the site of several waves of

> **Box 6.3**   Adding to the Portfolio: Creating Bonding Capital in the Absence of Bridging Capital
>
> ---
>
> 1. Do local people, on their own initiative, form a broad-based community coalition, including the formation of alliances between former enemies?
> 2. Do local residents engage in actions which demonstrate solidarity?
> 3. Do coalition members engage in actions which build trust?
> 4. Do outside organizations reject local environmental campaigns, viewing them at odds with their own organizational goals and agendas?
> 5. Do local activists reject outside assistance, viewing the tactics and politics of extra-local organizations and activists as incompatible with local culture?

human settlements. Initially the area had been rural, isolated, and sparsely populated. These early residents depended on each other for social support, friendships, and a modicum of collective life. A first wave of ex-urban development brought in families who were seeking a rural way of life without the strong social ties of their predecessors. While they were on a "hello" basis with their neighbors, mainly what they wanted was space and privacy. A second wave brought in younger families who wanted a more conventional suburban experience, including socializing with neighbors. While this wave began to change the social dynamic of the area, the overall sense of Legler as a community was not well developed until after the contamination incident. "Stores and other amenities, where neighbors might meet each other, were absent from the area."[41] Indeed, residents did not even know the area they lived in had the official designation of "Legler" until after the announcement of contamination problems.

Early environmental problems began in 1961 when the Glidden Corporation opened a 135-acre mining operation in the area. While the mine created some dust and noise problems, it also created jobs. In addition, residents were under the impression the site would be reclaimed as a park when the mine was played out. The possibilities this presented for improvements in quality of life and property values helped to offset some of the inconveniences of the mine. Reclamation as a park, however, was not to be the fate of this site.

[I]n 1971, when Glidden faced the prospect of closing the site and undertaking an expensive reclamation job, Jackson [Township] was seeking a new site for its municipal landfill. In a true marriage of convenience, they realized they both could benefit if Glidden deeded the site (for one dollar) to Jackson.[42]

Some Legler residents were alarmed when they learned of this plan, and a small group of residents organized to fight the landfill. Their primary concern was water pollution. There were 60-foot-deep pits at the mine site filled with water. The surrounding soil was sandy, presenting a porous medium through which pollutants could migrate. To compound the problem, the private drinking wells were shallow, with many less than 50 feet deep. Any pollution which migrated into the groundwater could easily migrate into the wells. The track record of the township with the existing landfill did not inspire confidence. It was shut down for several troubling reasons: it "had caused water pollution, it smelled, and it was a breeding ground for rats."[43]

The residents' fight to oppose the landfill was to no avail. Township officials, however, assured them that the landfill would be run properly, and furthermore promised to reclaim the site as a golf course once the dump had ceased operations, which was scheduled to occur after 10 years. Despite the failure of Glidden Corporation to keep its reclamation promise, some residents believed the township would keep its promise. It was never the case that all Legler residents opposed the landfill. Some viewed it as a convenience to have a dump nearby. Once operational, the landfill was not highly intrusive; families who moved into the area after the dump opened were often not aware of its existence.

"The municipal landfill operated in Legler from late 1971 until late 1980. As many as 50,000 gallons per day of human waste were deposited in the landfill through 1978."[44] Sporadic complaints about water quality and health problems began after the landfill opened, but residents dealt with these on an individual basis as "private troubles."[45] Lack of communication with neighbors on these issues meant Legler residents were unaware that other families in the area shared similar problems and concerns. The number of complaints over the years, however, finally led the Jackson Township Board of Health to request the New Jersey Department of Environmental Protection to test water in the area. The first test, conducted in the summer of 1978, did not detect any pollutants. A follow-up test, conducted in October of the same year, revealed the water was significantly polluted with organic chemicals.

Following this discovery, the Jackson Board of Health issued the following announcement: "It was recommended that because there was enough evidence for concern, area residents are advised *not* to use water for human consumption, but limit use for sanitary purposes only."[46] The advisement was later amended to caution residents "'not to soak for extended periods of time' when bathing."[47] While initially this recommendation did not cover the entire area, "by early 1979 all of Legler's approximately 150 families had received the warning."[48]

The discovery of organic chemicals in the water presented liability issues for Jackson Township, which ran the landfill. The most pressing need in the immediate aftermath of the board of health's announcement was that of supplying residents with an alternative water supply. Initially this was accomplished by parking two water tankers at accessible points on opposite sides of the subdivision. When residents needed water, they had to take the initiative to carry containers down to the tankers, fill them, and haul them back home. "After Liquid Plumber was inexplicitly found dumped in the outdoor tanks, the township began to use large metal civil defense containers to deliver water to each of the affected households."[49] Complaints about these containers eventually led to their replacement with plastic containers and spigots. When residents ran low on water, they had to remember to put a flag outside their house signaling the need for a delivery.

Regular water use is integral to the daily lives of contemporary Americans. When the tap can no longer just be turned on for use, it disrupts a host of routine activities. Ordinary household chores like brushing one's teeth, watering the garden, or cooking pasta for dinner required transporting water from the containers to the place it was needed. Many residents simply gave up their gardens; they were too much trouble to maintain. Bathing infants and children required hauling water from the container and heating it on the stove. Adults simply took fewer showers.

These ongoing disruptions of routine water use not only created enormous inconveniences but also served as constant reminders of the dangers that lurked in residents' private wells. Were there going to be long-term health effects from exposure to the chemicals? Since the final wave of settlement into the area had brought young families with children, parents had to worry about not only their own health but the potential for chronic, perhaps latent, health effects for their offspring. Many couples planned to have more children. They agonized over the uncertainty that their exposure might result in birth defects or other types of problems in the event of future pregnancies.

Many Legler residents became literally obsessed with these issues, so much so that they began to alienate relatives, friends, and coworkers living outside the subdivision who grew weary of the constant rehashing of these worries. As Legler residents failed to find the expected support from these sources, as they encountered instead impatience and a lack of sympathy and understanding, they retreated from their former social networks, cutting back on interaction time and withdrawing emotional support. Over time, it became apparent that most of those who were not sharing the nightmare were unable to understand what the citizens of Legler were going through.

Legler residents began to turn to their neighbors for support and empathy. Neighbors became more than passing acquaintances, as people stopped, commiserated, planned, and found common ground in their shared plight. Increasingly, residents turned to and relied on their neighbors, with whom they shared confidences, concerns, and support. In addition to creating social capital by increasing sociability, residents also forged social ties through activism. Indeed, shortly after the contamination was announced, the same group that had initially fought the landfill revived itself, changing its name to reflect a broader-based community representation: Concerned Citizens Committee of Legler (CCCL).

Local residents viewed the CCCL as their organization, their first and most authoritative collective voice. Among other activities, this group pressed for increased information about pollution problems and possible solutions to those problems, served as a conduit to disseminate that information to area residents, and filed a lawsuit against Jackson Township. In 1983, a New Jersey jury found in favor of the 330 plaintiffs who had filed the lawsuit, delivering a $15 million award covering emotional distress, diminished quality of life, and medical surveillance. As the result of subsequent appellate action, the reward for emotional distress was eventually dropped, leaving the final settlement in the lawsuit at $13 million.

Over the course of this controversy, and driven in part by oppositional activity, citizens of Legler invested increasing time and other resources in their relationships with one another. Circumventing the anonymity that comes with modern ex-urban life, they began to create meaningful social ties with those who lived around them. New social capital was created. Trust, mutual understanding, and coordinated social practices worked together to create a fund of working social capital within the boundaries of Legler. Not all Legler residents joined the lawsuit, nor did they all support the local CCCL. But residents did create sufficient stock of common sentiment, combined that with new community actions, and redefined Legler as a social (as well as an areal) community. In the process they overcame long-standing divisions between older and newer residents.

————————————— ❖ —————————————

Legler is a good example of the role oppositional groups can play in creating and enlarging, as well as undermining and reducing, social capital. Local activism engendered a newfound sense of neighborhood while encouraging families to break their ties with nonneighbors who refused to acknowledge their environmental miseries. Thus, oppositional activity pushed a subset of Jackson Township residents closer together, increasing the stock of active and purposeful connections as neighbors in the Legler area discovered one another and their shared goal of just compensation and potable water. Note also, however, that preexisting social networks with family, friends, and coworkers living in the general vicinity, but outside the Legler subdivision, waned. To reiterate, Legler residents embarked on courses of action which both created, and destroyed, bonding capital.

This is probably not an unusual outcome of local environmental conflicts. The very fact that we are looking at conflict and its cognates, acrimony, hostility, anger, and rage between two or more groups, suggests the potential inherent in these events to unravel the fabric of local social life. Oppositional activity, in other words, not only has the capacity to bring residents together—as we saw in the previous two sections—it may also alienate them one from the other. Indeed, the selfsame activity may simultaneously do both, building bonding capital in some areas while at the same time eroding it in others. This double-edged sword characteristic of oppositional activity—its ability to cut both ways—provides the lens through which we examine local environmental conflicts in this section.

Consider the oppositional activities which nurture bonding capital. Individuals join forces because they share concern about one or more local problems. As these individuals spend time talking among themselves, they establish meaningful social connections and reinforce their mutual understanding of the situation. As they plan and execute oppositional activity, they build up a fund of trust and goodwill. Yet activists' definition of the situation can be rejected by other residents. Even if other residents agree something is a problem, they may disagree with the strategies the activists use to seek redress.

Consider again the case of a mine fire burning underneath the town of Centralia, Pennsylvania.[50] In an effort to raise awareness about the dangers posed by the mine fire, one of the grassroots organizations which formed in the community (Concerned Citizens) organized a demonstration march to a Centralia Borough Council meeting. Far from raising the expected sympathy and support, the marchers' fellow residents greeted this action with considerable ire. Public demonstrations were just not something folks in Centralia did. These were the kinds of flamboyant and confrontational tactics used by wild-eyed youth in places like Berkeley, not the kinds of goings-on they wanted from respectable, decent, quiet folk.

Note here that the oppositional activity pursued by the activists was seen to threaten other residents' understanding of the *type* of community in which they lived. Indeed, the threat to community was even more deep rooted than this, for what activists sought was a government buyout of their town, a solution which would have allowed them to relocate to a safer location but would have spelled the end of the borough of Centralia. As is true of other forms of capital, bonding capital is valuable. When confronted

with attacks which devalue and diminish their stock of trust, mutual understanding, meaningful social connections, and goodwill, local residents are
likely to fight back.

Of course, disagreements over oppositional strategies may be based on
more prosaic concerns. For example, individual responses to local environmental campaigns may be driven by simple economic interests. Siting, conservancy, and exposure disputes often present local people with options
involving difficult trade-offs, what social psychologist Michael Edelstein
refers to as "double binds," a kind of "damned if you do, damned if you
don't" dilemma.[51] Consider an example of chemical contamination in the
soil of some residential subdivision (perhaps it was built on top of a former
industrial site). The best strategy residents can pursue if they want redress
(such as a government buyout) is to draw attention to their plight. They
would need to dramatize local problems, placing overwhelming emphasis
on the dangerous and negative aspects of the situation, in hopes this would
capture the attention of influential outsiders like media and government
officials. Residents who share this understanding of the situation, and work
together on a joint solution, would build social capital.

Yet this strategy also comes with a cost: in the very process of drawing
attention to local problems, the activists also create a stigmatized identity
for the local area. Who wants to live in a contaminated neighborhood?
Property values plummet; new businesses decide to locate elsewhere. Residents
who believe their economic investments are threatened by activists' efforts
may respond in a hostile fashion, especially if they do not share the activists'
beliefs in the dangers of contamination.

For a list of questions which will help students determine if they are examining a local environmental conflict where oppositional activity is simultaneously creating and destroying bonding capital, see Box 6.4. We turn now to
a concluding section which wraps up the material covered in this chapter.

A Concluding Word

This chapter has emphasized the close relationships between environmental
conflicts, local oppositional activities, and social capital. The three cases covered in some detail each demonstrate the importance of oppositional activity
to the creation of social capital. In the first two sections we saw how oppositional activity drawing on bridging capital can facilitate the formation of
bonding capital and how oppositional activity can create and strengthen
bonding capital in the absence of bridging capital. In the final section we
introduced contrary cases where citizen activists failed to inspire coordinated

---

Box 6.4   Adding to the Portfolio: Simultaneously Creating and Eroding Social Capital

---

1. Is there an environmental hazard which poses a threat to only part of a local community?

2. Does conflict result in a reconfiguration of local social connections, creating and strengthening some while undermining and eroding others?

3. Is the unifying and dividing process, facilitated by shared hardships and perceptions of danger which draw some residents together, at the same time alienating them from other residents who do not share, and cannot empathize with, their plight?

4. Does the process of planning and executing oppositional actions unify some residents at the same time other residents respond with hostility to efforts they regard as threatening the fundamental nature of their community?

5. Do double-blinds contribute to the unifying and dividing process?

---

actions and mobilize norms of reciprocity across constituencies. Indeed, the actions of these local activists and grassroots organizations appeared to have quite the opposite results, dividing, alienating, and angering residents, in the process eroding bonding capital. When it comes to social capital, then, oppositional activity often proves to be a double-edged sword, with the same activity simultaneously strengthening some social ties while undermining others.

As we pointed out in the introductory section, the concepts of oppositional activity and social capital provide valuable tools for pulling together the many ideas discussed over the course of this book. Many of these possible connections are presented in Box 6.1. In the following chapter we introduce the symbolic-realist position as a means to encourage more holistic thinking about how different conflict elements work together to influence the timing, nature, dynamics, and outcomes of conservancy, exposure, and siting disputes.

STUDENT EXERCISES

1. Illustrate how the concepts of bonding and bridging capital can be applied to the case of the Buffalo Creek flood (see text of the History as Harbinger section of Chapter 2).

2. In Chapter 4, the spotted owl controversy was used to illustrate the scientific uncertainty which pervades many environmental issues. This case vignette did not discuss conflict going on in particular communities. Using at least three questions from Box 1.4, create a profile of a hypothetical town located in the

habitat range of the spotted owl. This town can be as big or small, as homogenous or diverse, as you want. Speculate about how a controversy over the preservation of a spotted owl habitat might contribute to the creation and strengthening, or undermining and erosion, of bonding capital in this hypothetical community. Read back through Box 6.1 to glean insight into how materials covered in previous chapters can help you answer this question.

3. Compare and contrast the Orme Dam case (see Chapter 2) with the BASF/ Geismar case presented in this chapter. In the BASF/Geismar case, it was the evocation and strengthening of bridging capital which facilitated the creation of bonding capital. How does the chronological sequencing differ in the Orme Dam case? How would you account for these differences?

4. Review the Chicago Wilderness controversy (see Chapter 4). Which case vignette covered in the present chapter seems most similar to this controversy? Use ideas and concepts introduced in this chapter to defend your answer.

5. Review the case of radioactive fallout in the Cumbria sheep-farming region in England (see Chapter 4). Which case vignette covered in the present chapter seems most similar to this controversy? Use ideas and concepts introduced in this chapter to defend your answer.

Notes

1. Artist and civil disobedience advocate Jessie Shefrin, as quoted in Peterson (2002), 52–53
2. James (1956).
3. Hanifan (1916); see also Putnam (2000).
4. Putnam (1993), 200.
5. Putnam (2000), 22–23.
6. Allen (2003)
7. Case material from Minchin (2003).
8. Michin (2003).
9. Ibid.
10. Ibid.
11. Schnaiberg (1980).
12. Michin (2003).
13. Ibid., 139.
14. Ibid.
15. Putnam (2000).
16. Allen (2003), 2.
17. Case material from Peterson (2002); quotation from p. 40. The quotation marks around "low level," copied from the original source, are used to signify activists' perceptions that some of the material included in this category is too radioactive to qualify as "low-level" nuclear waste.

18. Peterson (2002), 28.

19. Ibid., 31–32.

20. Peterson (2002).

21. Ibid.

22. Ibid., 31.

23. Ibid., 75.

24. Local activist Mick Castle, as quoted in Peterson (2002), 98.

25. Walsh (1988); Walsh and Warland (1983).

26. Bryan and Wondolleck (2003).

27. Ibid., 64.

28. Wellock (1998).

29. Ibid.

30. Bryan and Wondolleck (2003).

31. Allen (2003).

32. Bryan and Wondolleck (2003).

33. Ibid.

34. Wellock (1998).

35. Ibid., 208.

36. Ibid.

37. Wellock (1998).

38. Ibid.

39. Since the coastline of California is an earthquake hot spot riddled with geological faults, building nuclear power plants there is actually a bad idea too, though this was not a point these activists mentioned (Wellock, 1998).

40. Case material from Edelstein (1988).

41. Edelstein (1988), 19.

42. Ibid., 22.

43. Ibid., 23.

44. Ibid., 23.

45. Mills (1956).

46. Jackson Board of Health notice cited in Edelstein (1988), 29; emphasis in original.

47. Edelstein (1988), 29.

48. Ibid., 30.

49. Ibid., 35.

50. Kroll-Smith and Couch (1990).

51. Edelstein (1988).

7

Social Facts and Brute Facts

Confounding the Social and the Physical

The quality of human life is inextricably interwoven with the kinds and variety of stimuli [we] receive from the earth and life it harbors, because human nature is shaped by ... external nature.

Rene Dubos[1]

There is an interchange between culture and environment, perhaps continuous dialectic interchange, if in adapting the culture transforms its landscape ... so it must respond anew to changes that it had set in motion.

Marshall Sahlins[2]

The first quote is from the biologist Rene Dubos; the second is from the anthropologist Marshall Sahlins. Each writer, the biologist and the anthropologist, addresses an incontrovertible condition of human existence: communities and environments are so entangled as to preclude imagining one without the other. And yet, each is constituted in an almost diametrically opposed manner. Humans are symbol making, symbol using, and as

Kenneth Burke noted, symbol misusing animals. Nature or environment, on the other hand, does not make, use, or misuse a symbol, though it does have agency, cycles, rhythms, and intricate patterns or ecologies that exist independent of our remarkable ability to symbol. Not that we can't alter environments. We have made so many profound alterations in nature that it is more precise to think of our contemporary environment as "postnatural."[3] But regardless of how many changes we introduce into the environment, it will always act independently of us, outside of, and at times in spite of, our symbols. This inescapable, if often bedeviling, confluence of community and environment is the topic for this, the final, chapter.

We placed our discussion of this more controversial approach in a concluding chapter for a reason. Chapters 2 through 6 provide a more canonic approach to the sociology of environments and community conflicts, fashioning a specifically sociological map of the tools and perspectives applicable to this genre of inquiry. In most respects, what we focus on—and embellish a bit—are well-established ideas rooted in mainstream sociology. Chapter 7, however, proposes an alteration in the principles of sociological mapping. (For a more detailed discussion of the relationship of this material to previous chapters, see Box 7.1.)

Box 7.1   Telling More Complicated Stories

In Chapter 1 we identified several goals in writing this book, one of which was to get readers started down a path of inquiry. We located our own approach within a fairly inductive and qualitative case study methodology. Beginning with basic descriptive questions, we moved readers to more analytic inquiries focusing on such key dimensions of local environmental conflicts as the role of history and uncertain knowledge. Each of the dimensions covered in Chapters 2 through 6 are complex topics worthy of investigation in their own right. Yet there is a further, even more challenging, step to be made in this analytic journey, one that we can only point the way to in this chapter. This step addresses the interrelationship among many factors present in a local environmental conflict.

The portfolio questions presented in Chapters 1 through 6 are intended to help students and scholars of local environmental conflicts profile the particular historical juncture of social, cultural, and environmental conditions present in any conservancy, siting, and exposure dispute. In kaleidoscope-like fashion, the exact configuration of factors shifts from case to case to case. To some extent, what we have are variations on a theme, which is why we can develop analytic models that transcend the specifics of any individual case. At the same time, each conflict constitutes a unique combination of events and players, perturbations and historical precursors, and so on. In our efforts to explain why a particular conflict happened when and where and how it did, we need to be able to account for the ways in which all the various elements of the conflict come together. To accomplish this, we trace the interplay of tensions, contradictions, and mutual reinforcements which shape the chronological unfolding of the controversy.

The symbolic realist perspective introduced in this chapter is intended to help students walk a bit further down this difficult leg of the investigative journey. By stretching the boundaries of conventional sociological inquiry, we illustrate how environmental conditions can influence the social and cultural dimensions of conflict. We do not do this to encourage determinism, or to suggest that environmental conditions should always be centrally located in every explanatory account. What we do argue for is a studied consideration of their relevance in understanding conservancy, siting, and exposure disputes. Whether environmental conditions play a large role, a small role, or perhaps no role at all in a particular controversy will depend upon the exact historical confluence of biophysical factors and other conflict elements. The challenge is to come up with an explanatory account which fits the specifics of any given case, in the process juggling with contingencies, human agency, and the unexpected. Symbolic realism and the inductive approach introduced through the portfolio questions provide a guidebook for this journey; we hope at least some readers have sufficient curiosity to walk a bit further down this road.

NOTE: For a good source on the role of contingency in case studies see Ragin (1987).

But don't panic; proposed here is not an anarchic dismantling of sociology. By alteration what we have in mind are border crossings, poaching, if you will, on nonsocial terrain. Indeed, one could reasonably argue that implicit in the study of environmental sociology is a certain sort of poaching license. It is, after all, interdisciplinary, seeking the relationships between two kinds of facts about the world: those that exist only by human agreement and those "natural" facts that exist independent of human consent.

About the first sort of facts, those of us who study the environment and society experience little difficulty. For example, the federal park system is the product of a complicated process of social and political work that created sufficient agreement among groups with a stake in the system. It originated through this consensus and continues today as an institutional reality. John Searle, a contemporary philosopher of language, calls this type of fact *institutional*.[4] Following Durkheim, we will call it, simply, a *social* fact.[5] A social fact for Durkheim was something that existed beyond the individual. Think of it as a force, a dynamic, an idea, or reality originating in society that imposes itself on human conduct and consciousness.

It is the second type, the natural fact, that is likely to raise an eyebrow or two among some sociologists who ascribe to Durkheim's famous aphorism that a social fact—the subject matter of sociology—can only be understood or explained in its relationship to other social facts.[6] Searle refers to the facts of nature somewhat colorfully as "brute" facts. Brute facts exist independently of human institutions. If institutional facts exist only because human beings collectively make them, brute facts have a tangible existence independent of human wishes, desires, and beliefs. Viruses are brute facts which affected human health for countless eons, even though humans had no knowledge of their existence until a little over a century ago. Canyons, deserts, and rivers are also brute facts, as are molecules, protons, the body's circulatory system, and the snail darter, that tiny fish that got in the way of the Tennessee Valley Authority's Tellico Dam project.

The snail darter is a brute fact, though it was first discovered in the early 1970s. The little critter exists, plain and simple. No reason to debate the obvious. But what about the ichthyological classification of the snail darter? Or, the habitat risk assessment of the snail darter? Or, local knowledge of the snail darter? These, of course, are social or institutional facts. They do not add an extra fin or scale to the snail darter. Rather, they add a web of descriptions, meanings, and relationships to the little fish. Moreover, one or more of these descriptions, meanings, and relationships might become a source of considerable controversy.

Perch and Seals: Confounding the Two Orders of Facts

Snail Darter Controversy

In 1967 the Tennessee Valley Authority began a monumental project to bring power to rural villages in Tennessee by building a dam to divert water from the Little Tennessee River.[7] The idea is a familiar one: cheap and abundant power would attract business and industry, and an "undeveloped" region would reap the benefits of economic growth. The dam would flood over 39,000 acres of bottom land in Loudon County, Tennessee. Though undeveloped commercially, this region was one of the most fertile agricultural areas in the American Southeast.

Opponents of the dam project were many, and included, not surprisingly, farmers and fishers, as well as owners of small businesses, hunters, and Cherokee Indians who viewed this land as part of their heritage. Through the early years of the dispute, opponents employed a variety of arguments to halt the project. Each interest group championed its individual claim, and at times, several interest groups merged their separate issues into a broader, more inclusive, argument to stop the project. Opponents of the dam, however, had no way of anticipating the discovery of ichthyologist Dr. David Etnier in August 1973.

Dr. Etnier, as the story is told, was observing schools of fish in the Little Tennessee River a few miles upriver from the Tellico Dam site. Excited by the discovery of what he knew to be a new species of perch, Dr. Etnier caught the attention of a passerby who allegedly asked him, "Wha'cha got there?" "Mister," he replied, "this is the fish that will stop Tellico Dam."[8] The good doctor's prophetic response would, in the end, prove overly optimistic. But his discovery of the snail darter would place this tan-colored, 3-inch fish at the center of a protracted and costly struggle.

Professor Etnier made his discovery in August 1973. In December of 1973 Congress passed the Endangered Species Act, or ESA. The intent of the ESA was designed to increase biodiversity and to protect vulnerable species from extinction. Although the proposed dam was opposed by Cherokee Indians who argued that flooding the region would destroy ancient burial sites, by local businessmen and women who viewed the dam as an economic liability, and farmers who did not want to see their way of life destroyed, it was the tiny snail darter that posed the greatest threat to the TVA's siting initiative.

In January 1975, the Secretary of the Interior listed the newly discovered snail darter as an endangered species. "[T]he snail darter," he concludes, "is a living entity which is genetically distinct and reproductively isolated from other fishes." More important, the Secretary found that the Tellico Dam would destroy the "critical habitat" of the snail darter.

> [T]he snail darter occurs only in the swifter portions of shoals over clean gravel substrate in cool, low-turbidity water. Food of the snail darter is almost exclusively snails which require a clean gravel substrate for their survival. The proposed impoundment of water behind the proposed Tellico Dam would result in total destruction of the snail darter's habitat.[9]

Environmentalists and others argued that the Tellico Dam would destroy the "critical habitat" of the snail darter, making its future existence all but impossible. In the ensuing court battles, the tiny fish as a brute fact was not at issue. Hotly debated was the kind and quality of an institutional fact, namely the ecological boundary within which the fish could survive.

Following the secretary's determination that the dam project threatened the "critical habitat" of the snail darter, controversies raged over just what the snail darter required by way of a critical habitat and whether or not this habitat could be found or reconstituted elsewhere. In the end, the dam was built. It was decided that a project that was 99% completed could not in principle be stopped by the discovery of a new species. Perhaps the decision by the Supreme Court to order the completion of the dam was directly related to the physical qualities of the snail darter. It was, after all, a tiny, rather nondescript fish, and, frankly, lacked the "cute appeal" of a koala bear or mountain lion cub. What if Professor Etnier had discovered a cuddly new species swimming about the Little Tennessee?

The Rats of the Sea

On a recent trip to Nova Scotia, Kroll-Smith chanced to see a number of harbor seals playing tag. There is arguably nothing cuter than a harbor seal, unless it's several harbor seals at play. He made this remark, or something like it, to a woman standing nearby who was also looking at the seals. Her response was unexpected. "Really? I hate 'um. If I had my way, they'd be extinct by now." Taken aback, he asked for an explanation. "Well, I'll tell you," she continued, "those seals you're looking at are the rats of the sea. Yes, rats. If it weren't for seals, we'd still have cod fishing in Nova Scotia." "No kidding. The harbor seals ate the cod?" "Right," she answered, with no apparent sign of irony.

Now, one might argue that the seals were around far longer than cod fishers. Moreover, while seals do eat cod, they also eat the cod's predators, achieving a natural balance common to healthy ecosystems. And for their part, cod fishers fished for years with no limit on their harvest, driving the number of fish below the threshold for reproduction. But, for this woman and many Canadians, the seal, the "rat of the sea," is the true culprit. Between 1995 and 2001, the Canadian government paid $20 million to subsidize seal hunting.

So, perhaps the discovery of a furry little pinniped in the Little Tennessee River might have stopped the Tellico Dam from being built, or it might not have, depending on the situated, historic intersection of the pinniped as both a brute, and a social, fact.

---------------- ❖ ----------------

Illustrated in this brief case is the intersection between social or negotiated realities and the brute reality of a tiny perch. Nobody contested the discovery of this fish. Dr. Etnier had indeed happened upon a new variety of perch. Its brute reality could not be denied. And the brute fact of this fish coincided with the discussion and passage of the federal ESA. Together, this fish and this act radically modified the history of the Tellico Dam construction project. (We can only imagine the outcome of the dam had a pinniped been discovered instead of a rather unremarkable little fish.)

The humble snail darter and the innocent-looking harbor seal are, in one sense, brute facts. Their presence in areas of environmental contention, and their entanglement with actual or proposed activities in those areas, demanded human attention. Yet to understand the social relevance of these brute facts we have to understand the particular meanings attached to them. Harbor seals become rats of the sea only when embedded in a web of relationships that include commercial fishers and cod, as well as shared cultural understandings of the despicable and undesirable character of rats. "Critical habitat needs" are institutional facts because they are not patently obvious; you cannot "see" critical habitat needs in the same way you "see" a snail darter. Rather, determinations of critical habitat needs require the application of abstract ecological models and, once established, have social implications for what sorts of activities are, or are not, possible. Any assertion of critical habitat needs cannot be understood apart from this web of social relationships.

Like all brute facts, the harbor seal and the snail darter have agency, but with respect to human projects, it is agency of a relatively limited kind. For this reason, these species are easily controlled and manipulated by social, cultural, and political machinations—social facts, as we are calling them here. At times, however, the brute facts of nature act back on communities and societies, often with a vengeance. Recall, for example, the history of the Army Corps of Engineers and its monumental (if hubristic) struggle to redirect the flow and current of the Mississippi River. A brute thing, like the Mississippi River, is surely independent of us; it doesn't require humans for its existence; it would be better off without us. For its part, however, the Mississippi River is anything but a passive victim, silently absorbing years of dredging, leveeing, and damming. In what looks at times like a choreographed dance, the Army Corps alters the character of this massive river, and the river, in turn, alters—at times dramatically—human landscapes and lives. In the end, we are told, the mighty Mississippi will go its own way in spite of the best efforts of the Army Corps.[10] Indeed, the catastrophic flooding that inundated New Orleans on August 29, 2005, is likely the result of errors the Army Corps made in building the levees surrounding the city. If the corps cannot protect the city from flooding canals and bayous, imagine how impossible it will be to "administer" indefinitely the fourth longest river in the world.

Symbolic Realism

Implicit in the ideas of brute facts, social facts, and their intersecting relationships is an underlying idea, one we can utilize to examine environmental conflicts from both a physical-organic and social-cultural perspective.

For want of a better term, we will call this idea *symbolic realism*.[11] Symbolic realism is *not* a theory per se. It is, rather, an orientation toward the social and material world. It has about it the quality of a stance, a certain posture we can assume when we want to view a scene or event from a particular vantage point, like tilting one's head to see something from a different angle.

More commonly used in sociologies of religion and the arts than in environmental sociology, symbolic realism is a heterodox orientation that challenges the boundaries of the discipline. For some readers, it might step too far afield of what is considered an appropriate sociological account. But we would argue that this overstepping is always a latent possibility in environmental sociology. By taking the environment seriously, sociologists opened a door into the provocative exchange between humans and nature. We ask you to step through that door, if only for a moment.

In one sense, if you have read the first six chapters, you've already walked through this portal. In organizing materials and discussions around three types of local environmental controversies, we strongly hint at the possibility that the *kind* of environmental disruption is likely to shape the ensuing community discord. Exposure, siting, and preservation controversies differ physically and organically one from the other. Perhaps these differences intersect with community activities and dynamics in unique ways. Moreover, perhaps the preconflict relationship of communities to environments prefigures the collective troubles that follow from a particular kind of environmental disruption.

In the discussion to follow, we make a modest case for a study of environments and community controversies, starting from the assumption that social facts are inescapably intertwined with brute facts. We are not the first sociologists who found occasions to challenge Durkheim's aphorism. We opened the first chapter with a quotation from William Catton reminding us of the intertwining of human communities and environments. In a now classic article coauthored with Riley Dunlap, this commonsense observation is turned on sociology itself: "ostensibly diverse and competing theoretical (approaches) in sociology are alike in their shared anthropocentrism."[12] In short, the diverse array of concepts and theories in sociology share one thing in common: they account for human affairs as if the physical and organic worlds that envelop them do not exist.

Catton and Dunlap offer a potent corrective to this human-centered view of the world: "Humans are influenced not only by social and cultural factors," they write, "but also by intricate linkages of cause, effect, and feedback in a web of nature."[13] In his more recent introduction to the study of sociology, Alan Irwin borrows from Bruno Latour, arguing for a "hybrid" approach to community and environment encounters, one that places some emphasis on the inescapable exchange between humans and their physical and organic milieu. [14]

We make our worlds, in other words, but not out of thin air. Put another way, there were more than words floating in Prince William Sound (see Chapter 2). This simple truth is illustrated in a memorable study of the psychosocial effects of the *Exxon Valdez* oil spill on native fishing villages surrounding the sound.[15] Developing the idea of the "renewable resource community," Picou and Gill make a persuasive case for the peculiar characteristics of human settlements "connected to the biophysical environment through resource harvests and uses" and the unique and devastating effects of the oil spill on the social and cultural organization of these villages.[16]

With this somewhat heady discussion in mind, we turn to our next case, one that allows us to examine the unique physioorganic differences between siting disputes and exposure disputes and their varying effects on community discord. Throughout we have drawn a distinction between three types of environmental disputes. We are aware of at least one case study that examines and compares in some detail two of these environmental disputes and their varying effects on local communities. The purpose of this study was to discern how the varying physical and organic realities of toxic exposure and hazardous waste siting might shape local patterns of social conflict. The results are instructive.

Siting Versus Exposure
Disputes in Rural Communities

Residents of Beaver Township, Pennsylvania, heard from friends, the media, and signs posted on poles, barns, and similar locations that a new landfill was being proposed for their area.

> In the fall of 1989, Beaver Valley Development, Inc., in Columbia County, Pennsylvania, applied to the state's Department of Environmental Resources for a permit to use 124 acres of township property for a sanitary landfill as ". . . a lot . . . used primarily for the disposal of garbage, refuse, and other discarded materials, including, but not limited to, solid and liquid waste materials resulting from industrial, commercial, agricultural, and residential activities."[17]

Not 27 miles southwest of Beaver Township "lies the borough of Centralia in Conyngham Township," the site of an exposure dispute discussed in some depth in Chapters 1 and 2.[18]

Centralia was a mining town . . . in the late 19th and early 20th centuries but declined steadily as gas, oil, and electricity gradually replaced coals as the principal sources of energy. The demise of Centralia, however, was not caused by the decline and fall of "king coal" but by an underground mine fire that vents poisonous gases through cracks in basement walls and floors and rents gaping holes in the ground that threaten to swallow anything standing on it.[19]

Described in these two short vignettes—one of a rural township, the other of a rural town—are two dissimilar environmental issues: one is a siting initiative, the other is a hazardous gas contamination problem. Two quite different patterns of social conflict emerged in these two geographically proximate settings. In Beaver Township residents formed the grassroots alliance SOIL, or Save Our Innocent Land. From 2 weeks of the group's founding, it grew to 404 members, or approximately 56% of the township residents. Moreover, the Township Board of Supervisors (TBS) joined the SOIL alliance in opposing the siting, and together the group raised $10,000 to hire attorneys and buy newspaper space and radio time to fight this initiative. Evident here is the construction of a potent and expressive horizontal nexus among citizens and local government. Forging a communal identity at the local level allowed for a coordinated and effective opposition to the industrial interests of Columbia County.

In Centralia, seven grassroots groups emerged in this village of just over 1,000 residents, each one with a different perception of the fire and a different idea about what should be done in response to it. The borough council added to the acrimony by favoring some groups and disparaging others. Neighboring customs in the village such as card games, quilting bees, and town picnics quietly died as former friends found it awkward to be in one another's company. Acts of property destruction and threats of violence "pierced the social fabric of the town and served as stark reminders of the growing loss of civility."[20] Here, obviously, is a quite different pattern of social conflict than that found in Beaver Township.

The horizontal struggle in Centralia is qualitatively different than the horizontal cohesiveness in Beaver Township and its vertical struggle with industry. The demographic compositions of the two populations are not dissimilar. Both populations faced local environmental troubles. The similarities appeared to outweigh the differences. Perhaps there are properties of the hazards themselves that might explain, in part, the different patterns of opposition.

In this comparative case study, one salient physical property stands out: in the siting case, the threat of contamination was not physically present in the township. It was a discursive threat, a topic for speculation, imagination, and conversation. In Centralia, of course, the mine fire was in the town. It was more than thoughts and words; it had a tangible, palpable physical quality to it.

> The people of Beaver Township were not forced to reappraise their relationship to the biophysical system but to collectively imagine the dangers that would follow if a landfill were placed within that system. [Their common] goal was to preserve the physical and social environment of their region.[21]

Without the fickle, volatile presence of toxins in their local habitat, in other words, residents of Beaver Township found it comparatively easy to imagine in unison the threats posed by the proposed landfill. Consensus or general agreement was achieved, in part, by the physical absence of the hazard.

Centralia, of course, was another matter. Here, residents knew that the toxins—in this case, poisonous gases—were physically present in the abandoned mine shafts and tunnels that formed a complicated filigree under their town. But these gases were, by and large, undetected by the ordinary senses. Colorless and odorless, they stalked the town. More important, not everyone was affected in the same way. The variable encroachment of these invisible toxic agents, affecting this street, ignoring that street, helped to ensure that the personal and familial experiences of this environmental hazard would be uneven and contradictory. "Where are the toxic gases?" "Where are they moving?" "Who is at risk and who isn't?"

Moreover, biomedical diagnostics are organized to respond to acute toxic exposures, not somatic risks from long-term, chronic exposures. The physical presence of the gases in the community meant that emotionally tinged questions about health and illness were likely to be answered in equivocal, uncertain terms. "Is a little methane exposure a problem for my asthma?" "The vision in my left eye is getting weaker. Do carbon gases affect the eyes?" "How?" And so on, through a litany of queries, most of which medical science cannot conclusively answer.

> The physical presence of contamination, then, adds an important and complicating factor to what is present in a siting dispute. Indeed, if hazard perceptions in siting disputes are solely a derivative of the structure of human relations and thus managed exclusively on a social terrain, hazard perceptions in exposure conflicts include both the pattern of human relations and the physical presence of the pollution in the community.[22]

❖

The conclusions drawn from this study are, in fact, quite modest. But it does advance the somewhat heretical idea that we should not necessarily dismiss the physical and organic qualities of the environment as extra-social, as falling outside the boundary of what students of society may legitimately examine. If the physical organic environment is *both* a brute fact—we know it is "out there"—and a social fact—we experience it through groups and organizations—it is more than a little tempting to consider how these two orders of facts might occasionally intersect to shape the contours of community conflict.

It is not only the fickle and volatile issue of the presence or absence of toxins in the biosphere that help to shape the quality and quantity of social conflict. Topography, certainly a more benign characteristic than poisons, may also intersect with local patterns of conflict. Indeed, topography itself might provide at least a partial account for the presence or absence of conflict. A comparative case study of two siting controversies illustrates this idea.

Topography and the Shape of Community Conflict: Offshore Oil Extraction on the Louisiana and California Coasts

In their quiet classic *Oil in Troubled Waters,* environmental sociologists Freudenburg and Gramling compare and contrast the local responses to offshore oil development in southern Louisiana and Northern California.[23] To make a long and interesting story short, communities in Northern California fought oil development with a stubborn tenacity. In stark contrast, communities in southern Louisiana were noticeably silent and overwhelmingly supportive in the face of a massive development project.

To account for these two quite divergent responses to comparatively extreme environmental change, the authors examine an array of social, cultural, and environmental differences between the two locales. Let's begin with Louisiana. Offshore oil extraction started early in this state—in the 1930s—and it was proceeded by several decades of onshore extraction, including in the extensive wetlands found in the southern part of the state. By the 1980s, offshore oil extraction had a pervasive presence in the central and western parts of the Gulf of Mexico. With respect to Louisiana, "by 1988 there were over three thousand platforms in federal waters, over three miles offshore, with many more in the state waters closer to shore."[24] This enormous undertaking had built up gradually, however, from fairly modest efforts begun decades before.

Furthermore, the Cajuns and other ethnic groups (including Filipinos, Canary Islanders, and Houma Indians) who lived along the Louisiana coast were already engaged in extractive activities. Spanish moss, cypress lumber, shrimp, and crawfish are among the many resources regularly harvested from the bayous, bays, and swamps of southern Louisiana. While some of these resources were used for subsistence purposes, coastal residents had been integrated into a regional and national market economy for a century prior to the first oil exploration in the area. The notion that a living could be made by removing resources from the swamps and selling them on the market was thus a vibrant part of local culture. Oil extraction readily fit into this cultural template.

In addition, oil extraction was not in competition with other possible uses of the area. With a few notable exceptions like Grand Isle, the Louisiana coast has never been a tourist destination spot. This is because Louisiana is virtually void of the kind of white, sandy beaches which provide sunbathing and other recreational potential. Instead, the Louisiana coast is comprised of wetlands. Long derogatorily dismissed as swamps, southern Louisiana has captured the public imagination as a place both unpleasant (especially in terms of bugs and humidity) and sinister. Even absent stereotypical voodoo priestess and Deliverance-like backwoods Cajuns, the Louisiana wetlands hold plenty of dangers. These include a confusing labyrinth of water passages, water moccasins, and alligators.

The wetlands present another barrier to recreation and tourism: lack of roads. Even in the early 21st century, there are few roads in southern Louisiana. Travel in the area is largely restricted to boats, which is why fishing is one of the few recreational activities which does occur in the area. This limited access affects not only outside tourism, but local travel as well. As one resident from Lafayette explained to Freudenburg and Gramling, "The Gulf is only about fifteen miles south of here, but there are probably more people in this town who've seen the Gulf from Florida than who've seen it from anyplace in Louisiana."[25]

Not only was there no tourist industry to be threatened by offshore oil extraction; at the time the industry was first developing in the 1930s there was also no offshore commercial fishing industry to speak of. "Shrimp, the most significant of the commercial species in the Louisiana Gulf today, were thought to be present only in the estuaries, and were not even known to be available in the deeper Gulf until the late 1940s."[26] Offshore oil extraction and commercial fishing thus "grew up" together.

There were also environmental conditions which reduced the potential for conflict. The Outer Continental Shelf (OCS) has a long, gradual slope off the Louisiana shore, with waters of a depth suitable for coastal commercial fishing extending out about 100 miles. This provides plenty of space for both oil platforms and fishing boats. In addition, the central Gulf area has a silty bottom, the result of millennia of deposits from the Mississippi River. Oil rigs create artificial reefs in an area with few natural, hard, substrate structures of this kind. In Louisiana, fishers often seek out rigs as prime fishing spots.

The oil industry also provided jobs and economic development in a region with few other viable options. Coastal Louisiana has long been isolated, and economically depressed. Yet at the height of the oil boom, in the mid-1970s, "a person could drop out of school, get training in a specialized trade (e.g., argon welding) and make $18–20 an hour."[27] Far from threatening local ways of life, many locals credit the oil industry with saving them.[28] Without the oil industries, many residents believe they (or at least their children) would have been forced to leave their hometowns to search for work elsewhere. This may go a long way toward explaining why, in their interviews with Louisiana coastal residents in the 1980s, Freudenburg and Gramling were hard pressed not only to find someone who opposed offshore oil extraction but to find anyone who even knew of someone who opposed offshore oil extraction.

The pervasive presence and positive image of the oil industry is written over the cultural landscape of the area. Even a first-time visitor can easily see signs of the long-term influence of offshore oil exploration in Lafayette and Morgan City. Someone who moves to town can buy a house from Oil City Realty, go shopping at the Oil Center Shopping Mall, and go to work at an office in the Oil Center. Until the bust came along, that same person could have visited the Oil Museum on the highway between the two cities, and even today, to drive between the two is to see not just a great deal of real oil technology—pipes, platforms, jack-up rigs, crew boats, heavy trucks, and helicopters—but even such nice touches as an office building that has been built in the size and shape of an actual offshore drilling platform.[29]

The situation in Northern California is markedly different. For starters, efforts at offshore extraction came much later to the area, and would have made its presence felt not in the terms of a gradual undertaking but rather as the apparently overnight sprouting of a technological leviathan. It also came at a time when other industries were established in the area. The three major ones were logging, fishing, and tourism; offshore oil would have been in competition with the last two.

To understand the competition with commercial fishing, we need to understand the differences in the marine environment in California and Louisiana. The depth of water suitable for coastal commercial fishing extends only a few miles off most of the Northern California coast. The

OCS here, in other words, is much more abbreviated in size, with a sudden rather than gradual drop-off. The Northern California seabed is also rocky rather than silty, precluding the need for artificial reefs. When these factors are combined with the threat to fisheries from the kind of massive oil spill that happened on an offshore platform at Santa Barbara in 1969, commercial fishers figure the risks are just not worth it.

The concerns for the tourist industry is limited not just to the potential for spills but also from the belief that the oil platforms would distract from the aesthetics of the place. The Northern California coast is considered one of the most beautiful coastlines in the country. A mountainous, rocky region with high-energy surge (waves crash with dramatic force against the shore), the term often used to describe the region is *awe inspiring*. Furthermore, roads and recreational areas make the coast highly accessible. While "only 12.26% of the Louisiana coast is accessible even by rudimentary roads, . . . the figure for California . . . [is] 90%."[30]

Local residents also fear offshore oil extraction will prove an eyesore, detracting from one of the primary benefits of living on the Northern California coast. In contrast to Louisiana, residents here consider the oil industry a threat to their way of life. In interviews with Freundenburg and Gramling, area inhabitants "worried openly about the social changes that . . . [offshore oil] might bring to what they considered to be peaceful, friendly, and largely rural communities."[31] Many residents had fled to the area from urban centers in search of a less harried way of life. There is, in fact, considerable opposition to further economic development of any kind in the area, but especially to offshore oil extraction, with its potential for environmental damage and boom-bust economic cycles.

In Northern California too, these negative sentiments toward the oil industry are displayed on the cultural landscape. Antioil materials—often featuring a red circle with a diagonal slash through a black oil derrick—are posted in windows, storefronts, and car windows. Motels and bed-and-breakfast establishments provide explanations of "why we opposed offshore oil development." General stores have antioil petitions on their bulletin boards, next to notices of "Kittens for Sale" and "Needed: Ride to San Francisco." Bumper stickers make clear that the owners of cars and pickups share the same sentiments.[32]

This two-case comparison presents us with an explanatory conundrum: Why is the exact same extractive activity regarded in such widely divergent ways on the southern Louisiana coast and the coast of Northern California?

Topography, it appears, should not be neglected in any reasonable response to this query. The coastal contours of southern Louisiana, the configuration of its estuaries, shallows, barrier reefs, and dune lands, do not allow for a wide range of land uses. The unique configuration of land, sand, and water in this region does not permit a wide range of growth initiatives. It is not conducive to tourism or industrial or residential development. Extractive activities of various kinds form the economic backbone of the region.

The oil industry is regarded by locals as compatible with other extractive industries like commercial fishing and shrimping. One reason for this compatibility is the biospheric conditions of the offshore area, including the silty nature of the central Gulf seabed. Because they can serve as artificial reefs, the oil platforms have proved beneficial to commercial fishers. Had offshore oil extraction been in competition with other uses of the marine environment, then it would have constricted the range of land and water use options. In this case, however, offshore production not only expanded local options, but it did so in a context where there were few other viable economic opportunities on the table.

Far from an ecological or development problem, the oil boom in the Gulf was correctly viewed by most locals as the critical resource in underwriting a comfortable middle-class life. This view was reinforced by the ubiquitous and uniformly positive messages about the oil industry written on the cultural landscape of southern Louisiana and repeated in conversations with families, friends, coworkers, and acquaintances.

In sharp contrast to the southern Louisiana coast, the coastal environment of Northern California invites a far broader array of possible uses. This coast is both accessible and breathtaking, encouraging a robust tourism. Commercial fishing and logging coexist (albeit uneasily) with tourism to create a multiuse, diverse, and flexible market. Most locals viewed offshore oil extraction as an unnecessary and potentially risk-prone industry that would endanger a vibrant regional land and water use economy.

They worried, in particular, about the potential negative effects of oil drilling and pumping on tourism and fishing. The incompatibility of fishing and offshore oil extraction can be traced, in part, to the topography of the Northern California seabed, including a geographically limited offshore area conducive to coastal fishing. This delimited fishing range would prevent fishers from simply shifting locations in the event of a spill.

Far from creating a desired way of life, Northern California residents viewed offshore oil extraction as a threat to their already diverse cultural and economic network. From the locals' perspective, oil industry intrusion into the area would constrict quality-of-life options presently provided by the local social, cultural, and environmental milieu. In contrast to the consistently positive messages written on the cultural landscape of southern Louisiana touting the benefits of an oil economy, the messages scrawled on Northern California billboards, reasoned in editorials, and loudly voiced in talk radio programs uniformly condemned the oil companies siting proposals.

A Concluding Word

There is what philosophers call a category difference in the configuration of ideas presented in this chapter and the ideas presented in Chapters 2 through 6. Ideas that are categorically different do not point to the same aspects of the world; they conjure or "see" the same world in substantively different ways. Chapters 2 through 6 work almost exclusively within the category of the social and the cultural. Assumed in these discussions is a classic sociological idea: environmental conflicts can be theorized in exclusively social and cultural terms. The biophysical characteristics of environments are not necessarily left out of the description of the problem. Indeed, they might be richly described. But—and here is the key—they are *not* conceptualized as part of the etiology of the conflict or its subsequent development and (perhaps) resolution.

The ideas and discussions in these five chapters might be usefully grouped under the heading Sociology of the Environment. Here, environment is a noun acted on by society. The focus here is on the machinations of people, groups, organizations, and institutions working, arguing, and agreeing on what should, might, or could be done about a problem or plan for the environment. A sociology of the environment accepts Durkheim's admonition to always account for the social in social terms.

Chapter 7, however, invites us to shift from an exclusively social and cultural category to one that joins what in fact are two categories: the social-cultural to the physical-organic. For purposes of discussion, we referred to these two classes of fact as brute and institutional and employed the term *symbolic realism* to indicate our intention to bring them together to see what kinds of insights and understandings we might win in our quest to make sense of local environmental conflicts. Symbolic realism asserts that "something—call it reality—exists outside our language and senses . . . [and] what we know about this reality is dependent upon the words we use to talk about it."[33]

Perhaps we can account for and make some sense of personal and social behaviors by examining their relationships to features of the biophysical world. By acknowledging the agentic quality of environments in accounting for the shape of community discord, this chapter might be thought of as an exercise in *environmental sociology.* Here, the noun *environment* is replaced by the adjective *environmental,* suggesting that the biophysical world can act on the world of people, groups, and communities.

An environmental sociology is, of course, fraught with a variety of hazards, not the least of which is being accused of environmental determinism. But it does open the door to a way of *seeing* the environment that makes sense both intuitively and biographically. Pressed, even the most staunch Durkheimian sociologist will admit that the biophysical world intersects with social things, affecting and modifying our personal and social lives. We know by experience, for example, that dense pollen leads to sneezing, which, in turn, leads to perfunctory, but socially meaningful, rituals of atonement (i.e., "Excuse me!") and reclamation (i.e., "God bless you!"). But a conventional, normal science approach to sociology demands the investigator approach these Goffmanesque exchanges as if sneezing was simply an expressive act with no connection of climatological rhythms. But a sociologist who took into account the seasonal cycle of pollen and the very real possibility that increased sinus irritation accompanied by increased sneezing in public created an accentuated, if temporary, flow of civic vim and vigor would be engaging in a variant of environmental sociology.

We encourage you not to engage in a stilted philosophical debate over brute and institutional facts, category differences, and the like. Rather, we invite you to take a more insouciant approach to symbolic realism. Try it out; toy with it. See if you can "see" what it invites you to look at. If you can, use it. If not, put it away for another time. It is simply another tool in your conceptual box.

STUDENT EXERCISES

1. Return to the spotted owl controversy presented in Chapter 4. Identify brute facts and social (or institutional) facts in this case, being sure to defend your choices.

2. Look back over the portfolio boxes in Chapters 1 and 4. Choose one portfolio question from each of these chapters you believe is suggestive of symbolic realism. Defend your answer.

3. Identify connections between the Tellico Dam case and the History as Tradition section of Chapter 2. Explain why traditions are examples of "social facts." Could we have developed an adequate explanatory account of the Tellico Dam case had we limited our attention to social facts? Defend your answer.

4. Excluding the Centralia case, choose one of the exposure disputes presented in a previous chapter and examine it from the standpoint of symbolic realism, being sure to identify relevant physical-organic and social-cultural factors, as well as the intersecting relationships between these.

5. Using the lens of symbolic realism, compare and contrast the Beaver Township siting dispute and the Centralia exposure dispute to one of the following conservancy disputes: (a) Scotia, California (Chapter 1), (b) turtle exclusion devices (Chapter 3), (c) Chicago Wilderness (Chapter 4), or (d) Wye Island (Chapter 5).

Notes

1. Dubos (1972), 38.
2. Sahlins (1964), 133.
3. See related discussion in Chapter 1 on the end of nature (McKibben, 1999) and socialized nature (Giddens, 1991).
4. Searle (1997).
5. Durkheim (1982).
6. Ibid.
7. Wheeler and McDonald (1986) and Etnier and Starnes (1993).
8. Wheeler and McDonald (1986), 156.
9. U.S. Supreme Court (1978).
10. Barry (1998).
11. Kroll-Smith, Gunter, and Laska (2000).
12. Catton and Dunlap (1980), 33.
13. Ibid., 34.
14. Irwin (2001); see also Latour (1995).
15. Picou and Gill (1996).
16. Picou and Gill (1996), 881.
17. Couch and Kroll-Smith (1994), 30.
18. Couch and Kroll-Smith (1994), 31.
19. Ibid.
20. Ibid., 32.
21. Ibid., 34.
22. Ibid., 35.
23. Freudenburg and Gramling (1994); for a more extensive discussion of the Louisiana experience, see also Gramling (1996).
24. Freudenburg and Gramling (1994), 8; emphasis in original.
25. Ibid., 79; emphasis in original.
26. Freudenburg and Gramling (1994), 76.
27. Ibid., 40.
28. It is possible these views have started to change in the years since Freudenburg and Gramling conducted their research, as coastal erosion, in part

caused by oil extraction activity, has placed coastal communities at extreme risk from subsidence and hurricanes. For an overview, see Tidwell (2003) and Hallowell (2001).

29. Freudenburg and Gramling (1994), 37.

30. Ibid., 81.

31. Ibid., 51.

32. Ibid., 47.

33. Kroll-Smith, Gunter, and Laska (2000), 54.

Postscript

Readers encountered dozens of case studies in this book. We fashioned these studies with a particular story line in mind. One case told a story of uncertain knowledge, another of oppositional activity, still another of the perception of fairness, and so on throughout. Joining sociology to story does have its detractors. A story, after all, could be a tall tale, a novel, or memoir, indeed, science fiction. Moreover, good storytelling brings the added complication of the persuasive force of the argument being carried by rhetorical and literary style. In other words, an author's work becomes convincing to others because, at least in part, the author is good with a turn of phrase, the pace and structure of the story, and other elements of writing that engage readers' attention.

Literary styles are a far cry from the objective approach scientific disciplines instill in their practitioners. Science is about the discovery of empirical facts. Those facts are to be produced through rigorous application of acceptable methods designed to eliminate bias. A scientist's job is to pull back the curtain to reveal the reality of the world currently hidden behind sensory and cognitive limitations. The naked fact is, simply put, what it is and should stand exposed before the world without being dressed up in flowery language.

But high-quality research can be joined with high-quality writing. We not only want to be storytellers, but good ones. Our goal is to present evidence in a way which engages our readers. Case studies present an especially hospitable medium for this goal, for they allow us to follow a series of events as these unfold over time. By paying attention to chronology, we create a time line for our story, which in turn provides possibilities for foreshadowing and suspense. We can even draw readers deeper into the story by challenging initial designations of the start and finish of a conflict, marshaling evidence that the roots of the conflict stretch far into the past, with consequences likely to reverberate far into the future. By paying attention to process we can analyze the dynamic forces which drive the conflict.

In the present book we have presented an analytic framework which helps investigators tell the story of local environmental conflicts. By way of concluding, we discuss some elements of good storytelling that may help students of environmental controversies convey the personal, social, and cultural drama of conflict. We begin with a particular setting, some context fixed in time and space, where momentous events are in the process of unfolding.

These events set particular characters into collision courses with one another. These courses are likely shaped by both present circumstances and historical events and patterns. Knowledge, a necessary and often volatile resource, is likely debated in the Manichean language of certainty and uncertainty. The human penchant for fairness puts this unstable and emotionally weighted value into play, ensuring that the combustible issue of justice will require expansive debate.

Moreover, the physical and biological environment itself, its topography, the presence or absence of toxins, the direction and quality of its water, are possibly confounded in a complex web of human and ecosystem relationships. The environment might enter into the story at some points as context, at other points as a momentous event, and at still other points as one of the characters in the drama.

Finally, good storytelling involves the revelation of initially hidden truths. This may take the form of ordinary people discovering unknown reserves of strength and courage in battles to protect their families, homes, and way of life (think Tolkien's *Lord of the Rings*). It may also take the form of dawning recognition that groups and individuals in positions of power who purport to work for the collective good have in fact betrayed the public trust through deceit and self-serving action (think Orwell's *Animal Farm*). Revelation might come about through sudden confrontation with unanticipated consequences of action (think Crichton's *Jurassic Park*). It may also come about through the unveiling of forces which shape characters' lives in ways they did not perceive (think Sophocles' *Oedipus Rex*).

Nowhere is the need to understand the volatility of humans and place greater today than in the ravaged city of New Orleans. New Orleans, of course, was born risk prone, and its subsequent development only intensified the dangers. But on August 29, 2005, dozens of levees failed to hold back the elevated waters of Lake Pontchartrain and—akin to Atlantis—within hours most of New Orleans was underwater. As the city slowly drained, a contested question quickly emerged in plain view of everyone: When water and culture collide, whose vision of the city will prevail? Black people, white people, rich people, poor people, social reformers, artists, oil companies, politicians, tourists, and more are marshaling resources to wage protracted struggles over the questions of culpability, fairness, what is safe and dangerous, over who should live where and in what kind of housing, and, finally, over what kind of city New Orleans can be in its precarious place between a river and a lake.

As we write, no one knows if New Orleans will rise from the ruins to provide a new model of urban development, one based on just and ecologically sustainable principles. It is a long shot, but it could happen. But whether it happens or not, one thing is sure: New Orleans will be adrift in environmental controversies for many years to come. Environmental controversies are now an inevitable part of the American landscape. They beg inquiry.

References

Alario, Margarita. 2000. "Urban and Ecological Planning in Chicago: Science, Policy and Dissent." *Journal of Environmental Planning and Management* 43:489–505.

Alaska Oil Spill Commission. 1990. *Final Report.* Retrieved from www.evostc.state.ak.us/facts/details.html.

Allan, Robert. 1992. *Waste Not, Want Not: The Production and Dumping of Toxic Waste.* London: Earthscan.

Allen, Barbara L. 2003. *Uneasy Alchemy: Citizens and Experts in Louisiana's Chemical Corridor Disputes.* Cambridge: Massachusetts Institute of Technology Press.

Anchorage Daily News. 1989. March 24.

Aronoff, Marilyn. 1993. "Collective Celebration as a Vehicle for Local Economic Development: A Michigan Case." *Human Organization* 52(4):368–379.

Aronoff, Marilyn, and Gunter, Valerie. 1992a. "Defining Disaster: Local Constructions for Recovery in the Aftermath of Chemical Contamination." *Social Problems* 39:345–363.

Aronoff, Marilyn, and Gunter, Valerie. 1992b. "It's Hard to Keep a Good Town Down: Local Recovery Efforts in the Aftermath of Chemical Contamination." *Industrial Crisis Quarterly* 6:83–97.

Barry, John M. 1998. *Rising Tide: The Great Mississippi River Flood of 1927 and How It Changed America.* New York: Simon & Schuster.

Barry, John. 1999. *Environment and Social Theory.* London: Routledge.

Barton, Allen H. 1969. *Communities in Disaster: A Sociological Analysis of Collective Stress Situations.* Garden City, NY: Doubleday.

Beamish, Thomas D. 2002. *Silent Spill: The Organization of an Industrial Crisis.* Cambridge: Massachusetts Institute of Technology Press.

Beck, Ulrich. 1995. *Ecological Enlightenment.* Atlantic Highlands, NJ: Humanities Press.

Beck, Ulrich. 1999. *What Is Globalization?* Cambridge, UK: Polity Press.

Bedford, Henry F. 1990. *Seabrook Station: Citizen Politics and Nuclear Power.* Amherst: University of Massachusetts Press.

Bell, Michael Mayerfeld. 1994. *Childerly: Nature and Morality in a Country Village.* Chicago: University of Chicago Press.

Bell, Michael Mayerfeld. 2004. *An Invitation to Environmental Sociology.* 2nd ed. Thousand Oaks, CA: Pine Forge Press.

Best, Joel, ed. 1995. *Images of Issues: Typifying Contemporary Social Problems.* 2nd ed. New York: Aldine de Gruyter.

Bogard, William. 1989. *The Bhopal Tragedy: Language, Logic and Politics in the Production of a Hazard.* Boulder, CO: Westview.

Bosso, Christopher J. 1987. *Pesticides and Politics: The Life Cycle of a Public Issue.* Pittsburgh, PA: University of Pittsburgh Press.

Bourdieu, Pierre. 1979. *Distinction: A Social Critique of the Judgment of Taste.* Cambridge, MA: Harvard University Press.

Brown, Phil. 1991. "The Popular Epidemiology Approach to Toxic Waste Contamination." In *Communities at Risk*, eds. Stephen R. Couch, and Steve Kroll-Smith, pp. 133–155. New York: Peter Lang.

Brown, Phil, and Mikkelsen, Edwin J. 1990. *No Safe Place: Toxic Waste, Leukemia, and Community Action.* Berkeley: University of California Press.

Bryan, Todd A., and Wondolleck, Julia M. 2003. "When Irresolvable Becomes Resolvable: The Quincy Library Group Conflict." In *Making Sense of Intractable Environmental Conflicts: Frames and Cases*, eds. Roy J. Lewicki, Barbara Gray, and Michael Elliott, pp. 63–90. Washington, DC: Island Press.

Buffalo Evening News. 1978. Editorial page. August 4, p. 19.

Burke, Kenneth. 1989. *On Symbols and Society.* Edited by Joseph R. Gusfield. Chicago: University of Chicago Press.

Busch, Lawrence, Tanaka, Kieko, and Gunter, Valerie J. 2000. "Who Cares If the Rat Dies? Rodents, Risks, and Humans in the Science of Food Safety." In *Illness and the Environment: A Reader in Contested Medicine*, eds. Steve Kroll-Smith, Phil Brown, and Valerie J. Gunter, pp. 108–119. New York: New York University Press.

Cable, Sherry, and Cable, Charles. 1995. *Environmental Problems, Grassroots Solutions: The Politics of Grassroots Environmental Conflict.* New York: St. Martin's Press.

Capek, Stella. 2005. "Time, Space and Birds: Cattle Egrets and the Place of the Wild." In *Mad About Wildlife: Looking at Social Conflict Over Wildlife*, eds. Ann Herda-Rapp, and Theresa L. Goedeke. Boston: Brill.

Carmean, Kelly. 2002. *Spider Woman Walks This Land: Traditional Cultural Properties and the Navajo Nation.* Walnut Creek, CA: AltaMira Press.

Catton, William R., and Dunlap, Riley E. 1980. "A New Ecological Paradigm for Post-Exuberant Sociology." *American Behavioral Scientist* 24:15–47.

Catton, William R. Jr. 1982. *Overshoot: The Ecological Basis of Revolutionary Change.* Urbana: University of Illinois Press.

Checker, Melissa. 2005. *Polluted Promises: Environmental Racism and the Search for Environmental Justice in a Small Southern Town.* New York: New York University Press.

Clarke, Lee. 1989. *Acceptable Risk? Making Decisions in a Toxic Environment.* Berkeley: University of California Press.

Clarke, Lee. 1999. *Mission Improbable: Using Fantasy Documents in a Toxic Environment*. Berkeley: University of California Press.

Colburn, Theo, Dumanoski, Dianne, and Myers, John Peterson. 1997. *Our Stolen Future: Are We Threatening Our Fertility, Intelligence and Survival? A Scientific Detective Story*. New York: Dutton.

Coles, Luke W., and Foster, Sheila R. 2001. *From the Ground Up: Environmental Racism and the Rise of the Environmental Justice Movement*. New York: New York University Press.

Copps, David H. 1995. *View From the Road: A Community Guide for Assessing Rural Historic Landscapes*. Washington, DC: Island Press.

Couch, Stephen R., and Kroll-Smith, Steve. 1985. "The Chronic Technical Disaster: Toward a Social Scientific Perspective." *Social Sciences Quarterly* 66:564–575.

Couch, Stephen R., and Kroll-Smith, Steve. 1994. "Environmental Controversies, Interactional Resources, and Rural Communities: Siting Versus Exposure Disputes." *Rural Sociology* 59:25–44.

Couch, Stephen R., and Kroll-Smith, Steve. 1997. "Environmental Movements and Expert Knowledge: Evidence for a New Populism." *International Journal of Contemporary Sociology* 34(2):185–210.

Crosby, Alfred W. 2003. *The Columbian Exchange: Biological and Cultural Consequences of 1492* (30th anniversary ed.). Westport, CT: Greenwood.

Culhane, Paul. 1981. *Public Lands Politics: Interest Group Influence on the Forest Service and the Bureau of Land Management*. Baltimore: Johns Hopkins University Press, for Resources for the Future.

Dizard, Jan E. 1999. *Going Wild: Hunting, Animal Rights, and the Contested Meaning of Nature*. Amherst: University of Massachusetts Press.

Dobbs, David. 2000. *The Great Gulf: Fishermen, Scientists, and the Struggle to Revive the World's Greatest Fishery*. Washington, DC: Island Press.

Domhoff, G. William. 1988. *Who Rules America?: Power and Politics in the Year 2000*. Mountain View, CA: Mayfield.

Dubos, Rene. 1972. *A God Within*. New York: Charles Scribner's Sons.

Dunlap, Riley E. 1992. "Trends in Public Opinion Towards Environmental Issues: 1965–1990." In *American Environmentalism: The U.S. Environmental Movement, 1970–1990*, eds. Riley E. Dunlap and Angela Mertig, pp. 89–116. Philadelphia: Taylor and Francis.

Dunlap, Riley E. 2002. "An Enduring Concern: Light Stays Green For Environmental Protection." *Public Perspective*. September-October: 10–12.

Durkheim, Émile. 1974. *Sociology and Philosophy*. New York: Free Press.

Durkheim, Émile. 1982. *The Rules of Sociological Method*. New York: Free Press.

Edelstein, Michael R. 1988. *Contaminated Communities: The Social and Psychological Impact of Residential Toxic Exposure*. Boulder, CO: Westview.

Encyclopedia of Sociology. 1974. Guilford, CT: Dushkin.

Environmental Justice. 2006. Retrieved from www.epa.gov/compliance/environmentaljustice.

Environmental Protection Agency. 1978. *Report: Love Canal, New York.* EPA Region 2, EPA ID#: NY D000606947. Washington, DC: Author.

Erikson, Kai T. 1976. *Everything in Its Path: Destruction of Community in the Buffalo Creek Flood.* New York: Simon & Schuster.

Espeland, Wendy Nelson. 1998. *The Struggle for Water: Politics, Rationality, and Identity in the American Southwest.* Chicago: University of Chicago Press.

Etnier, David A., and Starnes, Wayne C. 1993. *The Fishes of Tennessee.* Knoxville: University of Tennessee Press.

Fall, James A., Stanek, Ronald T., and Utermohle, Charles J., eds. 1995. *An Investigation of the Sociocultural Consequences of Outer Continental Shelf Development in Alaska, II Prince William Sound.* OCS Study MMS 95-011. Anchorage, AK: U.S. Department of the Interior.

Fine, Gary Alan. 2004. "The When of Ethnographic Theory." *Perspectives* 27:4.

Fowlkes, Martha R., and Miller, Patricia Y. 1982. *Love Canal: The Social Construction of Disaster.* Report Code: EMW-1-4048. Washington, DC: Federal Emergency Management Agency.

Francis, Leslie Pickering, and Silvers, Anita, eds. 2000. *Americans With Disabilities: Exploring Implications for Individuals and Institutions.* New York: Routledge.

Freeman, Milton M. R., Bogoslovskaya, Lyadmila, Caulfield, Richard A., Egede, Ingmar, Krupnik, Igor I., and Stevenson, Marc G. 1998. *Inuit, Whaling and Sustainability.* Langham, MD: AltaMira.

Freudenburg, William R. 1988. "Perceived Risk, Real Risk: Social Science and the Art of Probabilistic Risk Assessment." *Science* 242(October 7):44–49.

Freudenburg, William R. 1993. "Risk and Recreancy: Weber, The Division of Labor, and the Rationality of Risk Perception." *Social Forces* 71:909–932.

Freudenburg, William R., and Gramling, Robert. 1994. *Oil in Troubled Waters: Perception, Politics, and the Battle Over Offshore Drilling.* Albany: State University of New York Press.

Frey, Scott. 2001. *The Environment and Society Reader.* Boston: Allyn & Bacon.

Futrell, Robert. 1999. "Performative Government: Impression Management, Teamwork, and Conflict Containment in City Commission Proceedings." *Journal of Contemporary Ethnography* 27:494–529.

Gallie, Walter B. 1956. "Essentially Contested Concepts." *Proceedings of the Aristotelian Society* 56:167.

Gaventa, John. 1980. *Power and Powerlessness: Quiescence and Rebellion in an Appalachian Valley.* Oxford, UK: Claredon.

Gibbons, Boyd. 1977. *Wye Island.* Baltimore: Johns Hopkins University Press, for Resources for the Future.

Gibbs, Louis Marie. 1982. *Love Canal: My Story.* Albany: State University of New York Press.

Giddens, Anthony. 1987. *Social Theory and Modern Sociology.* Stanford, CA: Stanford University Press.

Giddens, Anthony. 1991. *Modernity and Self-Identity: Self and Society in the Late Modern Age.* Cambridge, UK: Polity Press.

Giddens, Anthony. 1994. *Beyond Left and Right: The Future of Radical Politics.* Stanford, CA: Stanford University Press.

Giddens, Anthony. 2000. *Runaway World: How Globalization Is Reshaping Our Future.* New York: Routledge.

Gill, Duane A., and Picou, J. Steven. 1997. "The Day the Water Died: Cultural Impacts of the *Exxon Valdez* Oil Spill on Alaskan Natives." In *The Exxon Valdez Disaster: Readings on a Modern Social Problem*, eds. J. Steven Picou, Duane A. Gill, and Maurie J. Cohen, pp. 167–191. Dubuque, IA: Kendall/ Hunt.

Glanz, James. 2002. "Almost All in U.S. Have Been Exposed to Fallout, Study Finds: Low-Level Radiation Could Cause Up to 11,000 Deaths." *New York Times* March 1:A14.

Glaser, Barney G., and Strauss, Anselm L. 1967. *The Discovery of Grounded Theory: Strategies for Qualitative Research.* Chicago: Aldine.

Glazer, Penina Migdal, and Glazer, Myron Peretz. 1998. *The Environmental Crusaders: Confronting Disaster and Mobilizing Community.* University Park: Pennsylvania State University Press.

Gobster, Paul, and Hull, Bruce R., eds. 2000. *Restoring Nature: Perspectives From Humanities and Social Sciences.* Washington, DC: Island Press.

Goodwin, Jeff, Jasper, James M., and Polletta, Francesca, eds. 2001. *Passionate Politics: Emotions and Social Movements.* Chicago: University of Chicago Press.

Gottlieb, Robert. 1993. *Forcing the Spring.* Washington, DC: Island Press.

Gottlieb, Robert. 2001. *Environmentalism Unbound: Exploring New Pathways for Change.* Cambridge: Massachusetts Institute of Technology Press.

Gould, Kenneth A., Schnaiberg, Alan, and Weinberg, Adam S. 1996. *Local Environmental Struggles: Citizen Activism in the Treadmill of Production.* New York: Cambridge University Press.

Gramling, Robert. 1996. *Oil on the Edge: Offshore Development, Conflict, Gridlock.* Albany: State University of New York Press.

Gray, Barbara. 2003. "Framing of Environmental Disputes." In *Making Sense of Intractable Environmental Conflicts: Frames and Cases*, eds. Roy J. Lewicki, Barbara Gray, and Michael Elliot, pp. 11–34. Washington, DC: Island Press.

Gunter, Valerie, Aronoff, Marilyn, and Joel, Susan. 1999. "Toxic Contamination and Communities: Using an Ecological-Symbolic Perspective to Theorize Response Contingencies." *Sociological Quarterly* 40:623–640.

Hallowell, Christopher. 2001. *Holding Back the Sea: The Struggle for America's Natural Legacy on the Gulf Coast.* New York: HarperCollins.

Hanifan, Lyda Johnson. 1916. "The Rural School Community." *Annals of the American Academy of Political and Social Science* 67:130–138.

Hannigan, John A. 1995. *Environmental Sociology: A Social Constructionist Perspective.* London: Routledge.

Harper, Charles L. 2003. *Environment and Society.* Englewood Cliffs, NJ: Prentice Hall.

Harr, Jonathan. 1995. *A Civil Action.* New York: Random House.

Harris, David. 1996. *The Last Stand: The War Between Wall Street and Main Street Over California's Ancient Redwoods*. San Francisco: Sierra Club.

Hart, John, Holdren, Cheryl, Schneider, Richard, and Shirley, Christine. 1991. *Toxics A to Z: Everyday Pollution Hazards*. Berkeley: University of California Press.

Helford, Reid M. 2000. "Constructing Nature as Constructing Science: Expertise, Activist Science, and Public Conflict in the Chicago Wilderness." In *Restoring Nature: Perspectives From the Social Sciences and Humanities*, eds. Paul H. Gobster, and R. Bruce Hall, pp. 119–142. Washington, DC: Island Press.

Homrighaus, Barbara, Couch, Stephen R., and Kroll-Smith, Steve. 1985. "Building a Town but Preventing a Community: A Social History of Centralia, Pennsylvania." In *Proceedings of the Canal History and Technology Symposium*, pp. 69–91. Easton, PA: Center for Canal History and Technology.

Hufford, Mary. 2002. "Reclaiming the Commons: Narratives of Progress, Preservation, and Ginseng." In *Culture, Environment and Conservation in the Appalachian South*, ed. Benita J. Howell, pp. 100–120. Champaign: University of Illinois Press.

Irwin, Alan. 1995. *Citizen Science: A Study of People, Expertise and Sustainable Development*. London: Routledge.

Irwin, Alan. 2001. *Sociology and the Environment: A Critical Introduction to Society, Nature and Knowledge*. Cambridge, UK: Polity Press.

James, William. 1956. *The Will to Believe and Other Essays in Popular Philosophy*. New York: Dover.

Jasper, James M., and Nelkin, Dorothy. 1992. *The Animal Rights Crusade: The Growth of a Moral Protest*. New York: Free Press.

Kasindorf, Martin. 2002. "Tribe Seeks Uranium Enrichment." *USA Today*, August 12:A04.

Kasperson, Roger E., and Pijawka, K. David. 1985. "Societal Response to Hazards and Major Hazard Events: Comparing Natural and Technological Hazards." *Public Administration Review* 45:7–18.

Kazis, Richard, and Grossman, Richard L. 1982. *Fear at Work: Job Blackmail, Labor, and the Environment*. New York: Pilgrim Press.

Kline, Benjamin. 2000. *First Along the River: A Brief History of the U.S. Environmental Movement*. 2nd ed. Lanham, MD: Rowman & Littlefield.

Kriesberg, Louis. 2003. *Constructive Conflicts: From Escalation to Resolution*. 2nd ed. Lanham, MD: Rowman & Littlefield.

Kroll-Smith, J. Stephen, and Couch, Stephen Robert. 1990. *The Real Disaster Is Above Ground: A Mine Fire and Social Conflict*. Lexington: University Press of Kentucky.

Kroll-Smith, J. Stephen, and Floyd, H. Hugh. 1997. *Bodies in Protest: Environmental Illness and the Struggle Over Medical Knowledge*. New York: New York University Press.

Kroll-Smith, Steve. 1995. "Toxic Contamination and Loss of Civility." *Sociological Spectrum* 15:377–396.

Kroll-Smith, Steve, Gunter, Valerie, and Laska, Shirley. 2000. "Theoretical Stances and Environmental Debates: Reconciling the Physical and the Symbolic." *American Sociologist* 40:623–640.

Kuehn, Robert, ed. 1991. *Citizen's Guide to Environmental Protection in Louisiana.* New Orleans, LA: Tulane Environmental Law Clinic.

Labyrinth. 1999. Video released by Jim Henson Home Entertainment, Lucasfilm Ltd., Sony Pictures, and Columbia Tri-Star Home Video.

Latour, Bruno. 1995. *We Have Never Been Modern.* Cambridge, MA: Harvard University Press.

Lerner, Steve. 2005. *Diamond: A Struggle for Environmental Justice in Louisiana's Chemical Corridor.* Cambridge: Massachusetts Institute of Technology Press.

Levine, Adeline Gordon. 1982. *Love Canal: Science, Politics and People.* Lexington, MA: Lexington Books.

Lewicki, Roy J., Gray, Barbara, and Elliot, Michael, eds. 2003. *Making Sense of Intractable Environmental Conflicts: Frames and Cases.* Washington, DC: Island Press.

Lord, Nancy. 1997. "Oil in the Sea: Initial Biological Impacts of the *Exxon Valdez* Disaster." In *The Exxon Valdez Disaster*, eds. J. Steven Picou, Duane A. Gill, and Maurie J. Cohen, pp. 95–115. Dubuque, IA: Kendall/Hunt.

Loseke, Donileen R. 1999. *Thinking About Social Problems: An Introduction to Constructionist Perspectives.* New York: Aldine de Gruyter.

Loseke, Donileen R. 2003. *Thinking About Social Problems: An Introduction to Constructionist Perspectives.* 2nd ed. New York: Aldine de Gruyter.

Lowry, William R. 2003. *Dam Politics: Restoring America's Rivers.* Washington, DC: Georgetown University Press.

Lukes, Steven. 1974. *Power: A Radical View.* London: Macmillan.

Maples, David R., and Snell, Victor G. 1988. *The Social Impact of the Chernobyl Disaster.* New York: Palgrave Macmillan.

Margavio, Anthony V., and Forsyth, Craig J. 1996. *Caught in the Net: The Conflict Between Shrimpers and Conservationists.* College Station: Texas A&M University Press.

Mauss, Armand L. 1975. *Social Problems as Social Movements.* Philadelphia: Lippincott.

Mazmanian, Daniel A., and Morell, David. 1992. *Beyond Superfailure: America's Toxic Policy for the 1990's.* Boulder, CO: Westview Press.

Mazur, Allan. 1998. *A Hazardous Inquiry: The Rashomon Effect at Love Canal.* Cambridge, MA: Harvard University Press.

McKibben, Bill. 1999. *The End of Nature.* New York: Anchor Books.

McSorley, J. 1990. *Living in the Shadow: The People of West Cumbria and the Nuclear Industry.* London: Pluto.

McWhoter, Diane. 2001. *Carry Me Home: Birmingham, Alabama: The Climatic Battle of the Civil Rights Revolution.* New York: Simon & Schuster.

Michigan Agricultural Experiment Station. 1988. *Report to the Michigan Legislature on the Impact of the Farm Financial Crisis and the 1986 Flooding* on *Michigan Agricultural and Rural Communities*. Submitted by the Michigan Agricultural Experiment Station, College of Agricultural and Natural Resources, Michigan State University.

Milbrath, Lester W. 1984. *Environmentalists: Vanguard for a New Society*. Albany: State University of New York Press.

Mileti, Dennis S., Drabeck, Thomas A., and Haas, J. E. 1975. *Human Systems in Extreme Environments: A Sociological Perspective*. Boulder: Institute of Behavioral Science, University of Colorado.

Mills, C. Wright. 1956. *The Power Elite*. London: Oxford University Press.

Minchin, Timothy J. 2003. *Forging a Common Bond: Labor and Environmental Activism During the BASF Lockout*. Gainesville: University Press of Florida.

Morrison, Eric. 1993. "Tatitlek." In *Minerals Management Service, Social Indicators Study of Alaskan Coastal Villages: IV, Postspill Key Informant Summaries, Schedule C Communities, Part I*, OCS Study MMS 92–0052, pp. 427–436. Anchorage, AK: Department of Interior.

Mott, Paul E. 1974. "Bureaucratic Community Planning." In *The Community: Approaches and Applications*, ed. Marcia Pelly Effrat, pp. 311–323. New York: Free Press.

Nash, Roderick. 1967. *Wilderness and the American Mind*. New Haven, CT: Yale University Press.

Nelson, Richard K. 1997. *Heart and Blood: Living with Deer in America*. New York: Knopf.

New York Times. 1985. "U.S. Company Said to Have Had Control in Bhopal." January 28.

Olson, E., and Cameron, D. 1995. *The Dirty Little Secret About Drinking Water*. New York: Natural Resources Defense Council.

Ott, Riki. 1994. *Sound Truth: Exxon's Manipulation of Science and the Significance of the* Exxon Valdez *Oil Spill*. Anchorage, AK: Greenpeace.

Palinkas, Lawrence A., Peterson, John S., Russell, John, and Downs, Michael A. 1993. "Community Patterns of Psychiatric Disorders After the *Exxon Valdez* Oil Spill." *American Journal of Psychiatry* 150(10):1517–1523.

Pellow, David Naguib. 2002. *Garbage Wars: The Struggle for Environmental Justice in Chicago*. Cambridge: Massachusetts Institute of Technology Press.

Peterson, Thomas V. 2002. *Linked Arms: A Rural Community Resists Nuclear Waste*. Albany: State University of New York Press.

Picou, J. Steven, and Gill, Duane A. 1996. "The *Exxon Valdez* Oil Spill and Chronic Psychological Stress." In *Proceedings of the* Exxon Valdez *Oil Spill Symposium* (Vol. 18), eds. F. Rice, R. Spies, R. Wolfe, and B. Wright, pp. 879–893. Bethesda, MD: American Fisheries Society.

Picou, J. Steven, and Gill, Duane A. 1998. "Technological Disaster and Chronic Community Stress." *Society and Natural Resources* 11:795–815.

Picou, J. Steven, Gill, Duane A., and Cohen, Maurie J., eds. 1997. *The* Exxon Valdez *Disaster: Readings on a Modern Social Problem*. Dubuque, IA: Kendall/ Hunt.

Picou, J. Steven, Marshall, Brent K., and Gill, Duane A. 2004. "Disaster, Litigation, and the Corrosive Community." *Social Forces* 82:1497–1526.

Pring, George W., and Canan, Penelope. 1996. *SLAPPs: Getting Sued for Speaking Out*. Philadelphia: Temple University Press.

Putnam, Robert D. 1993. *Making Democracy Work: Civic Traditions in Modern Italy*. Princeton, NJ: Princeton University Press.

Putnam, Robert D. 2000. *Bowling Alone: The Collapse and Revival of American Community*. New York: Simon & Schuster.

Quarantelli, E. L., and Dynes, Russell R. 1976. "Community Conflict: Its Absence and Presence in Natural Disasters." *International Journal of Mass Emergencies and Disasters* 1:139–152.

Ragin, Charles C. 1987. *The Comparative Method: Moving Beyond Qualitative and Quantitative Strategies*. Berkeley: University of California Press.

Ritchie, Liesel Ashely. 2004. *Voices of Cordova: Social Capital in the Wake of the Exxon Valdez Oil Spill*. Ph.D. dissertation, Mississippi State University.

Robbins, Lynn A. 1993. "Kenaui." In *Social Indicators Study of Alaskan Coastal Villages, IV*, pp. 445–514. Technical Report No. 155. Postspill Key Information Summaries. Schedule C Communities, Part 2. HRAF, Alaska OCS Region. Anchorage, AK: U.S. Department of the Interior, Minerals Management Service.

Roberts, J. Timmons, and Toffolon-Weiss, Melissa M. 2001. *Chronicles From the Environmental Justice Frontline*. Cambridge, UK: Cambridge University Press.

Rosaldo, M. 1984. "Toward an Anthropology of Self and Feeling." In *Culture Theory: Essays on Mind, Self and Emotion*, eds. R. Shweder and R. Levine, pp. 137–157. New York: Cambridge University Press.

Rothman, Jay. 1997. *Resolving Identity-Based Conflict in Nations, Organizations, and Communities*. San Francisco: Jossey-Bass.

Russell, J. 1991. "Culture and the Categorization of Emotions." *Psychological Bulletin* 11:426–450.

Sachs, Aaron. 1996. "Dying for Oil." *Worldwatch* 9(3):10–21.

Sahlins, Marshall. 1964. "Culture and Environment: The Study of Cultural Ecology." In *Horizons in Anthropology*, ed. Sol Tax, pp. 136–147. Chicago: Aldine.

Satterfield, Terre. 2002. *An Anatomy of a Conflict: Identity, Knowledge, and Emotion in Old-Growth Forests*. Vancouver: University of British Columbia Press.

Schnaiberg, Alan. 1980. *The Economy: From Surplus to Scarcity*. Oxford, UK: Oxford University Press.

Schnaiberg, Alan, and Gould, Kenneth. 1994. *Environment and Society: The Enduring Conflict*. New York: St. Martin's Press.

Searle, John. 1997. *The Construction of Social Reality*. New York: Free Press.

Selected Environmental Law Statutes 1995–1996. 1995. (Educational ed.) St. Paul, MN: West.

Shirley, Shirley. 1994. *Restoring the Tallgrass Prairie*. Iowa City: University of Iowa Press.

Shulman, Seth. 1992. *The Threat at Home: Confronting the Toxic Legacy of the U.S. Military*. Boston: Beacon Press.

Simon, Herbert Alexander. 1997. *Administrative Behavior: A Study of Decision-Making Processes in Administrative Organizations*. New York: Free Press.

Singer, Peter. 1998. *Ethics Into Action: Henry Spira and the Animal Rights Movement*. Lanham, MD: Rowman & Littlefield.

Stanley, Joe S. 1986. *Broad Scan Analysis of Human Adipose Tissue, Executive Summary*, Vol. 1. EPA Contract B560/5-86/035. Springfield, VA: National Technical Information Service.

Stern, Paul C., and Fineberg, Harvey V., eds. 1996. *Understanding Risk: Informing Decisions in a Democratic Society*. Washington, DC: National Academy Press.

Swidler, Ann. 1986. "Culture in Action: Symbols and Strategies." *American Sociological Review* 51 (April):273–286.

Szasz, Andrew. 1994. *Ecopopulism: Toxic Waste and the Movement for Environmental Justice*. Minneapolis: University of Minnesota Press.

Thoits, Peggy A. 1989. "The Sociology of Emotion." *Annual Review of Sociology* 15:317–342.

Thomas, Evan. 2005. "How Bush Blew It." *Newsweek*, September 15:30–40.

Thoreau, Henry David. 1952. *Walden*. New York: W. W. Norton.

Tidwell, Mike. 2003. *Bayou Farewell: The Rich Life and Tragic Death of Louisiana's Cajun Coast*. New York: Pantheon.

United States Supreme Court. 1978. *TVA v. Hill*, 437 U.S., 153 Sixth Circuit No. 76-1701. Retrieved from http://laws.findlaw.com.us/437/153.html.

Vale, Thomas R., ed. 2002. *Fire, Native Peoples, and the Natural Landscape*. Washington, DC: Island Press.

Vyner, Henry. 2000. *Invisible Trauma*. Lexington, MA: Lexington Books.

Walsh, Edward J. 1981. "Resource Mobilization and Citizen Protect in Communities Around Three Mile Island." *Social Problems* 29:1–21.

Walsh, Edward J. 1988. *Democracy in the Shadows: Citizen Mobilization in the Wake of the Accident at Three Mile Island*. New York: Greenwood Press.

Walsh, Edward J., and Warland, Rex. 1983. "Social Movement Involvement in the Wake of a Nuclear Accident: Activists and Freeriders in TMI Area." *American Sociological Review* 48:764–780.

Walton, John. 1992. *Western Times and Water Wars: State, Culture, and Rebellion in California*. Berkeley: University of California Press.

Weisaeth, Lars. 1991. "Psychosocial Reactions in Norway to Nuclear Fallout From the Chernobyl Disaster." In *Communities at Risk*, eds. Stephen R. Couch, and Steve Kroll-Smith, pp. 53–80. New York: Peter Lang.

Wellock, Thomas Raymond. 1998. *Critical Masses: Opposition to Nuclear Power in California, 1958–1978*. Madison: University of Wisconsin Press.

Wheeler, Richard S. 1998. *The Buffalo Commons*. New York: St. Martin's Press.

Wheeler, William Bruce, and McDonald, Michael J. 1986. *TVA and the Tellico Dam 1936–1979: A Bureaucratic Crisis in Post-Industrial America*. Knoxville: University of Tennessee Press.

Wynne, Brian. 1992. "Misunderstood Misunderstanding: Social Identities and Public Uptake of Science." *Public Understandings of Science* 1(3):381–394.

Wynne, Brian. 1996. "May the Sheep Graze Safely? A Reflexive View of the Expert-Lay Knowledge Divide." In *Risk, Environment and Modernity*, eds. Scott Lash, Bron Szerszynski, and Brian Wynne, pp. 44–83. London: Sage.

Yaffee, Steven Lewis. 1994. *The Wisdom of the Spotted Owl: Policy Lessons for a New Century*. Washington, DC: Island Press.

Yin, Robert. 1994. *Case Study Research: Design and Methods*. 2nd ed. Beverly Hills, CA: Sage.

Zwart, Ivan. 2003. "A Greener Alternative? Deliberative Democracy Meets Local Government Environmental Politics." *Environmental Politics* 12(2):23–48.

Index

About the Authors

Valerie J. Gunter is an Associate Professor in the Department of Sociology at the University of New Orleans. Following the ravages of Hurricane Katrina, she spent a year as a Visiting Associate Professor at Michigan State University, from which she had received her PhD in sociology in 1994. She has spent over 20 years researching the controversial processes by which environmental issues become registered on community and national political agendas. Articles reporting the results from this research have been published in such journals as *Social Problems, The Sociological Quarterly, The American Sociologist, Sociological Inquiry,* and *Rural Sociology.* She is a coeditor of *Illness and the Environment: A Reader in Contested Medicine.*

Steve Kroll-Smith is the Head of the Department of Sociology at the University of North Carolina in Greensboro. He was formerly Research Professor of Sociology at the University of New Orleans. He has edited and written five books on environmental hazards and disasters, health and the environment, and sociologists as expert witnesses. He is the current editor of *Sociological Inquiry* and the 2004 recipient of the American Sociological Association's Distinguished Contribution Award in the study of environment and technology. His current work is the problem of race, class, and water in New Orleans in the aftermath of Hurricanes Katrina and Rita. He also regularly contributes to the growing scholarship on the sociology of sleep.